STUART'S CAVALRY

IN THE

GETTYSBURG CAMPAIGN

BY

JOHN S. MOSBY

*"I give thy harp heroic theme,
And warm thee with a noble name."*
—Scott.

NEW YORK
MOFFAT, YARD & COMPANY
1908

Copyright, 1908, by
MOFFAT, YARD & COMPANY
NEW YORK

All rights reserved

Published, February, 1908

The Plimpton Press Norwood Mass. U.S.A.

This scarce antiquarian book is included in our special *Legacy Reprint Series*. In the interest of creating a more extensive selection of rare historical book reprints, we have chosen to reproduce this title even though it may possibly have occasional imperfections such as missing and blurred pages, missing text, poor pictures, markings, dark backgrounds and other reproduction issues beyond our control. Because this work is culturally important, we have made it available as a part of our commitment to protecting, preserving and promoting the world's literature. Thank you for your understanding.

MAJOR-GENERAL J. E. B. STUART

STUART'S CAVALRY
IN THE
GETTYSBURG CAMPAIGN

This volume is inscribed as a tribute of devotion to the memory of
GENERAL J. E. B. STUART
"the champion of a cause more interesting than prosperous — one of those causes which please noble spirits but do not please destiny — which have Cato's adherence but not Heaven's."

CONTENTS

	PAGE
PREFACE	v
INTRODUCTION	vii

I

BRANDY

Hooker and the Army of Northern Virginia — Culpeper — Pleasanton crosses the Rappahannock — Beverly Ford — Stuart repulses Buford — Kelley's Ford — Winchester — Brandy Station . 1

II

GETTYSBURG

General Lee moves to the Potomac — General Stuart — Union officers captured — Aldie — Col. Duffie defeated — Hooker at Fairfax — Rodes crosses the Potomac — Defeat of Reynolds — General Ewell — Meade issues orders — July 1st — Bristoe Station — General Robertson — General Lee's Report — . . 58

ILLUSTRATIONS

	PAGE
MAJOR-GENERAL J. E. B. STUART . . . . *Frontispiece*	
COLONEL JOHN S. MOSBY	72
MAP OF THE GETTYSBURG CAMPAIGN	222

PREFACE

THESE pages have been written as a duty I owe to a soldier to whom great injustice has been done. The statements in the two reports of the commanding general in regard to his orders and the management of the cavalry in the Gettysburg campaign have been generally accepted without question; and the criticisms of his staff officers and biographers on the conduct of the Chief of Cavalry have assumed them to be true. It seems never to have occurred to these critics to analyze and compare the two reports with each other, and with the contemporaneous correspondence, to ascertain if they agree, or in what respect they differ. This I have done and have found it impossible to reconcile their differences. It was my fortune to serve under the direct orders of General Robert E. Lee and General Stuart, and for both I have always felt a deep affection. General Lee mentioned my name when I was a private in a general order to the army, and the last communication I received from him put me in command of all Northern Virginia. I have tried to explain how his name is signed to papers that do so much injustice as well to himself as to General Stuart. The following letter to me from General Beauregard shows that my theory of the Gettysburg campaign is far more flattering to General Lee as a commander than his own report.

NEW ORLEANS, Jan. 6, —92.

MY DEAR COLONEL: —

I read with much pleasure your two articles in *Belford's Magazine* on the Gettysburg Campaign, which I had always condemned as dangerous and ill advised, but as explained by you, I withdraw my condemnation of it. It is on the contrary to be regretted that General Lee's plan was not carried out as he intended.

I am yours very truly,
(Signed)   G. T. BEAUREGARD.

General Stuart's report of the campaign shows what were my relations with him at that time; and as I brought the information that induced him to ask permission to cross the Potomac in rear of the enemy when he was ordered to the Susquehanna, and was chosen to command the advance of his column, I think I have a right on my own account as an actor in the great tragedy as well as on his, to be heard. The fatal shears cut the thread of his life before the end of the conflict came, and he was denied the opportunity to speak for himself. The time has come to apply the test of reason to the Gettysburg legend to discover who is responsible for bringing upon us the *Dies irae!—dies illa!*

The equestrian statue of the great leader of the Southern cavalry which was lately unveiled at Richmond is a testimony of the love and admiration of the men who followed him in battle and wept over his bier:

> "So sinks the day-star in the Ocean bed,
> And yet anon repairs his drooping head,
> And tricks his beams and with new spangled ore
> Flames in the forehead of the morning sky."

JNO. S. MOSBY.

WASHINGTON CITY,
   August 21, 1907.

INTRODUCTION

For the true laurel-wreath which glory weaves,
Is of the tree no bolt of thunder cleaves.
        BYRON, *Childe Harold.*

THE battle of Chancellorsville was fought on May 3, 1863; it was a prelude to Gettysburg. Considering the numerical inferiority of the Southern army and the fact that it took the offensive and drove its antagonist out of his entrenchments over the river it had just triumphantly crossed,[1] I consider it the boldest deed of arms and the most wonderful achievement in the history of war.

[1] GENERAL ORDERS, No 47.
        HEADQUARTERS ARMY OF THE POTOMAC,
            CAMP NEAR FALMOUTH, VA.
                April 30th, 1863.

It is with heartfelt satisfaction the commanding General announces to the army that the operations of the last three days have determined that our enemy must either ingloriously fly, or come out from behind his defences and give us battle on our own ground where certain destruction awaits him. . . .

By command of Major-General Hooker,
        S. WILLIAMS,
            A. A. G.

In contrast with the above is the following despairing despatch from Hooker to President Lincoln.

"MAY 3, 1863, 3.30 P.M.

"We have had a desperate fight yesterday and to-day, which has resulted in no success to us, having lost two lines which had been selected

I once expressed this opinion to General Sherman; he agreed with me. General Warren, an engineer officer, referring in his report to Jackson's flank march and surprise of Hooker's right wing on the evening of the 2d, says: "I was near this part of the field about 5 P.M., when heavy firing of musketry began on our right and I hastened to the spot. The Eleventh Corps on their left had made no stand at all behind its breastworks, but ran away while yet the enemy's bullets scarcely reached them, and while their own artillery heroically served, still held the enemy in check. I tried in vain to assist some of the officers in rallying their men, but soon saw it was a waste of precious time. This flank move in our very presence, which General Lee had decided upon, and the execution of which he had entrusted to General Jackson, was one of great risk under any circumstances." . . .

At Austerlitz the Allies attempted to do the same thing that Jackson did and met a great disaster. But General Lee knew that he did not have Napoleon in his front. At 4.10 P.M., on May 2, when Jackson was almost in touch with his flank and was forming his lines for attack, Hooker, unconscious of Jackson's presence and of the impending blow, said in a despatch to Sedgwick:

for our defence. It is now 1.30 o'clock and there is still some firing of artillery. We may have another turn at it this P.M. I do not despair of success. If Sedgwick could have gotten up there could have been but one result. It is impossible for me to know the exact position of Sedgwick as regards his ability to advance and take part in the engagement. I cannot tell when it will end. We will endeavor to do our best. My troops are in good spirits. We have fought desperately to-day. No general ever commanded a more devoted army."

INTRODUCTION

"Capture Fredericksburg with everything in it and vigorously pursue the enemy. We know that the enemy is fleeing to save his trains. Two of Sickle's divisions are amongst them."

But at 9 P.M., after Jackson had struck the blow that created a panic and rout, Hooker ordered Sedgwick to "at once take up his line of march on the Chancellorsville road until you connect with us. You will probably fall upon the rear of the forces commanded by General Lee and between us we will use him up. Send word to General Gibbon to take possession of Fredericksburg." Gibbon was on the opposite side of the river at Falmouth.

On April 29, Sedgwick with 22,000 men had crossed the Rappahannock below Fredericksburg. This was only a feint by Hooker to deceive Lee while the main body of his army was marching out of sight to the upper fords. Lee soon penetrated his design and, with Jackson's corps, went to meet Hooker, but left Early behind with 10,000 men as a rear-guard and containing force to hold Sedgwick in check and protect his flank.[1] Hooker had not antici-

---

[1] "A containing force is a body of troops charged with the duty of holding in check a body (generally numerically superior) of the enemy, while the main efforts of the army are directed against another portion of the hostile force." — *Wagner.*

Colonel Hamley, in his work on the operations of war, says:

"To bring an army from the order of march to the order of battle is a work of time. Therefore it may, in most cases, be checked by a force deployed in order of battle, only a little superior to the heads of the advancing columns. And the uses to be made of this circumstance are manifold; it is not too much to say that, rightly employed, it is the most effective weapon in the military armory. . . . If a body of troops were to remain drawn up to oppose the advance of a superior force on

INTRODUCTION

pated this bold move of his adversary. He had expected him to retreat toward Richmond to fight a defensive battle; his orders to Sedgwick were to pursue him in that direction. Hooker's plans were upset by Jackson's unexpected turning of his flank; his army was divided and he was now on the defensive. Such a sudden transformation of scene was never seen before. Jackson's untimely fall in the first act of the great tragedy has put him amongst the deified heroes of antiquity, and his name is so blended with the great victory that the world has taken little

a plain where the whole conformation were visible, the attempt would be futile and disastrous. The enemy would at once attack with superior forces and compel a costly retreat under penalty of rout or destruction. But skilfully disposed in a good position across the path of an adversary advancing in an ordinarily broken country, the risk is greatly reduced. If the armies have been manœuvering near each other, with numbers and positions constantly changing, and plans and combinations only to be guessed at, the leader who comes on such an obstacle in his path cannot at first know the amount of force which bars his way sufficiently well to begin an immediate battle. He will generally pause, reconnoiter and feel his way; and will defer a general attack till he shall be ready to deploy a force sufficient to render him confident of success. In the meanwhile the commander of the smaller force must watch carefully the disposition of his adversary, and combine in an unusual degree resolution with prudence. For if he were to engage the whole of his troops throughout the extent of their front, it would be out of his power to withdraw when the adversary had deployed a superior force, and he would be out-flanked and heavily defeated. On the other hand, if he were to give way before the enemy had made a considerable deployment, the advance, which it was his business to check, would not be retarded. He must occupy his ground to the last moment possible without committing himself to a general action, and must then effect an orderly retreat. At the first opportunity offered by the ground, he must repeat the manœuver. . . . The sole use of a containing force is to prevent a reunion of the enemy's parts."

account of the fact that Stuart took Jackson's place on the field and finished the work which Jackson had begun. If Homer had painted this battle scene of the Wilderness he would have represented Jackson and Stuart as the Twin-Gods riding on the lightning and directing the storm.

I do not mean that Stuart accomplished all that Jackson would have done if he and his next in command, A. P. Hill, had not been wounded. Jackson fell about 8 P.M.; Hill about the same time. He was pressing to cut the enemy off from the United States Ford, their line of retreat. Stuart, on whom the command of Jackson's corps now devolved, was several miles away on the flank near Ely's Ford on the Rapidan. The advance of Jackson's troops had been arrested by his fall for they had no commander. Stuart did not arrive on the field to take command until midnight.[1] The panic had then subsided;

---

[1] GENERAL LEE TO PRESIDENT DAVIS, RICHMOND, VA.

HEADQUARTERS NEAR CHANCELLORSVILLE, VA.

MAY 2nd, 1863.

MR. PRESIDENT:—

I find the enemy in a strong position at Chancellorsville and in large force; his communications extend to the Rapidan at Germanna and Ely's Fords, and to the Rappahannock at United States Ford. He seems determined to make the fight here and, from what I learn from General Early, has sent up troops from his position opposite Fredericksburg. Anticipating such a movement on his part, I directed General Early last evening, if it occurred, to leave a guard at his position and join me with the rest of his forces. I have repeated the orders this morning. It is plain that if the enemy is too strong for me here I shall have to fall back, and Fredericksburg must be abandoned. . . . I have no expectations that any reinforcements from Longstreet or North Carolina will join me in time to aid in the contest at this point. . . .

INTRODUCTION

Hooker's army had recovered from the shock of the attack and his lines had been re-formed to protect his rear. The opportunity to destroy him was gone.

It is impossible even for the greatest master of a profession to execute another's conceptions without specific directions. It was said of Apelles that no artist could be found to complete a picture which he left unfinished. Of all the great commanders of history, Jackson was probably the most reticent about his plans. Even if Stuart had been present on the field when he fell, the transfer of command would have involved a delay that might have been fatal to victory.

Colonel Henderson, an English soldier, in his "Stonewall Jackson and the American War," says:

"These arrangements made, Jackson proceeded to join his advanced line. At the point where the track to the White House and United States Ford strikes the plank road, he met General Lane seeking his instructions for the attack. They were sufficiently brief: 'Push right

GENERAL LEE TO GENERAL STUART

MAY 3rd, 1863, 3 A.M.

GENERAL J. E. B. STUART:—

GENERAL; it is necessary that the glorious victory thus far achieved be prosecuted with the utmost vigor and the enemy given no time to rally. As soon, therefore, as it is possible they must be pressed, so that we can unite the two wings of the army. Endeavour, therefore, to dispossess them of Chancellorsville, which will permit the union of the whole army. I shall myself proceed to join you as soon as I can make arrangements on this side, but let nothing delay the completion of the plan of driving the enemy from his rear and from his positions. I shall give orders that every effort be made on this side at daylight to aid in the junction.

ahead Lane, right ahead.' As Lane galloped off to his command, General Hill and some of his staff came up and Jackson gave Hill his orders: 'Press them, cut them off from the United States Ford, Hill; press them.' . . .

"The skirmishers on both sides were now engaged and the lines of battle in the rear became keenly on the alert. Some mounted officers galloped hastily back to their commands. The sound startled the Confederate soldiers, and an officer of the 18th North Carolina, seeing a group of strange horsemen riding towards him through the darkness — for Jackson, hearing firing, had turned back to his own lines — gave the order to fire. The volley was fearfully effective. Men and horses fell dead and dying on the narrow track. Jackson himself received three bullets, one in the right hand and two in the left arm, cutting the main artery and crushing the bone below the shoulder, and as the reins dropped upon his neck, 'Little Sorrel,' frantic with terror, plunged into the woods and rushed towards the Federal lines. An overhanging bough struck his rider violently in the face, tore off his cap and nearly unhorsed him; but, recovering his seat, he managed to seize the bridle with his bleeding hand and turned into the road. . . . When Stuart reached the front he found the troops still halted, Rodes and Colston re-forming on the open fields near Dowdall's Tavern, and the Light Division deployed within the forest, and the generals anxious for their own security.

"So far the attack had been completely successful, but Lee's lack of strength prevented the full accomplishment of his design. Had Longstreet been present, with

INTRODUCTION

Pickett and Hood to lead his splendid infantry,[1] the Third Corps and the Twelfth would have been so hardly pressed that Chancellorsville, Hazel Grove and the White House would have fallen an easy prize to Jackson's bayonets. . . .

"In Stuart, however, Hooker had to deal with a soldier who was no unworthy successor of Stonewall Jackson.

[1] GENERAL LEE TO PRESIDENT DAVIS

FREDERICKSBURG, April 30th, 1863.

. . . General Stuart is supposed to have crossed Rapidan last night to interrupt enemy's column at Germanna. He cut it in the afternoon near Madden's, north of Rapidan. Enemy was still crossing the Rappahannock at 5 P.M. yesterday. . . . Object evidently to turn our left. If I had Longstreet's divisions — Hood's and Pickett's — would feel safe.

RICHMOND, VA., April 30th, 1863.

GENERAL LONGSTREET, SUFFOLK, VA.: —

Move without delay to this place to effect a junction with General Lee.

S. COOPER,
A. and I. G.

GENERAL LEE TO GENERAL JACKSON

HEADQUARTERS, May 3rd, 1863.

GENERAL: I have just received your note informing me that you were wounded. I cannot express my regret at the occurrence. Could I have directed events I should have chosen for the good of the country to be disabled in your stead. I congratulate you on the victory which is due to your skill.

GENERAL LEE TO GENERAL LONGSTREET

May 7th.

My letter of the 1st instant to which you refer, was intended to apprise you of my intended movement and to express the wish rather than the expectation that one of your divisions could cooperate in it. I did not intend to express the opinion that you could reach me in *time*, as I *did* not think it practicable.

INTRODUCTION

Reluctantly abandoning the idea of a night attack, the cavalry general, fully alive to the exigencies of the situation, had determined to reduce the interval between himself and Lee, and, during the night, the artillery was brought to the front and the batteries deployed wherever they could find room. Just before the darkness began to lift, orders were received from Lee that the assault would be made as early as possible. The right wing, swinging around in order to come abreast of the center, became hotly engaged. Away to the southeast, across the hills held by the Federals, came the responding thunder of Lee's guns; and 40,000 infantry, advancing through the woods against front and flank, enveloped in a circle of fire a stronghold which was held by over 60,000 muskets. . . . It must always be an interesting matter of speculation what the result would have been if Jackson had accomplished his design on the night he fell, of moving a large part of his command up the White House road and barring the only line of retreat left open to the Federals.

"Undoubtedly to those who think more of numbers than of human nature, of the momentum of the mass rather than the mental equilibrium of the general, the fact that a superior force of comparatively fresh troops was at Hooker's disposal will be sufficient to put the success of the Confederates out of court. Yet the question will always suggest itself, would not the report that a victorious enemy of unknown strength was pressing forward in the darkness of the night towards the only line of retreat, have so demoralized the Federal soldiers, already shaken by the overthrow of the Eleventh Corps, that they would have thought only of securing their own safety? Would Hooker, whose tactics the next day, after he had had the night given him in which to recover his senses, were so inadequate, have done better if he had received no respite? . . . He must be a great leader indeed, who, when his flank is suddenly rolled up and his line of retreat threatened, preserves sufficient coolness to devise a general counterstroke."

The Count of Paris says: "From earliest dawn, Stuart, anxious to show his comrades that he was not only a brilliant cavalry officer, but that he is likewise able to lead an army corps, is occupied in rectifying his lines and in making the Second Corps take the most favorable positions for renewing the attack. . . . It is five o'clock in the morning; provisions were about to be distributed to the soldiers of these three brigades, who had fully earned them by twenty-four hours of marching and fighting, but at the cry 'Let us remember Jackson,' they are all in motion without waiting for anything, for they are no longer ignorant of his wound, and are burning with desire to avenge upon the enemy the fatal accident that has robbed them of their chief. This cry is repeated by the rest of the division, which is advancing on the left of the road under Stuart's lead, and the two other lines that have passed beyond the clearing of Dowdall's Tavern in order to get back in the woods. . . .

"The plateau is soon covered with soldiers flying in disorder, and the abatis, filled with the dead and wounded, catch fire. The conflagration is soon communicated to the Chancellor dwelling, which has been converted into a hospital; with it perished all the victims of this frightful conflict who had sought a protecting shelter under its roof. Hooker mounts his horse again with difficulty and proceeds in sadness and in silence in the direction of the new line which he had caused to be formed in the Bullock crossing. During this time Lee is in the vicinity of the Chancellor dwelling; his soldiers are in possession of the whole plateau. It is ten o'clock in the morning. . . . The [third] Federal line was well defined; each organization fell readily into its place in the same order as around Chancellorsville. The position, which was very bad for an army desiring to get out of the forest, was easy to defend. Yet Lee, giving his troops only the time strictly necessary to breathe and form again, was already preparing to attack it. . . . But at this moment came alarming news to put a stop to his movement, obliging him to form a resolution even more daring, perhaps, than that which the day previous had brought Jackson upon the flank of the enemy."

This news was that Sedgwick after a short combat had captured Fredericksburg and the surrounding heights — that Early had retreated on the Telegraph road towards Bowling Green (Richmond), and had left the plank road to Chancellorsville open to Sedgwick, who was advancing on Lee's rear which was now uncovered. No doubt General Lee intended to leave the road to Richmond open. If Sedgwick accepted the invitation, then Early, having the interior line and central position could easily have united with Lee at Chancellorsville to crush Hooker while Sedgwick was far away. In that event Sedgwick would never have re-crossed the Rappahannock. If, on the contrary, Sedgwick took the plank road he would have been checked by Wilcox while Lee with the reinforcement of Early was driving Hooker into the river. Early had thus become separated from Lee's army. Lee had intended that Early should guard his rear and keep between him and Sedgwick. Fortunately Wilcox, who was at Bank's Ford, a few miles above Fredericksburg, without orders, moved back to Salem Church on the plank road and formed his brigade in the dense thicket across it. This compelled Sedgwick to halt and deploy, and, temporarily, barred his advance until the arrival of McLaws. Lee had suspended the attack he was about making on Hooker's new position when he heard that Sedgwick was in his rear, and sent McLaws to check the movement. He followed with Anderson's division — attacked and drove Sedgwick back over the river. The Count of Paris says: "While McLaws' [division] and Mahone's brigade were marching in the direction of Fredericksburg, Wilcox was establishing himself at Salem Church, and Early, believing the enemy to be moving on the Bowling Green [Richmond] road, was making useless preparations to dispute it to him far away from the real battle-field."

When Lee turned against Sedgwick he left Stuart to hold Hooker; after finishing Sedgwick, he moved back to strike Hooker another blow with his united army. Early had then joined him. But Hooker had gone. Lee had successfully repeated Napoleon Bonaparte's tactics in his first campaign in Italy. An English officer,

INTRODUCTION

Captain Cecil Battine of the 15th King's Hussars, has given in his book, "The Crisis of the Confederacy," a graphic sketch of Stuart, and of his brilliant leadership in this battle. He says:

"James Stuart, or Jeb, as he was called in the army, from his first initials, proved himself, in his short career, the greatest warrior amongst the great men who have been so called. Whether or not he was really descended from Robert the Bruce, he certainly inherited the kingly talent for leading men and making war. He won the great battle of May 3, which was decisive in this campaign, by skilful and gallant leading. He was but twenty-eight years old when he took Jackson's place at the head of the Second Corps; and it would have perhaps been well for the Southern cause if Lee had retained him at his side to share in the supreme command as he had used Jackson, instead of at once again transferring him to the command of the cavalry which Fitz-Lee, W. Lee, or Hampton was qualified to hold.[1] Stuart had, like Sedgwick, served under

[1] WASHINGTON, D. C.
December 10, 1907.

COLONEL MOSBY:—

Complying with your request for a brief account of how Wilcox and his command stood between Sedgwick and the rear of Lee's army on the 3d of May, 1863.

Coming from Bank's Ford in the forenoon, Wilcox with his Alabama Brigade, four pieces of Lewis' Battery and forty or fifty of the 15th Va. Cavalry under Major Collins, in three successive skirmishes, first near Taylor's house, then near Downman's, and then at the toll-gate, so delayed Sedgwick's advance that his final attack was not made upon us at Salem Church, three and a half miles from Fredericksburg, until five o'clock, P.M.

INTRODUCTION

Lee in the cavalry of the United States army, and the knowledge possessed by their former colonel of the two men's characters and capacity stood the Southern general in good stead on this critical field; he could take liberties with the over-cautious Sedgwick, and give rein to the offensive skill of Stuart. Soon after the outbreak of the

Wilcox's Brigade was formed across the road. After shelling us heavily, two divisions, Brooks' and Newton's, comprising six brigades, were massed and assaulted us. The attack was mainly on our brigade, but as General Lee reports it, "partially involved the two brigades" on our left, Semmes' and Mahone's, which had come to our help. After a hot and bloody battle we drove the enemy back to the shelter of their artillery, three quarters of a mile three of Semmes' regiments advancing with us. Losses on our side about 1000; on the enemy's side over 2500.

A notable and singularly happy sequel was this: May 3, 1907, the survivors of the gallant 23d New Jersey, one of the foremost regiments in that bloody fight, erected a monument at Salem Church on which were two plates, one inscribed

"To the Memory of our Heroic Dead Comrades Who Gave Their Lives for their Country's Honor on this Battle-field, This Tablet is Dedicated."

On the other plate was this:

"To the Brave Alabama Boys, Our Opponents on this Field of Battle, Whose Memory we Honor, This Tablet is Dedicated."

As the oldest surviving officer of the Alabamians in that fight, I acknowledged gratefully this magnanimous compliment and received from Colonel E. Burd Grubb a noble letter, which I much regret you have not space to publish.

Very truly yours,
HILARY A. HERBERT,[1]
Last Colonel, 8th Ala. Regt.

COLONEL JOHN S. MOSBY,
Washington, D. C.

[1] Secretary of the Navy 1893–1897.

INTRODUCTION

war Stuart distinguished himself as a cavalry leader, and his strategical work in blindfolding the enemy and in enlightening his own army has never been surpassed. As a cavalry tactician he is not only the first, but hitherto the only leader of the army who understood how to combine the effects of fire and shock, how to render effective service in fighting on foot without losing the power to strike on horseback when opportunity offered, though his Federal opponents imitated his strategy and tactics with some success in the next campaign."

"On Sunday, May 3, the dawn was obscured by the river mist so frequent on the banks of the Rappahannock. By five o'clock in the morning the Confederate regiments had got under arms and, scarcely waiting to eat the food which Stuart had caused to be distributed, the soldiers of Hill's division, now forming the first line, were clamoring to be led into action. While it was yet dark Stuart had brought up the artillery of the Second Corps to the Lewis creek in order to enfilade the hostile position, but before it came into action his infantry threw themselves upon the Federal soldiers still remaining in the wood which had been the scene of last night's engagement, with vengeful cries of 'Remember Jackson.'

"Sickles in the meanwhile had begun to execute Hooker's orders for the evacuation of the ground west of Lewis creek when the furious charge of the gray riflemen compelled him to turn and defend himself. The fierce and costly fight which followed left the contested wood and the heights of Hazel Grove in the possession of the assailants. Stuart lost no time in dragging his artillery forward on to the heights; he established a battery of thirty guns opposite Fairview Hill and cemetery which could fire across the high road at a range of only eleven hundred yards. . . .

"The troops at Lee's disposal were too few to enable him to strike home when Stuart began his advance on both sides of the main road, but he closed his brigades towards their left, leaving skirmishers to keep the enemy's left wing amused, and pushing forward artillery wherever an opening in the trees gave it range. Thus skilfully disposing his forces, he began gradually to press upon the Federal breastworks, threatening them right along their line and so keeping them in doubt as to his real point of attack. The Confederate artillery, under the orders of both Stuart and Lee, greatly assisted the attack; the fire of the batteries of the First and Second corps crossed and inflicted death and wounds in the space around the Federal headquarters, crowded as it was with troops, trains, and field-hospitals. Of the seven Federal divisions seriously attacked, three defended the Fairview plateau, two faced westward along the Lewis creek ravine, and two held Lee at bay, facing east on the plank and old pike roads which once again diverged at Chancellorsville.

"When he judged the fire of his guns to have produced some effect, Stuart hurled his line across the ravine and a hard fight followed on its eastern bank; at the same time, two brigades attacked from the south and repeatedly charged the defenders of the cemetery with the bayonet. In the lull of the fighting Stuart rode through his troops and helped to re-form them for another attack, while he caused the artillery to increase its fire against the enemy's position and to sweep the high road. Lee was doing the same thing and the effect of this bombardment was to inflict still greater loss and confusion in the enemy's ranks. Hooker himself was wounded and stunned by the falling masonry at Chancellor's house, which was set on fire; many wounded soldiers were burnt alive and the dry branches in the barricades and entanglements also caught fire. All order had ceased in the clearing north of Fairview; no succor came to the decimated defenders. At this critical moment Lee himself brought Perry's Florida brigade from the woods south of the plank road down the ravine until he joined hands with Archer's brigade which formed Stuart's extreme right. The five Confederate divisions were thus united in a continuous line of battle. The sight of Lee roused the utmost enthusiasm among Jackson's soldiers, who shouted, 'God bless your noble head!' as he passed. The signal was then given for an assault right along the line. While the guns swept the road and the clearing on either side of it, Stuart led his infantry once more across the ravine, singing at the top of his voice and waving his sword. His blonde beard, blue eyes, and noble figure on horseback recalled the Norman heroes who led the van at Hastings, singing the songs of Roland. With a fury the Federals were no longer able to resist, the converging troops from the west, south, and east thronged across the ravine cheering and waving their tattered colors. The brigades and regiments were mixed up and many hundreds of the men were dabbled with blood from wounds given or received, but, undeterred by previous failure, the whole line lowered their bayonets and fell upon Sickles' corps, which bravely contested every yard of the ground, repeatedly charging with cold steel, but were finally swept away.

"By ten o'clock the whole mass of the three Federal corps was recoiling before the victorious assailants. Sickles' corps, which had sustained the brunt of the conflict, had also suffered most and was in the greatest disorder; the Twelfth Corps fell back fighting, and on the Federal left Hancock withdrew his division in masterly style, checking McLaws' advance as he did so. In this manœuver Colonel Miles, afterwards commander-in-chief of the United States army, first became distinguished. The scene around Chancellorsville, when Lee on horseback, amid his victorious soldiers, reached the cross-roads, showed how severe had been the struggle and how destructive had been the fire of the Southern artillery. The ground was littered with injured men and horses and with the smoking debris of carts and equipments; an immense mass of military stores became the prize of the victors, who crowded around their well-beloved chief with enthusiastic cheers, while the retreating mass and the sound of firing slowly rolled northward. But little time was wasted in self-congratulation. Lee was determined to finish off Hooker without giving him time to recover from the stunning blow under which his army was reeling, and orders were issued to re-form the decimated gray divisions with the intention of resuming the attack.

"The victory was indeed a brilliant achievement. . . . News, however, reached the Confederate commander soon after one o'clock which compelled him to countermand the fresh attack for which troops had already been drawn up, and to leave Hooker in his intrenchments, over which a mass of black smoke rolled from the burning woods. A message from General Early informed Lee that the Federal Sixth Corps had stormed Marye Heights and was in possession of the Orange plank road; Lee's countenance showed no change at these evil tidings; he promptly suspended the preparations for the attack, and commanded that four divisions instead should invest Hooker while McLaws marched to meet the Federals menacing the rear of his army. These orders were forthwith executed. . . . Engrossed by the tremendous events at Chancellorsville, Lee had omitted to inform Early of the new situation which had arisen, and which made the road to Chancellorsville, and not the road to Richmond, the important one to bar.

"[Lee's orders to Early were to protect his rear; his report says; 'General Early had been instructed, in the event of the enemy withdrawing from his front and moving up the river, to join the main body of the army with so much of his command as could be spared from the defence of his lines. . . . The enemy then began to advance up the plank road, his progress being gallantly disputed by the brigade of General Wilcox, who had moved from Bank's Ford as rapidly as possible to the assistance of General Barksdale, but arrived too late to take part in the action. General Wilcox fell back slowly until he reached Salem Church on the plank road, five miles from Fredericksburg. Information of the state of affairs in our rear having reached Chancellorsville, as already stated, General

McLaws, with his three brigades and one of General Anderson's, was ordered to reinforce General Wilcox. The next morning General Early advanced along the Telegraph road and recaptured Marye's and the adjacent hills without difficulty, thus gaining the rear of the enemy's left.']

"A single brigade could have sufficiently delayed Sedgwick's advance to the South if he had rashly taken that direction; but he had no such intention, and a close observation of the Federal dispositions and the swifter manœuver of the slender forces at his disposal would have enabled Early, if not to deny the Chancellorsville road entirely to the enemy, yet to hold him in check long enough to prevent interference with Lee's army. Moreover, Lee's headquarters were but ten miles distant by road, and the sound of heavy firing all the morning attested the violence of the struggle in which the main army was engaged, and gave a clue to the situation. . . . Early rallied his division on the Telegraph road leading to Richmond; Wilcox, who had made a rapid march from Bank's Ford, which he was guarding to assist in the defence, fell back along the plank road with the intention of guarding Lee's rear as long as possible by checking any Federal troops that might try to march along it. . . The two divisions which had been engaged piled their arms until Brook's, the third division, which had formed Sedgwick's left wing, was brought on the plank road and deployed across it in front of them. The manœuver was not unmolested by Wilcox, who managed to delay the Federals another hour before they advanced in two lines covered by skirmishers and followed by the Sixth Corps in column. . . . A running fight to Salem Church, then a determined stand followed; before the Federals could bring their strength to bear, however, McLaws men, tramping from the battle-field of Chancellorsville, had heard the firing and had hastened their march. A solid line of battle was soon formed by McLaws' two leading brigades and a determined advance threw the Federals on the defensive in their turn and recovered a quarter of a mile of the road. . . . By his presence of mind and a correct tactical insight, Wilcox had gained a very important advantage for the Confederate army in checking the Sixth Corps seven miles from the principal scene of action. Early would have done better if he had perceived the real objective of Sedgwick's advance and if he had massed some of his troops so as to fall on the flank of the Federals advancing on the plank road. . . . The staunchness of the Confederate soldiers of the First Corps who fearlessly fought overwhelming numbers, and who swiftly strode from one sanguinary battle-field to another, cannot be too highly praised nor too faithfully imitated, for no infantry ever fought better; while the constancy of their Federal opponents in returning again and again to the struggle in spite of reverses of fortune caused by feeble leadership established their claim to the highest consideration and enhances the fame of both combatants. . . . But there was yet a third group of Confederates, the five brigades under Early, 8,000 men, lying in the fields beside the Richmond road only five miles from the bivouac of the Sixth Corps. During the night Early had established touch with McLaws and realized how matters stood. Somewhat ashamed of the blunder he had made in leaving open the road to Sedgwick, he now determined to retrieve it by attacking the Federals in the rear without waiting for orders, and as soon as it was light, his brigades were marching to sweep from the heights of Fredericksburg the feeble hosts which occupied them. . . . While these movements were in process of execution, Lee betook himself to Salem Church to take command in the battle while Stuart remained to sit on guard over the mass of the enemy's army. Profiting by the inaction of the Unionists and making good use of the curtain of forest which narrowly bounded its horizon, Stuart ably and successfully carried out Lee's instructions. A reconnaissance in force against his left was driven in with a loss of 500 men to the Federals, leaving Hooker more than ever convinced that he was surrounded by superior forces. . . . Soon there came word that Sedgwick's army corps had disappeared in the night; and the report was followed by a message from Marye Heights announcing that the enemy had retreated from them, evacuating the right bank of the Rappahannock and the town of Fredericksburg. The Confederate general had now greatly simplified the task of his army; there only remained the forces of Hooker, cooped up in their entrenchments, on the river bank, and at them he resolved to strike at once. . . . The Federal commander had already resolved to retreat, and in the morning when it began to rain he summoned a council of war to share the responsibility of the decision. . . . The passage of the stream was successfully accomplished, though it seemed at one time as though the current might

INTRODUCTION

carry away the bridges and leave the army cut in twain. The whole day was spent by the Federals in gloomily retracing their steps to the winter cantonments; wet, weary and discouraged, the troops could see no end to their task, while the loss of comrades and kinsfolk in what seemed to be an impossible attempt weighed heavily on every one. Little as they seemed to have gained in the sanguinary campaign, however, an accident had given them an advantage which, perhaps, alone made possible the ultimate triumph of the North, when, in the confusion of the forest fighting, a chance bullet laid low their most dangerous foe. In a very different frame of mind the Southern soldiers marched back from the scene of their glorious victory to their old quarters around Fredericksburg, for Lee had found it impossible to follow his enemy over the river, much as he would have liked to strike another blow at him." [1]

[1] GENERAL LEE TO PRESIDENT DAVIS

May 5th, 1863.

At the close of the battle of Chancellorsville on Sunday, the enemy was reported advancing from Fredericksburg in our rear. General McLaws was sent back to arrest his progress and repulsed him handsomely at Tabernacle Church. Learning that this force consisted of two corps under General Sedgwick, I determined to attack it. Leaving a sufficient force to hold General Hooker in check, who had not re-crossed the Rappahannock, as was reported, but occupied a strong position in front of the United States ford, I marched yesterday with General Anderson, and uniting with McLaws and Early in the afternoon, succeeded by the blessing of heaven in driving General Sedgwick over the river. We have re-occupied Fredericksburg and no enemy remains south of the Rappahannock in its vicinity.

General Lee's report says: "At 5.30 A.M. on April 28, the enemy crossed the Rappahannock in boats near Fredericksburg and driving off the pickets on the river, proceeded to lay a pontoon bridge a short distance below Deep Run. Later in the afternoon another bridge was constructed about a mile below the first. A considerable force crossed on these bridges during the day and was massed out of view under the high banks of the river. The bridges as well as the troops were effectually protected from our artillery by the depth of the river bed and the narrowness of the stream, while the batteries on the opposite heights completely commanded the wide plain between our lines and the river. . . . No demonstration was made opposite any other part of our lines at Fredericksburg, and the strength of the force that had crossed, and its apparent indisposition to attack, indicated that the principal effort of the enemy would be made in some other quarter. This impression was confirmed by the intelligence received from General Stuart that a large body of infantry and artillery were passing up the river. During the forenoon of the 29th, that officer reported that the enemy had crossed in force near Kelly's ford on the preceding evening. Later in the day he announced that a heavy column was moving from Kelly's towards Germanna Ford on the Rapidan and another towards Ely's ford on the same river. The routes they were pursuing after crossing the Rapidan converge near Chancellorsville, whence several roads lead to the rear of our position at Fredericksburg. . . . The enemy in our front near Fredericksburg continued inactive and it was now apparent that the main attack would be made upon our rear and flank. It was, therefore, determined to leave sufficient troops to hold our lines and with the main body of the army to give battle to the approaching column. . . .

"Jackson's troops followed Anderson on the plank road. Colonel Alexander's battalion of artillery accompanied the advance. The enemy was soon encountered on both roads and heavy skirmishing with infantry and artillery ensued, our troops pressing forward steadily. A strong attack on General McLaws was repulsed with spirit by Semmes' brigade, and General Wright by direction of General Anderson, converging to the left of the Plank road, marched by way of the unfinished railroad from Fredericksburg to Gordonsville and turned the enemy's right. His whole line thereupon retreated rapidly, vigorously pursued by our troops until they arrived in about a mile of Chancellorsville. Here the enemy assumed a position of great natural strength, surrounded on all sides by a dense forest filled with tangled undergrowth, in the midst of which breastworks of logs had been constructed with trees felled in front so as to form an almost impenetrable abatis. His artillery swept

INTRODUCTION

the few narrow roads by which his position could be approached from the front, and commanded the adjacent woods. The left of his line extended from Chancellorsville toward the Rappahannock, covering the Bark Mill Ford where he communicated with the north bank of the river by a pontoon bridge. His right stretched westward along the Germanna Ford road more than two miles. Darkness was approaching before the strength and extent of his line could be ascertained, and, as the nature of the country rendered it hazardous to attack by night, our troops were halted and formed in line of battle in front of Chancellorsville, at right angles to the plank road, extending on the right to the Mine road and to the left in the direction of the Catherine Furnace. Colonel Wickham, with the Fourth Virginia cavalry and Colonel Owen's regiment, was stationed between the Mine road and the Rappahannock.

"The rest of the cavalry was upon our left flank. It was evident that a direct attack upon the enemy would be attended with great difficulty and loss, in view of the strength of his position and his superiority in numbers. It was therefore resolved to endeavor to turn his right flank and gain his rear, leaving a force in front to hold him in check and conceal the movement. The execution of this plan was entrusted to Lieutenant-General Jackson with his three divisions. The commands of Generals McLaws and Anderson, with the exception of Wilcox's brigade which, during the night, had been ordered back to Bank's Ford, remained in front of the enemy. Early on the morning of the 2nd, General Jackson marched by the Furnace and Brock roads, his movement being effectually covered by Fitzhugh Lee's cavalry, under General Stuart in person. . . . After a long and fatiguing march, General Jackson's leading division, under General Rodes, reached the old turnpike, about three miles in rear of Chancellorsville, at 4 P.M. As the different divisions arrived they were formed at right angles to the road — Rodes in front, Trimble's division under Brigadier-General Colston in the second, and A. P. Hill's in the third line.

"At 6 P.M. the advance was ordered. The enemy was taken by surprise and fled after a brief resistance. General Rodes' men pushed forward with great vigor and enthusiasm, followed closely by the second and third lines. Position after position was carried, the guns captured and every effort of the enemy to rally defeated by the impetuous rush of our troops. In the ardor of pursuit through the thick and tangled woods, the first and second lines at last became mingled and moved on together as one. The enemy made a stand at a line of breastworks across the road at the house of Melzie Chancellor, but the troops of Rodes and Colston dashed over the entrenchments together, and the flight and pursuit were resumed and continued until our advance was arrested by the abatis in front of the line of works near the central position at Chancellorsville. It was now dark and General Jackson ordered the third line, under General Hill, to advance to the front and relieve the troops of Rodes and Colston, who were completely blended and in such disorder, from the rapid advance through the intricate woods and over broken ground, that it was necessary to reform them. As Hill's men moved forward, General Jackson, with his staff and escort, returning from the extreme front, met his skirmishers advancing and, in the obscurity of the night, were mistaken for the enemy and fired upon. Captain Boswell, chief engineer of the corps, and several others, were killed and a number wounded. General Jackson himself received a severe injury and was borne from the field. The command devolved on Major-general Hill, whose division, under General Heth, was advanced to the line of intrenchments which had been reached by Rodes and Colston. A furious fire of artillery was opened upon them by the enemy, under cover of which his infantry advanced to the attack. They were handsomely repulsed by the Fifty-fifth Virginia regiment under Colonel Mallory, who was killed while bravely leading his men. General Hill was soon after disabled and Major-general Stuart, who had been directed by General Jackson to seize the road to Ely's Ford in the rear of the enemy, was sent to take command. . . .

"Upon General Stuart's arrival soon afterwards (midnight), the command was turned over to him by General Hill. He immediately proceeded to reconnoitre the ground and make himself acquainted with the disposition of the troops. The darkness of the night and the difficulty of moving through the woods and undergrowth rendered it advisable to defer further operations until morning, and the troops rested on their arms in line of battle. . . . As soon as the sound of cannon gave notice of Jackson's attack on the enemy's right, our troops in front of Chancellorsville were ordered to press him strongly on the left to prevent reinforcements being sent to the point assailed. . . .

"Early on the morning of the 3rd, General Stuart renewed the attack upon the enemy, who had strengthened his right during the night with additional breastworks, while a large number of guns, protected by entrenchments, were posted so as to sweep the woods through which our troops had to advance. . . . As the troops advancing upon the

INTRODUCTION xxxiii

enemy's left and right converged upon his central position, Anderson effected a junction with Jackson's corps and the whole line pressed irresistibly on. The enemy was driven from all his fortified positions with heavy losses in killed, wounded and prisoners, and retreated towards the Rappahannock. By ten in the morning we were in full possession of the field."

GENERAL CARL SCHURZ TO GENERAL O. O. HOWARD

May 21st, 1863.

The arrangement spoken of between yourself and the Secretary of War with regard to my transfer to another army is not acceptable under present circumstances. . . . My reasons are these: I have been most outrageously slandered by the press. Ridiculous as it may seem, my division has been made responsible for the defeat of the corps; my officers and men have been called cowards. If we go now will it not have the appearance that we were shaken off by the army of the Potomac? Would it not to a certainty confirm the slanders circulated about me? Would it not seem as if I voluntarily accepted the responsibility of the disaster of the 2nd of May?

I

BRANDY

AFTER the battle of Chancellorsville and the death of Jackson, General Lee reorganized the Army of Northern Virginia, that had been divided into two corps under Longstreet and Jackson; three corps were formed; Longstreet, Ewell, and A. P. Hill were assigned to the command of them.

On June 23 the first step in the campaign that culminated at Gettysburg was taken, although General Lee at that time had no intention of going there. McLaws' division broke up its camp near Fredericksburg and led the advance; the two other divisions of Longstreet's corps, Hood's and Pickett's, that had been at Suffolk, went direct from Richmond to the Rapidan and united in Culpeper. Ewell's corps from its camp at Hamilton's Crossing followed McLaws the next day by way of Spottsylvania Court-house and Verdiersville in Orange, and crossed the Rapidan at Somerville Ford some fifteen or twenty miles above its junction with the Rappahannock. General Lee's object in sending his troops by this route was to conceal the movement from the observation of the enemy on the Rappahannock.

A. P. Hill's corps was left in observation at Fredericksburg as a mask to screen the operation and create the impression on Hooker that Lee's whole army was still in front of him. It seems that Hooker's man in the balloon had detected the disappearance of some Confederate camps, which caused uneasiness. In his testimony before the Committee on the Conduct of the War, Hooker said that on June 6 he directed two bridges to be thrown across the Rappahannock, and ordered Sedgwick to make a reconnaissance for the purpose of developing the enemy's forces;[1] but the "enemy was found in full force and apparently no movement was under way at that time." On the 5th Hooker had telegraphed to the President: "Yesterday morning appearances indicated that during the night the enemy had broken up a few of his camps and abandoned them. These changes were observed on the right of the line in the vicinity of Hamilton's crossing. So far as I am enabled to judge with all my means of information, it was impossible for me to determine satisfactorily whether this movement had been only a change of camp, or the enemy had moved in the direction of Rich-

[1] Scott's Military Dictionary says: "To gain information it is therefore necessary to push a reconnaissance through the curtain of light troops by which an enemy has enveloped himself and drive back and cut off outposts so as to enable the officer charged with the reconnaissance clearly to see the army of the enemy, and note the advantages and disadvantages of his position, count his battalions, and judge of his means of resistance. . . . By this means the general is assured of the true state of the enemy before giving his last orders. . . . The commander of a reconnaissance ordinarily receives written instructions. He should well understand the object before him and demand such explanations as he may require. . . . The line of the enemy is soon pierced and his corps will soon be deployed to repulse the attack. When once this object has been gained, a retreat must be sounded, even in the midst of a combat. . . . The object of a reconnaissance is to gain information."

mond, or up the river; but taken in connection with the fact that some deserters came in from the divisions of Hood and Pickett, I concluded that those divisions had been brought up to the front from their late positions at Gordonsville and Taylorsville [Hanover Junction], and that this could be for no other purpose but to enable the enemy to move up the river with a view to the execution of a movement similar to that of Lee's last year."

As Hood and Pickett were nowhere near the Rappahannock that day, no doubt these pretended deserters were sent over to mislead Hooker and make him believe that their divisions had joined General Lee on the river. He further said: "Under instructions from the Major-General, commanding the army, dated January 31, I am instructed to keep in view always the importance of covering Washington and Harper's Ferry, either directly, or so operating as to be able to punish any force sent against them. In the event the enemy should move as I anticipate he will, the head of his column will probably be headed towards the Potomac, via Gordonsville or Culpeper, while the rear will rest on Fredericksburg.

"After giving this subject my best reflection, I am of the opinion that it is my duty to pitch into his rear, although, by so doing, the head of his column may reach Warrenton before I return."

On the 5th of June Hooker telegraphed the President about a reconnaissance he had just made. ". . . As soon as we got to work they began to assemble in great numbers from all quarters, and the more remote are still arriving. I took about 50 prisoners and they report that the changes remarked in their camp proceed from the reorganization of their army and the assignment of them to new camps. All of Longstreet's command are now with Lee, but no part of the Charleston forces. They have no infantry force higher up the Rappahannock than its junction with the Rapidan. Their cavalry is assembled around Culpeper [Court-house], but the threat to make a crossing [here] may bring them back." General Lee did not leave Fredericksburg until the 6th.

What the prisoners reported to Hooker about the forces on the river confronting him was just the opposite of the truth, and was intended to deceive him, as it evidently did; Hooker, by reporting this information to Mr. Lincoln, showed that he believed it. General Lee was still there with only Hill's corps; Hooker thought his whole army was before him.

General Lee left the next day for Culpeper. But President Lincoln did not approve of Hooker's plan to cross the river and pitch into Lee's rear. He replied — "In one word, I would not take any risk of being tangled up on the river like an ox jumped half over a fence, and liable to be torn by dogs front and rear without a fair chance to gore one way, or kick the other."

On June 5, Halleck from Washington sent a telegram to Hooker, saying: "Prisoners and deserters brought in here state that Stuart is preparing a column of from 15,000 to 20,000 men, cavalry and artillery, for a raid. They say it will be ready in two or three days." Later on the same day, Hooker telegraphed to Halleck that Buford, whose division of cavalry was at Warrenton

Junction, had just informed him that a refugee reported Stuart to be in Culpeper with 20,000 cavalry, and that it was understood that he intended to make a raid. The truth is, Stuart's cavalry had been sent to Culpeper, not to make a *raid*, but to prevent a repetition of the Stoneman raid of a few weeks before. There was also another reason. Culpeper was good grazing ground for the cavalry and forage was scarce at that season. Jones' cavalry brigade had just been brought from the Shenandoah Valley and Robertson's from North Carolina. Stoneman had been relieved after Chancellorsville, and Pleasanton had succeeded him as Chief of Cavalry. Pleasanton was, in my opinion, the ablest Chief of Cavalry the Army of the Potomac ever had.

In a letter to Stuart on May 9, General Lee said: "Hampton has probably joined you. Get your cavalry together and give them breathing time, so that, when you strike, Stoneman may feel you." Pleasanton with the cavalry corps was now in Fauquier on the Orange and Alexandria railroad, which was his line of supply; his outposts were on the Rappahannock River. In a letter dated May 11, instructing Stuart to rendezvous with his cavalry in Culpeper, General Lee said: "I regret to inform you that the great and good Jackson is no more. He died yesterday at 3.15 P.M., of pneumonia, calm, serene, and happy. May his spirit pervade our whole army; our country will then be secure."

When Buford's cavalry division was ordered to the railroad he was directed; "On arriving at Bealeton, should you find yourself with sufficient force, *you will drive the enemy out of his camps near Culpeper and across the Rapidan, destroying the bridge at that point.*" [Italics mine.] On May 28, Hooker told Secretary Stanton that "The enemy has all of his cavalry force [five brigades] collected at Culpeper [Court-house] and Jefferson [ton]."

[Culpeper in the Northern dispatches means the town; in the Southern it means the county.]

"This would indicate a movement in the direction of the Orange and Alexandria railroad. If Stoneman had not almost destroyed one-half of my serviceable cavalry force, I would pitch into him in his camps, and would now if General Stahel's cavalry were with me for a few days."

To this Stanton replied: "There is no other cavalry force about Washington but that of General Stahel, which is now engaged in scouting duty towards Bull Run and Occoquan River. If it be removed, there will be no force in front to give notice of enemy's raids on Alexandria and Washington." In his testimony before the Committee on the Conduct of the War, Hooker said: "I may here state that while at Fairfax Court-house [moving to the Potomac] my cavalry was reinforced by that of Major-General Stahel. The latter numbered 6100 sabres and had been engaged in picketing a line from Occoquan River to Goose creek. The line was concentric and a portion of it within the line held by my army. The force opposed to them was Mosby's Guerrillas, numbering about 200 [50] and, if the reports of the newspapers are to be believed, this whole party was killed two or three times over during the winter. From the time I took command of the Army of the Potomac there was no evidence that any force of the enemy, other than the above named, was within a hundred miles of Washington City, and yet the planks on the Chain bridge were taken up at night during the greater part of the winter and spring. It was this cavalry force, it will be remembered, I had occasion to ask for [Brandy Station], that my cavalry might be strengthened when it was numerically too weak to cope with the superior numbers of the enemy."

Hooker's headquarters were at Fairfax in June when his army was moving North; Stahel's division of cavalry was then assigned to his command. The following dispatches are evidence of the trouble he had in keeping open his line of communication:

HALLECK TO HEINTZELMAN

WASHINGTON, May 29th, 1863.

It is reported that the enemy's cavalry is collecting in force on the upper Rappahannock. I think General Stahel should be cautioned to be exceedingly vigilant against raids to cut the Orage and Alexandria Railroad into Alexandria. If made, they will be quick and rapid. The utmost vigilance must be kept up at all the posts. Staff and other officers must be detailed to see that the troops are continually on the alert.

BUFORD TO PLEASANTON:

WARRENTON JUNCTION, May 31st, 1863.

... On assuming command yesterday I saw a note from Colonel Mann stating that a railroad bridge had been burned about four miles from here. I moved the whole command up the railroad to near the place. No bridge was burned, but a train of cars with supplies was destroyed by some 100 [40] of Mosby's cavalry. The party was pursued and routed by some of General Stahel's troops, who captured and killed some 16 men [1 killed; 2 captured] and took a piece of artillery. I am removing the wreck of the train from the tracks and suppose a construction train will be sent to repair the road. The wires were cut yesterday at 7.30 A.M. and no communication was had until 8 A.M. to-day. The train was destroyed four or five miles beyond my department and in General Stahel's. The guard on the train [Vermont men] ran to the woods and returned to see the train burn. . . .

Colonel Mann of the 7th Michigan Cavalry, reported: "Mosby, with 200 [40] men and one howitzer attacked our train near Catlett's; guard fled; Mosby burned train. Heard firing in camp and went in search with First Vermont, Fifth New York, and a detachment of the Seventh Michigan. Came up with Mosby in strong position two miles southwest of Greenwich and charged him. He gave us grape; boys never faltered; took his gun [after my last round of ammunition had been fired]; Captain Hoskins mortally wounded, and Lieutenant [Sam] Chapman, severely, and several privates."

Stahel reported four killed and fifteen wounded, also eleven horses killed. No one on our side was killed except Captain Hoskins, an English officer; he had the Crimean medal. That no independent raid by the cavalry corps was contemplated, as Hooker and Halleck imagined, is shown by a letter from General Lee to Stuart, of June 2, in which he discourages such an enterprise. He says: "I have read with much attention General Hampton's letter of 1st instant, giving results of his reconnaissance of the enemy's line on the Rappahannock. I should like very much to capture the division of the enemy he speaks of and am much pleased at the gallantry of the proposition. It is what I would expect of an officer of his boldness and daring. But at this distance I do not feel so confident as he does that it can be so easily done, and I fear the loss that would fall on our brave men."

To forestall Stuart in making his expected raid, Hooker determined to take the initiative and attack his camps, which he thought were at Culpeper Court-house, disperse the cavalry force collected there and drive them over the Rapidan. He thought all of Lee's army except the cavalry was still on the lower Rappahannock. On June 5 Buford telegraphed to Hooker from Warrenton Junction that — "I have just received information which I consider reliable, that all the available cavalry force of the enemy is in Culpeper County. Stuart, the two Lees, Roberston, Jenkins, and Jones are all there. [All except Jenkins, who was in the Shenandoah Valley.] Robertson came from North Carolina, Jenkins from Kanawha, and Jones from the Valley. Jones arrived at Culpeper after the others on the third. Since the Chancellorsville fight the cavalry has been much increased from the infantry; 800 Texans from Hood's command have been recently mounted on horses from Richmond. [Not true: Hood's division with his infantry brigade of Texans was then camped on the Rapidan.] My informant, a refugee from Madison County, says Stuart has 20,000; can't tell his intentions but thinks he is going to make a raid."

A dispatch from Hooker to Halleck shows his object in crossing the Rappahannock to attack Stuart:

June 6th, 1863, 3 P.M.

MAJOR GENERAL HALLECK: —

As the accumulation of the heavy rebel force of cavalry about Culpeper may mean mischief, I am determined, if practicable, to break it up in its incipiency. I shall send all my cavalry against them, stiffened by about 3000 infantry. It will require until the morning of the 9th for my forces to gain their positions, and at daylight on that day it is my intention to attack them in their camps. As many of my cavalry are unserviceable from the effects of Stoneman's raid, I am too weak to cope with the numbers of the enemy if as large as represented. It would add much to my efficiency if some of Stahel's forces could advance and hold the fords at Beverly and Sulphur Springs sometime during the forenoon of the 9th. If this should be done, I desire that the officer in command should not be informed of the object of his march, but merely to hold these fords. It is next to impossible to confine information to its proper limits. I have 2500 sabres on a reconnaissance to-day in the vicinity of Jefferson [ton]. Jones' brigade, which has been hovering about Milroy all winter, numbering 1600, is among them; also an additional brigade from North Carolina.

JOSEPH HOOKER, Major-General.

HOOKER TO HALLECK

June 6th, 1863, 8 P.M.

I request that I may be informed whether or not I am to receive assistance in my attack on the rebel forces at Culpeper from any portion of Major-General Heintzelman's forces [Stahel's cavalry] and if so, what?

The aid was not furnished. The capture of the train on the railroad near Catlett's a few days before had created great uneasiness at Washington. It required all of Stahel's cavalry to guard the road. In his dispatch to Halleck informing him of his intention to attack the cavalry in Culpeper, nothing is said about making a reconnaissance and getting information. As Pleasanton was defeated, he tried afterward to make it appear that the affair was only a reconnaissance; and that he got the information he wanted and voluntarily withdrew from the combat. It is strange that Southern writers should have been misled into putting the same construction upon Pleasanton's expedition. The object of a reconnaissance is not to fight, but to get information; whatever fighting is necessary is only an incident. An officer conducting a reconnaissance avoids fighting as much as possible. A sufficient force is applied to compel an enemy to develop his strength and position, but no more. When this has been accomplished the reconnoitering force retires even in the midst of a combat; which gives a reconnaissance in force even when successful the appearance of a defeat.[1]

Hooker thought he knew the location of every corps in Lee's army. He was not seeking information, he relied on spies for that; his instructions to Pleasanton did not order him to make reconnaissance, or ask for information. His telegram to Lincoln about his intended attack on Stuart's camps, and his orders to Pleasanton, do not mention any object except to break up what he thought was a contemplated raid, by dispersing the cavalry assembled in Culpeper. He told Pleasanton expressly that there was no infantry there; he knew that the cavalry was

---

[1] Voyle's Military dictionary says: — "Reconnaissances are made for the purpose of procuring information of the position and strength of the enemy. The commander of a reconnaissance ordinarily receives written instructions. [Pleasanton had written instructions to attack and drive Stuart back over the Rapidan.] He should well understand the object before him and demand such explanations as he may require. When the reconnaissance is finished, the commanding officer makes a written report to the general when his verbal account is not sufficient. . . . This kind of a reconnaissance is conducted by a general officer, who, at the head of a considerable force, marches towards the enemy, driving in his outposts, and forces him to discover his position."

there. Of course, he would not have sent Pleasanton to find out what he already knew. Pleasanton did, or rather tried to do, what he was ordered to do — he crossed the Rappahannock at Beverly Ford — drove in the pickets — moved forward until he ran unexpectedly into a strong force of cavalry and several batteries — halted — and then re-crossed the river on the same day. McDowell might as well have called his Bull Run campaign a reconnaissance. The Court-house, ten miles away, where he supposed Stuart's cavalry were camped, was his objective point; he had anticipated no serious resistance before he got there; and had arranged to unite at Brandy with Gregg's division that had crossed six miles below at Kelly's. The plan was for the united columns then to move on to the Court-house, attack the cavalry in their camps, and pursue them to the Rapidan. Gregg had detached Duffie's division after crossing the river to go to Stevensburg on his left and *join him at Culpeper*. Although Pleasanton crossed the river at daylight with Buford's division he never got within sight even of Brandy; Duffie only got as far as Stevensburg, where he met two cavalry regiments under Colonel Butler and Colonel Wickham. Gregg retreated when he got in seven miles of Culpeper Court-house. After a skirmish in which Colonel Butler (afterward a Senator from South Carolina) lost a leg, and Colonel Frank Hampton was killed, Duffie went home satisfied to be let alone. To cover up Pleasanton's defeat it was given out that he was only making a reconnaissance; that his expedition was a success, and that he voluntarily returned after accomplishing his purpose.—

Southern writers adopted this account as true. His instructions and report to Hooker had not then been published. They now appear in the War Records and contradict any such theory. He went after a fight. Its principal effect was to mislead the authorities at Washington, and was really the cause of Milroy's rout and disaster at Winchester. It was assumed at Washington that, if Longstreet and Ewell had been in Culpeper, Pleasanton would have found it out. He made no reference to it in his report to Hooker on the night he returned. He spoke of cars coming to Brandy with infantry to account for his retreat, but gave no estimate of the number, or where they came from. The story about a train load of infantry was a fiction. On the day after the combat, June 10, Ewell, who had been several days in Culpeper with his corps, started to the Valley. General Lee remained there with Longstreet several days longer. The cavalry was also kept in Culpeper to mask Ewell's movement and to conceal Longstreet. It had received no orders to cross the Rappahannock. If they had gone with Ewell it would have been notice to Milroy that a forward movement had begun. Jenkins' cavalry brigade was watching and waiting for Ewell on the Shenandoah. Milroy did not suspect any other force in his front.

No warning had been received from Washington. On the 13th he was surprised to find Ewell's corps surrounding him. No doubt Hooker was as much surprised as Milroy when on the 14th he got this dispatch from Mr. Lincoln: "Do you consider it possible that 15,000 of

Ewell's men can now be at Winchester?" Later in the day Stanton told him: "No doubt is entertained here that Milroy is surrounded at Winchester and so closely invested that no scout or other information has been had from him later than 11 o'clock Saturday night [13th]."

At 11 P.M., on June 9, when Stuart and Gregg were charging and counter-charging around Brandy, Hooker sent the following telegram to General Dix at Fortress Monroe, telling him the news that a spy had just brought him: "We have reliable information that Pickett's division, which was lately at Taylorsville, near Hanover Junction, has come up this way and gone towards the Rapidan. Hood's preceded it in the same direction. . . . Our scouts penetrated to Hanover Junction and we believe the above reliable from previously reported information concerning it and the character of the scouts." So it was a spy on June 9, and not Pleasanton, who informed Hooker that Pickett and Hood had gone toward the Rapidan.

This is Hooker's letter of instructions to Pleasanton; it was sent by a staff officer, Captain Eric Dahlgren:

CAMP NEAR FALMOUTH, VA.
June 7th, '63.

COMMANDING OFFICER CAVALRY CORPS : —

I am directed by the Major-General commanding to inform you as follows: Brigadier General Ames left here yesterday and Brigadier General Russell left to-day, and it is expected that their brigades, consisting [each] of 1500 men and a horse battery, will be in position to-morrow night. The latter marches with rations for three days and will require to be replenished before they cross the river from Bealeton. As they march without wagons, it will be advisable to have them sent to Kelley's ford in season to be distributed to-morrow night. Two boats have also been forwarded to facilitate the passage of the last named ford. As it is held by the enemy's pickets it may be advisable to throw over a small party above and below the ford to knock them away without resorting to artillery, as the first gun would be heard by the enemy at Culpeper [Court-house] and vicinity. From the most reliable information at these headquarters, it is recommended that you cross the Rappahannock at Beverly's and Kelley's fords and march directly to Culpeper [Court-house]. *For this you will divide your cavalry to carry into execution the object in view, which is to disperse and destroy the rebel force assembled in the vicinity of Culpeper and destroy its trains and supplies of all descriptions to the best of your ability.*

Shortly after crossing the two fords the routes you will be likely to take intersect, and the Major General commanding suggests that you keep your infantry force together, as in that condition it will afford you a moving *point d'Appui* to rally on at all times, which no cavalry force can be able to shake. *It is believed the enemy has no infantry.* Should you find this to be the case, by keeping your troops well in hand, you will be able to make head in any direction. The General recommends also that you make use of the forest and the cavalry to mask the movements of the infantry from the enemy's forces, and keep the enemy in ignorance of their presence as long as possible, in order that, at the proper time, you may be able to cut off and destroy great numbers of them. The General also suggests that you throw out strong pickets at Ely and Germanna fords, and that you hold Stevensburg with not less than a regiment and section of artillery, with special instructions to look after Raccoon ford [on the Rapidan]. All the fords on the Rappahannock below Kelley's ford and including it are held by our forces. If you should succeed in routing the enemy, the General desires that *you follow him vigorously as far as it may be to our advantage to do so.*

The officer in command [Barnes] holding Kelley's ford will be instructed to lend you such aid as may be in his power, and it is hoped will be able to throw out on the Culpeper road a sufficient force, in conjunction with your cavalry at Stevensburg, to secure your flank from any force in that direction. Captain Dahlgren, aide-de-camp, will deliver this to you, and it is desired that he will remain with you until you cross the river and that you communicate with headquarters as often as is practicable. He will hand you some maps of the direction in which you are operating. Have received no word from Washington as to the force [Stahel's] to be sent to your assistance from General Heintzelman's command; you will not be able to count on any assistance from there.

Very Respectfully,
DANIEL BUTTERFIELD.
Major-General Chief of Staff.

These instructions contain no hint or suggestion of making a reconnaissance. If Hooker had wanted Pleasanton to find out if Lee had taken one or two army corps to Culpeper, he would have told him so. *On the contrary, Pleasanton was told that there was no infantry there.* He speaks of the road to Culpeper on which Pleasanton would go after crossing the Rappahannock. As he would be in Culpeper County as soon as he got over the river, this clearly refers to the road to the Court-house.

Pleasanton's instructions show that Hooker did not suspect that Ewell and Longstreet were in Culpeper County, or that Stuart's camps and headquarters were so near the river. At 2 P.M. on the 7th, Pleasanton sent a dispatch to Hooker, saying: "The enemy have an idea that our army is to advance by the railroad, and the Rapidan is to be their line of defense. This comes from the country people. Culpeper County is the best grazing in Virginia and they use it for their animals. Its loss will be a great one to the rebels."

This letter is the key to the operations on the 9th; the intention was to drive the Confederate cavalry from their grazing ground in Culpeper and break up a raid. Barnes' division of the Fifth Corps was at Kelly's. Two infantry brigades were to accompany Pleasanton. They were told that they would be absent from camp four or five days — "rations in haversacks, empty knapsacks, one blanket and 150 rounds of ammunition to be carried on pack mules and on the person. The pack mules, to transport the ammunition and the shelter tents of the officers, should come from reserve mules supplied by the Chief-Quarter-Master for contingent uses, to avoid, if possible, taking any from the wagon-trains. Pack-masters, ambulance attendants, etc., should accompany the detachment so that its effective fighting force may not be less than that indicated above." Such preparations do not look like it was expected that these troops would cross the Rappahannock in the morning and return in the evening — march up a hill and then march down again. As before stated, Pleasanton, in person, at daylight on the morning of the 9th, with Buford's cavalry division, supported by Ames' infantry brigade, crossed the Rappahannock at Beverly Ford, while Gregg, with his own and Duffie's cavalry divisions, and Russell's infantry brigade, crossed six miles below at Kelly's. They had marched during the night from their camps at Bealeton and Warrenton Junction. General Lee and Stuart knew that Hooker's cavalry had moved their camps to Fauquier two weeks before and that their outposts were on the Rappahannock. There was a heavy fog on the river that morning that favored the operation. All the fords were picketed on the Southern bank; Captain Gibson's company of the Sixth Virginia Cavalry was at Beverly's Ford and gallantly contested the crossing. The column was led by the Eighth New York Cavalry; it was commanded by Colonel "Grimes" Davis, a Mississippian, and a West Point graduate. He fell soon after he reached the opposite bank of the river. Jones' cavalry brigade, with Beckham's four batteries of horse artillery, was camped a mile and a half from the ford. For some reason, the artillery camp was between the cavalry and the river. Stuart's headquarters were four miles away — near Brandy.

Jones was a graduate of West Point and was regarded as the best outpost officer in the army.[1] He had resigned from the United States army and was captain of the company in which I was a private the first year of the war. The camps were aroused by the firing at the ford; there was saddling and mounting in hot haste. It is said that many of Jones' men rode bareback in the charge, and that Jones led them without coat or boots on. Jones' and Beckham's accounts give a vivid description of the engagement. While Jones with two regiments was holding the enemy in check, Beckham was hitching the horses to his guns, and removing them back a few hundred yards to a hill near St. James' Church. One of the guns was drawn by hand into the road; it opened fire and stopped the advance of the enemy's column. This was a great surprise to Pleasanton; he had expected to find only a few pickets on the river, and to go on and meet Gregg at Brandy; and to be at the Court-house before noon. In what appeared to be a desperate situation both Jones and Beckham displayed the self-command and courage of Cæsar, when his camp was surprised by the Nervii. Jones says:

"At daylight the report of small arms in the direction of Beverly Ford indicated a serious attack. Knowing the

[1] Jones was killed in 1864.

park of division artillery was without other protection than the pickets in front, its safety was doubtful. The Sixth Virginia Cavalry was on picket at the time and the Seventh Virginia was grand guard. Going to the scene of action at top speed, the Sixth and Seventh regiments were found rapidly approaching the position of the enemy, only a few hundred yards beyond the artillery.

"The batteries being neither ready for action nor movement, it was a matter of the utmost importance to gain time. Major Flournoy, in command of the Sixth, was ordered down the Beverly road and to its right, and Colonel Marshall on his left. Both were directed to attack with vigor whatever force they encountered. At the same time directions were sent to the artillery to withdraw as quickly as practical from the edge of the woods. The cavalry did its work well, but with considerable sacrifice. The artillery took position near the brick church. Captain W. K. Martin, Assistant-Adjutant-General, having ordered up the Eleventh and Twelfth regiments, and the Thirty-Third Virginia cavalry, they were posted in support of the artillery. When the Sixth and Seventh regiments could no longer withstand greatly superior numbers of footmen in the woods, they retired right and left of the position held by the remainder of the brigade. By this time the enemy had penetrated through the woods, showing himself in some force in the open ground. A little shelling having caused a withdrawal, an attack was deemed expedient. Colonel Harman leading with his regiment [Twelfth Virginia], moved along the road, supported on the left by the Thirty-Fifth Battalion [Colonel E. V.

White] and the Eleventh Regiment [Colonel Lomax]. As the head of Colonel Harman's regiment reached the woods, it received a severe fire and was immediately charged by cavalry. The prompt arrival of supports soon turned the tide of battle in our favor. The enemy lost here very considerably in killed and wounded, and heavily in prisoners.

"About this time General Hampton [arrived] and took position on my right [from his camp near Brandy], and General W. H. F. Lee [who had camped near Wellford's Ford on Hazel River] notified me he was on my left. He was requested to keep up connection with me, which for some time was done, our line making a right angle at the Junction. The enemy now made his appearance in our rear at Brandy Station and Miller's house. This was the force [Gregg's] which early in the day was reported by Captain Grimsley through me to General Stuart as advancing from Kellysville.[1] . . . My brigade bore the brunt

[1] CULPEPER, VA.
February 16, 1907.

Colonel JOHN S. MOSBY,
    Washington, D. C.

DEAR SIR:—On the 9th of June, 1863, when the Battle at Brandy Station was fought, I was Captain of Company B, Sixth Virginia Cavalry, Jones' Brigade.

This command had recently come from the Shenandoah Valley to Culpeper, reaching the latter place on or about the 7th of June. After the Cavalry Review on the 8th, Jones' Command, with Beckham's Battalion of Artillery, went into camp near St. James' Church, picketing the Rappahannock River for a few miles in its front. On the night of the eighth, Company 'A' (Captain Gibson), of the Sixth Regiment, was on picket at Beverly's Ford, Company 'B' at the Rappahannock

Bridge (not then destroyed), and the ford immediately below. Some time during the night, the picket at the bridge notified me that he could hear the movement of troops on the north side of the river. I went down to the bridge and lying down on the track with my ear to the rail could hear distinctly horses passing over the railroad on the north side, and the 'cluck' of the artillery wheels as they came in contact with the rails. I immediately sent a courier to General Jones informing him of this fact. I do not recall exactly the time of night this occurred, but I apprehend it was but a short while before daybreak. The enemy crossed at Beverly's Ford about day light, and the battle was on. I threw out a line of videttes communicating with the field of battle and sent out scouts towards Kelley's Ford, who shortly reported the enemy crossing in large force at that point, and I so informed General Jones.

General Robertson, with his North Carolina Brigade was sent in the early morning towards Kelley's Ford, by way of Elkwood, and after he had passed me, I ceased to look to the condition of affairs in that direction.

From Culpeper to Brandy is about six miles, from Brandy to Fleetwood Heights is about one mile, and to Beverly's Ford and Rappahannock Bridge about four miles. From Brandy to Stevensburg is about three and a half miles southeast. Rappahannock Bridge is about two miles below Beverly's Ford, and about five miles above Kelley's Ford. From Jones' Camp at St. James' Church to Beverly's Ford is about one and a half miles, a large body of woods intervening. The picket firing at Beverly's was distinctly heard in Jones' Camp, as well as by me at Rappahannock Bridge. I could also hear the firing at Kelley's Ford.

Company 'A' (Captain Gibson), resisted the advance of the enemy from Beverly's with great persistency and gallantry, and the 6th and 7th Regiments (the latter, the Grand Guard), of Jones' Brigade, were soon mounted and hurled against the advancing columns of the enemy in the woods, and checked their advance. Beckham's Artillery Camp was near that of Jones', and his guns were brought immediately into action, one of them being put in position by hand and brought into action before the horses were harnessed and hitched up. They were finally put in position on the ridge in front of and to the right of the church. Hampton's Brigade coming up on the right of Jones' and William F. H. Lee's on the left, the battle was joined with great fury, and Buford was held in the woods as if in a vice, although he made repeated efforts to advance therefrom, apparently bringing into action his entire force, infantry as well as cavalry. The day thus far was with the Confederates. Buford had been foiled and defeated, and would have been driven pell mell across the river but for the appearance of Gregg at Fleetwood Hills, near Brandy Station, who had eluded Robertson, and passing by his right flank, reached the latter point.

You will observe from the map accompanying Stuart's report, that two roads led from Brandy to Kelley's Ford, one by way of Elkwood, nearer the river, and the other, the more direct, from Brandy to Kelley's Ford. These roads at the farthest points are distant one from the other about one and a half or two miles. You will also observe from the same map, and from Robertson's reports, that he met the enemy at or near Brown, laid down on the map, about two miles south of Kelley's Ford, and from the same map and reports it will be observed that Gregg, taking the more direct route, passed to the right of Robertson, and reached Brandy Station in his rear.

Gregg was, however, soon driven from Fleetwood and Brandy, where a fierce conflict took place between his command and that of Jones and Hampton, and swinging around to the east and north joined on to Buford, near St. James' Church, where the entire Federal force was united. After the union of the enemy's forces, and the re-arrangement of our lines, an ineffectual effort was made by General Merritt, with his brigade of regulars, to turn our left on the road from Brandy to Wellfords, but this movement was met by the 9th and 10th regiments of William H. F. Lee's and the 6th regiment of Jones' brigade, and effectually checked, and Merritt's command was driven in confusion from this part of the field. The enemy began then their retrograde movement, and re-crossed the river. Fitz Lee's brigade encamped the night before near Oak Shade, some seven miles north of Brandy, and did not reach the field in time to take part to any extent in the action.

General R. E. Lee reached the battle-field some time during the day, and in the evening occupied the Barbour House, situated on an elevation, about one mile west of Brandy, from which point he had a plain view of the battle-field. His Headquarters at this time were at Eastern View, three quarters of a mile east of the town of Culpeper. Ewell's Corps was in Culpeper County. His advance division (Rhodes') was encamped at Chestnut Fork, about two and a half miles north of Culpeper, and his other two divisions, nearer the town, on the Sperryville turnpike.

Two divisions of Longstreet's corps (Hood's and McLaw's), were encamped on the road between Raccoon Ford on the Rapidan River, about sixteen miles above its confluence with the Rappahannock River, and the Town of Culpeper, on the west side of Mt. Pony. Mt. Pony is about two and a half miles from Culpeper, and extends south some two or three miles towards the Rapidan River. I have been unable to identify the particular locality of the encampments of these two divisions. I am satisfied no train came from Culpeper towards Brandy on this occasion with infantry aboard. Rhodes' division of Ewell's corps left its encampment at Chestnut Fork and, marching across the country, in the direction of Brandy Station, reached the Botts farm, about two miles southwest of Brandy, but following the line of depression along Jonas' Run were concealed from view at Brandy. On our side this was a battle of the cavalry alone; on the Federal side both infantry and cavalry.

Yours very truly,
Dan'l S. Grimsley.

P. S. — Excuse delay in answering your letter, but I have been so much engaged lately I have not really had time. I hope this covers all points of your inquiry.

D. S. G.

of the action both in the morning and evening and lost severely in killed and wounded, but had the satisfaction of seeing the enemy worsted in every particular more than ourselves. We ended the fight with more horses and more and better firearms than we had in the morning. We took two regimental colors, many guidons, and a battery of three pieces."

Major Beckham reports:

"I have the honor to report that on the morning of June 9 four companies of the horse artillery were encamped on the Beverly Ford road about one and a half miles from the river. The Fifth Company [Breathed's] had been detached and was at this time higher up the river with General W. H. F. Lee's command. [Lee's brigade was near Wellford's ford on the Hazel River not far from its junction with the Rappahannock River.] Just before sunrise I received information to the effect that our pickets had been driven in and that the enemy was advancing in large force. I immediately directed Captain Hart to place one piece by hand in the road, and ordered others to be hitched up as promptly as possible and take position on the high ground about 600 or 700 yards south of the camp. The enemy approached rapidly and boldly, and had it not been for the delay of a few minutes caused him by the arrival of a regiment under General Jones, it is more than probable that we would have been compelled to abandon the pieces. As it was, several of the horses were wounded before we could move camp.

"The position first taken was just opposite St. James Church on the east of the road. This was held with ease against the enemy's columns for two hours or more; and could, I think, have been held all day had not the appearance of the enemy in our rear rendered it necessary to abandon this point in order to regain Pettis Hill [Fleetwood], which the enemy had occupied with his cavalry. In this first position taken up three of the pieces had become disabled from the shock of the recoil; one had been detached with Colonel Butler on the Stevensburg road; two were on the Kellysville road, and two had been placed by order of the major-general commanding on Pettis Hill. This left only five pieces, now nearly exhausted, of ammunition within reach to be brought into action. Three of these by General Stuart's order were left with General

Jones, and the remaining two [McGregor's] were moved to the rear to assist in driving the enemy from the position north of Brandy. Captain Hart also succeeded in getting into position one of the guns whose carriage had already been greatly damaged, and fortunately succeeded in firing two or three effective shots before the carriage was completely disabled. The pieces first placed on Pettis Hill were under command of Lieutenant [Tuck] Carter, of Chew's battery, and had been repeatedly charged by the enemy and re-taken by our cavalry, and at the time that the two guns were brought towards the crest of the hill, it was very doubtful which party had possession of it. The guns, however, moved off rapidly, and scarcely had they reached the top, and before they could be put into position, a small party of the enemy charged them. The charge was met by the cannoneers of the pieces. Lieutenant Ford killed one of the enemy with his pistol; Lieutenant Hoxton killed another, and private Sully [Sudley] of McGregor's battery, knocked one off his horse with a sponge staff. Several of the party were taken prisoners by the men at the guns. Fire was then opened from these guns upon the enemy towards Brandy Station, and soon afterwards I was enabled to get together the guns which had been sent on the Kellysville road, or left with General Jones, and to place them in position for clearing the plain about the hill, firing slowly until the enemy had re-crossed the river and I received an order to withdraw. During all the morning the firing had been quite regular, but not very rapid, and in the first position directed nearly all the time at the skirmishers of the enemy and the masses concealed in the woods. I was not able to judge positively of the effect of the firing owing to the covered ground the enemy occupied, he rarely showing more than his line of sharpshooters. However, I learn since that a large number of horses were left dead in the woods, and no doubt he suffered severely in men also. The firing done in regaining Pettis Hill was very accurate and powerful in its results, scattering the columns of the enemy advancing to the charge. Captain Breathed, whose battery was with General W. H. F. Lee, in the vicinity of Freeman's Ford, reports that about 8 P.M., of the 7th instant, one section, under Lieutenant Johnston, crossed the Hazel River and took position guarding the road leading from Beverly towards Wellford Ford; the other section was near Starke's Ford." There is no explanation of the artillery being placed between the cavalry camps and the ford.

Beckham was a West Pointer and a fine officer. When Pelham was killed a few months before and on the same field as the fight of June 9, he succeeded him in command of the horse artillery.[1]

Stuart's headquarters were at Fleetwood, half a mile from Brandy Station and between the latter place and the Rappahannock. He was apprised early in the morning by the picket firing that the enemy were crossing the river at two fords. He promptly disposed his forces to meet them. Hampton's and W. H. F. Lee's brigades were ordered toward Beverly to support Jones; Robertson's brigade and a battery were sent on the road to Kelly's to hold in check the column advancing from that direction.

[1] Beckham was killed in 1864.

Robertson had sufficient force to do it. Everything at headquarters was packed up and sent off with the wagons of the division to the Court-house. Stuart then went at full speed to take command of the troops on the field near St. James' Church, that were holding back Buford's division in the woods. He found Pleasanton already on the defensive. Pleasanton's dispatches from the field betray his surprise at the strong force he had met at the crossing, and his despair of overcoming it. He was evidently alarmed about the possibility of Stuart's getting in his rear and cutting him off by crossing at a ford above him.

PLEASANTON TO STAHEL, KETTLE RUN

BEVERLY FORD, June 9th, 1863.

The enemy has his whole cavalry force here, and I have had a severe fight. He may try to cross above me before Gregg joins from below.

Gregg joined Buford on the Rappahannock on the retreat that evening. Pleasanton and Gregg were moving from different bases in two widely separated columns that were not in communication with each other. Such a movement is called a double line of operations. It is always hazardous when the point of concentration is in the presence of an enemy. It gives him an opportunity to attack and destroy the separate forces before the combination can be effected. It proved to be so in this case. Buford's and Gregg's divisions were marching on roads so far apart that there could be no co-operation between them. Stuart's cavalry had the interior line and had this advantage. The lines of the two columns converged on Brandy Station.

The plan was for them to unite at that point and then go on to Culpeper Court-house. They would have had to pass through Stuart's camps to get there. At that place they expected to join Duffie's division, which Gregg had detached after crossing at Kelly's to go by Stevensburg. Stuart with the inspiration of genius did exactly what Bonaparte did when he discovered the Austrians surrounding him at Rivoli.[1]

[1] Napoleon always regarded Rivoli as one of his masterpieces in both strategy and tactics. In his dying hour at St. Helena he handed his watch to Count Bertrand, saying, "It struck two in the morning when I ordered Joubert to attack at Rivoli." Colonel Sargent in his "Napoleon Bonaparte's First Campaigns" in Italy says: "By these dispositions Alvinzie expected to surround the French and by making simultaneous attacks upon their front and both flanks, to overwhelm and crush them. On January 13, these fractions of Alvinzie's army were marching towards Rivoli. They camped that night in sight of the battle-field. . . .

"During the night while the Austrians were sleeping, Joubert was returning to occupy the plateau, Massena and Rey were hurrying forward, and Bonaparte himself, having pushed ahead of Massena's column, was riding rapidly toward Rivoli. He arrived there after midnight; he saw the lights from the Sixth Austrian corps; he saw that Alvinzie had separated his columns by impassable obstacles; and he saw that if he could collect his own forces and hold the plateau, he could probably prevent the Austrian columns from arriving simultaneously upon the battle-field, and by so doing he could defeat them in detail. In his front were twenty-eight thousand Austrians; he had only Joubert's division of ten thousand; but Massena would soon bring eight thousand more upon the battle-field, and perhaps Rey might arrive with his four thousand in time to take a part in the struggle. At once Bonaparte began to arrange the troops and artillery for battle. Early in the morning Joubert advanced; the Austrians in his front having no artillery, he succeeded in driving them back, and by directing part of his artillery upon Quasdanovich's column, he held it in check. But the Austrians soon rallied; the fighting became desperate. An Austrian column attacked furiously the French left and succeeded in turning it. Bonaparte himself re-

He struck Buford in the morning a stunning blow that sent him reeling back toward the river and stopped him; then turned and concentrated his force against Gregg at Brandy and drove him back to the Rappahannock. Pleasanton's separated columns were thus beaten in detail. After a skirmish at Stevensburg with the Fourth Virginia and the First South Carolina Cavalry, Duffie was called off by Gregg to support him at Brandy. He started but found Gregg on the road retreating. Pleasanton's telegram to Hooker from the field shows that he had lost heart, was beaten early in the morning, and that his enterprise was a failure.

PLEASANTON TO HOOKER

BEVERLY FORD, June 9th, 1863.

The enemy is in strong cavalry force here. We had a severe fight. *They were aware of our movement and prepared.* [Italics mine.]

arranged his shattered left, then hurried to the town of Rivoli to bring up Massena's division which had just arrived there. These troops were hurried forward and Massena hurled them against the Austrian right, drove it back and succeeded in re-establishing the French left. But the French right was hotly engaged. Quasdanovich, after hard fighting, had overcome the resistance in his front and was urging his column up the winding road to the battle-field. Already his advance troops were deploying on the plateau. Lusignon, too, could be seen in the distance deploying in Bonaparte's rear. In fact Bonaparte was surrounded; twenty-eight thousand Austrians were advancing upon him. He had but eighteen thousand soldiers. For a moment success seemed impossible, defeat inevitable; but his clear eye took in the whole field; he saw that none of the Austrians columns had yet united; he saw at a glance where the blow must be struck in order to turn disaster into victory, and with remarkable coolness he gathered his troops and prepared to throw them in succession against the several Austrian columns. . . . On all sides the Austrians were defeated. Alvinzie's army was almost destroyed."

It is clear that Pleasanton was more surprised than the Confederates were. He had not then gone a mile from the river; he stayed where he was nearly all day. It was the commanding ability of Stuart that "from the nettle danger plucked the flower safety," and won the battle of Brandy. There were many able officers under him, but as a distinguished writer, Colonel Dodge, says of Napoleon, "Every captain owes much to his lieutenants. But the creative force which fashions an army, or an engine, as well as the motive power which drives either, have their origin in the heart and head of the chief: both depend on him. The engine has a driver, every division must have a lieutenant, but the role of each is subordinate."

BUTTERFIELD, CHIEF OF STAFF TO PLEASANTON
BEVERLY FORD,
June 9th, 1863, 12.10 P.M.

Dispatch 7.40 received. If you cannot make head against the force in front of you, return and take your position on the north bank of the river and defend it. At this distance it is impossible for the General [Hooker] to understand your circumstances. Exercise your best judgment and the General will be satisfied.

Which shows that Hooker, too, was in despair; he sent this telegram to Halleck:

June 9th, 1863, 12 M.

Brigadier-General Pleasanton reports that after an encounter with the rebel cavalry over the Beverly Ford, he has not been able to make head against it. *He reports that his movement was anticipated.* [Italics mine.]

At 12 M. Pleasanton, still near Beverly Ford, asks Hooker to reinforce him with infantry. He says, "For fear the enemy should receive reinforcements during the night, had you better not order 1000 of the Fifth Corps to Brandy Station?" If he had then supposed that Longstreet and Ewell were in Culpeper he would not have asked Hooker to send 1000 infantry to meet them. He thought that reinforcements might be brought to Stuart by rail from a distance. On June 11 he told Hooker, "I am informed the enemy can bring troops by railroad from Gordonsville to Brandy Station in two hours. They can also send infantry by rail from Fredericksburg in from six to eight hours." At 2.40 P.M., on the 9th, when Gregg was fighting at Brandy, and when he did not pretend that he had heard of any Confederate infantry in Culpeper, Pleasanton tells Stahel, who was at Kettle Run, "I will re-cross this P.M., I send my trains to Bealeton. Please give them protection." Bealeton is five or six miles from Beverly. Who ever heard of taking a wagon train on a scout? Earlier in the day he said to Stahel, "Please send some cars down this side of Bealeton for our wounded. Have crossed. Enemy in some force of cavalry."

If he had expected to have a fight so near camp he would have provided transportation for his wounded before he started, unless he expected to hold Culpeper County. But Meade did not, as requested, send the 1000 infantry to Brandy, because Pleasanton returned. He said to Barnes, "The order to hold 1000 men in readiness to move and supply their places from the reserve was based on the supposition that General Pleasanton was at Brandy Station and might require them. His return has done away with this exigency." Stuart arrived on the field at St. James' Church after Buford had been repulsed, and was about taking the offensive to drive him over the river when the surprising news came that Gregg had passed Robertson and was approaching his rear at Brandy Station without opposition. Leaving W. H. F. Lee's brigade, which was on Buford's flank, to hold him in check, Stuart, with Jones, Hampton, and the artillery, went a gallop to Brandy. Munford's brigade, which was on the other side of Hazel River, was expected on the field every minute. His delay in not arriving earlier had been caused, it is said, by ambiguous orders.

Stuart arrived in time to meet Gregg, drive him off, and capture his guns; but in the open plain around Brandy there was probably the fiercest mounted combat of the war — in fact of any war. Gregg's battery was captured and re-captured several times. First by Colonel Elijah White, who was overpowered and driven away, and finally Lomax, with the Eleventh Virginia Cavalry, swept the field, took the guns and held them.[1]

---

[1] Captain Martin, who commanded the Sixth New York battery, in his report says: "Immediately on arriving at the position where Lieutenant Clark was engaged with his remaining pieces, I formed the section on his right and immediately commenced firing at the house which I before mentioned as having been occupied by General Stuart as his headquarters, and which was completely surrounded by a dense mass of the enemy's cavalry. Almost simultaneously the enemy commenced their attack by repeated charges on the guns, but it was not until they had been twice repulsed that their efforts were successful, and I am confident that even then they would have been discomfited had their final charge not been made almost simultaneously front and rear. It took but one of canister shot from each piece to repulse their charges, and could I have reversed my pieces in sufficient time on their last effort to have

Stuart ought to have been surprised to hear that Gregg was in his rear, and at first he would not believe it. When firing was heard at Kelly's early in the morning, he had ordered Robertson to go with his brigade and some guns on that road and hold in check any force of the enemy he might meet. His plan was first to concentrate against Buford; drive him over the river, and then turn on Gregg. In some way Robertson seems to have gotten lost; he allowed Gregg's column to pass unmolested in Stuart's rear to Brandy. Robertson reports: "Although in sight of the enemy for several hours and exposed to the fire of his artillery, my command was not at any time actively engaged. With the exception of four horses mortally wounded or totally disabled, I have no casualties to report." Robertson and Gregg seem to have taken different roads both in the morning and evening and so they missed each other. As parallel lines meet in infinity there might have been a collision between them if the fight had lasted long enough. Stuart at Beverly's Ford was now in the same position that Lee was in at Chancellorsville when

given them a round before they were in the battery, they should never have taken the guns. Once in the battery it became a hand-to-hand fight with pistol and sabre between the enemy and my cannoneers and drivers, and never did men act with more coolness and bravery and show more of a stern purpose to do their duty unflinchingly and, above all, save their guns; and while the loss of them is a matter of great regret to me, it is a consolation, and great satisfaction, to know I can point with pride to the fact that of that little band who defended the battery, not one of them flinched for a moment from his duty. Of the 36 men I took into the engagement but 6 came out safely, and of these 30, 21 were either killed, wounded or missing, and scarcely one of them but will carry the honorable mark of the sabre or the bullet to his grave."

the surprising news came that Sedgwick was moving up the plank road in his rear, and that Early had retreated on the Bowling Green road toward Richmond. Lee suspended the attack he was making on Hooker who was cooped up on the river, and moved back against Sedgwick. Stuart left a small force in front of Pleasanton to hold him in check and then concentrated on Gregg. General Gregg says in his report: "that after hearing from Pleasanton of the severity of his engagement with a superior force at Beverly's, he determined to recall Duffie from Stevensburg and direct him to join him at Brandy." When the head of the Third division arrived near Brandy Station, Gregg says, "It was discovered that the enemy were in great force." He was disappointed that Buford's command did not join him at Brandy; no doubt that was his reason for recalling Duffie. Evidently he had not calculated on meeting anything but a picket there. Of the fight around Brandy, Gregg says: "Thus for an hour and a half was the contest continued, not in skirmishing, but in continued charges. The contest was too unequal to be long continued. The second division [Duffie's] had not come up; there was no support, and the enemy's numbers were three times my own. I ordered the withdrawal of my brigades. In good order they left the field, the enemy not choosing to follow." Duffie says that while he was engaged at Stevensburg he received an order from Gregg to move to his support. He started, but met Gregg's division going back and covered its retreat. After stating that he ordered a retreat because he was greatly outnumbered by Stuart's cavalry, General Gregg says, "When engaged with the enemy at Brandy Station, cars loaded with infantry were brought from Culpeper."

No other report on either side speaks of cars with infantry coming to Brandy that day; *and none came.* Neither Wyndham or Kilpatrick, who commanded Gregg's two brigades and fought around the station, speaks of seeing any infantry. Wyndham says: "Observing the enemy breaking away on the left, I ordered a portion of the First Maryland Cavalry, led by Major Russell, to charge the Station, which they did in fine style, capturing a number of the enemy and bringing away an ambulance and four horses captured by our advance guard. . . . My command being now much scattered by the charges it had made, Colonel Duffie not coming to my support as I expected, and seeing that the enemy was strongly reinforced, I was compelled to withdraw."

If Wyndham and Kilpatrick had seen a train-load of infantry coming up they would have been glad to have given it as a reason for their retreating. As General Gregg had Russell's brigade of infantry in supporting distance, why did he not order it to attack this infantry, instead of leaving the field? If he was making a reconnaissance he ought to have compelled the force to at least deploy and display its strength. It might be only an isolated train-guard. The last charge that drove the enemy from Brandy Station was made by Colonel Lomax with his regiment, the Eleventh Virginia Cavalry. His report says: "Observing a force of the enemy at Brandy Station, I moved towards that point and found three regiments of cavalry under Sir Percy Wyndham plundering and destroying the property there. I charged and drove them from the station, taking a stand of colors, and many privates (amongst them a colonel), and pursued them some distance on the Stevensburg road. This ended the fight at Brandy." Lomax says nothing about any infantry being there.

Colonel Newhall, who was an aide to Pleasanton and on the field that day, in an article in the *Philadelphia Times* of November 10, 1877, says: "Culpeper Courthouse is some ten miles south of the river, and there was no expectation on General Pleasanton's part of encountering Stuart's troopers when crossing the fords of the Rappahannock. General Pleasanton having no reason to suspect the presence of the enemy in force this side of Culpeper Court-house, his plan contemplated a movement of at least two columns on Brandy Station, an intermediate point on the Orange and Alexandria railroad between Culpeper and the Rappahannock. The Orange and Alexandria railroad crosses the river at Rappahannock Station. Beverly Ford is, perhaps a mile above, and for the purpose of his reconnaissance General Pleasanton determined to pass his troops over both these fords. The consequences of this plan proved to be to some extent unfortunate, because when the river was crossed on the morning of the 9th, and the troops became engaged, the operations of the widely severed connections were independent of each other and could not at that distance, and in a wooded and irregular country, be brought promptly into harmony. . . . Be it as it may, General Pleasanton was destined to reap some of the occasional disadvantages of a broken military chain. The force dispatched to Kelley's Ford was composed of Gregg's and Duffie's cavalry and a small brigade of infantry, perhaps 1500 men, commanded by the gallant General David Russell, who was subsequently killed in the battle of the Opequon in the Shenandoah Valley. The force to cross at Beverly Ford was accompanied by General Pleasanton in person, and was composed of Buford's cavalry and a small brigade of infantry commanded by General Adelbert Ames [afterwards distinguished in leading the assault on Fort Fisher, and notorious later as the carpet-bag Governor of Mississippi]. To effect the contemplated junction near Brandy Station, the Beverly Ford column would bear to the left, the Kelley's Ford column to the right—the Orange and Alexandria railroad lying between them as they marched. As an aide-de-camp to General Pleasanton it was my fortune to be thrown with the Beverly Ford column, and all that I saw of what occurred after the crossing of the river on the morning of the 9th was connected with the operations of the right. . . . There was no word yet of the Kelley's Ford column and our progress towards Brandy Station had been greatly delayed; but nothing could be done to get on faster until our right was relieved of the pressure of the enemy towards Beverly Ford. . . . Leaving General Buford to push on as rapidly as possible, General Pleasanton now rode to St. James' Church where all was quiet with no enemy in sight. Towards Brandy Station [which was two or three miles away] a high hill confronted us, shutting off all view in that direction; but Buford's success now made it possible to resume the march, which was about to be done when General Gregg rode into our lines from the left, reporting the results of the Kelley's Ford column as far as he was aware of them. . . . Before reaching Brandy Station, General Duffie had turned to the left, hoping to accomplish something in the enemy's rear. . . .

"General Gregg had advanced directly upon Brandy Station without opposition, and thence to Fleetwood Hill, where Stuart made hasty preparations to receive him. Fleetwood is a ridge of ground half a mile from Brandy Station towards the Rappahannock and west of the railroad. St. James' Church is on the river side of the hill and General Buford was working his way up to it from that side also; hence, while the Beverly Ford column was approaching it from one side, Gregg had been moving on it from the other, neither column having knowledge of the other's movements, whereby Stuart escaped the consequences supposed to arise from being between two fires . . . Gregg gained this hill and the house that surmounted it, and a fierce fight was brought on with charges and counter-charges, at the end of which Gregg found himself over-matched and withdrew to the lower ground, losing, as he fell back, three pieces of artillery after a desperate effort to save them, as Major McClellan [Stuart's staff officer] says. . . . It was after his own repulse that he was rejoined by Colonel Duffie, and meantime the enemy were pouring infantry into Brandy Station by railroad from Culpeper Court-house [a pure invention], introducing a new and not unexpected element to General Pleasanton's consideration. When Gregg reported all this to General

Pleasanton at St. James' Church, all that was necessary to the purpose of General Hooker had been accomplished; the information required had been secured with unmistakable accuracy from personal observation and from the official documents captured on the field as related by Major McClellan." Pleasanton had told Stahel some hours before he met Gregg that he would re-cross that evening.

Buford and Gregg had both been successively repulsed; they had found out they could go no further; therefore they went back — that was all. Major McClellan in his Life and Campaigns of Stuart says: "There are two points in connection with this battle which, although proven incorrect, have been persistently repeated. It is asserted that General Stuart's headquarters, his baggage and his papers, were captured; that Confederate infantry was seen debarking from the cars in the vicinity of Brandy Station while the fight with Gregg's division was in progress. As regards the asserted capture of Stuart's baggage and papers, it is to be noticed that no official report on the Federal side makes any such claim; and it cannot be supposed that so important a fact would have passed without notice had it occurred. . . . If necessary, the testimony of every surviving officer of Stuart's staff can be produced showing that long hours before Gregg's attack on the Fleetwood Hill all of the headquarters wagons had been sent to Culpeper Court-house. The assertion that Confederate infantry was seen debarking from the cars in the vicinity of Brandy Station has no better foundation. If any such papers had been captured, Pleasanton would have sent them to Hooker and they would have been published." Colonel Newhall speaks of Pleasanton's advance to St. James' Church late in the day as if it were owing to the Confederates being defeated. This was the position held by Jones' brigade and Beckham's artillery in the morning. When Pleasanton reached it no enemy was there; Colonel Newhall omits to give the reason why; he leaves it to be inferred that Buford had driven the Confederate cavalry away. It is true that Stuart had left; he had withdrawn his guns and all his cavalry, except W. H. F. Lee's brigade, to meet Gregg at Brandy Station. He had thought the containing force he had sent under Robertson toward Kelley's Ford would hold Gregg in check — Napoleon thought the same of Grouchy at Waterloo. W. H. F. Lee's brigade was pressing on Buford's flank and threatening his rear; Munford with a brigade was just coming up. Pleasanton became alarmed; he was afraid that Lee and Munford would get between him and the ford. It was for this reason that he sent Stahel the dispatch I have quoted about the enemy crossing the river above and intercepting him. Stahel construed it as a cry for help, and replied: "Your telegram, 2.40 P.M., has just been received and I will comply with your request at once. Colonel Mann is already moving up." This dispatch shows that Pleasanton was looking with more anxiety to his rear than to his front.

Colonel Newhall claims that this was a *reconnaissance in force* to ascertain if Lee was moving across the Blue Ridge to the Shenandoah Valley; and that it was then known that a part of his army was in motion in a "dangerous direction," and that Stuart's cavalry was in Culpeper. If that was Pleasanton's object his expedition was worse than a failure, it was a great blunder. When Colonel Newhall was writing he had an *ex post facto* knowledge of the position of each corps of Lee's army that day; but neither Hooker, Halleck, Milroy, or Pleasanton had even a suspicion on June 9 that Lee was then at Culpeper with the corps of Longstreet and Ewell; or that a blow was meditated in the Shenandoah Valley. *Pleasanton was not even instructed to inquire about them.* All that Pleasanton claimed in his dispatch that he had done was that he had so crippled Stuart that he could not go on his raid. Stuart had no intention of going on a raid. Pleasanton was simply ordered to attack and break up Stuart's camps in Culpeper to prevent a cavalry raid. If Pleasanton learned anything of importance on his so-called reconnaissance, why was it not communicated to Milroy so that he could pack up and leave?

If what Colonel Newhall says about the information Pleasanton got is true, then Milroy was the victim of Stanton and Hooker, and was placed under arrest for other people's sins. Milroy's report says that on June 12 he sent out from Winchester a reconnoitering force on the Front Royal pike. It met the advance of Ewell's corps at Cedarville, and had a skirmish. Milroy was only looking out for a cavalry raid against which he had been warned; he had no reason to be looking for anything more. He discredited the report of the commanding officer that he had encountered a large force; he thought it was only some of the forces that had been a long time in the Valley. He says: "The reconnaissance on the Front Royal road was abortive. The expedition consisted of the Twelfth Pennsylvania Cavalry, about 400 strong, under command of Lieutenant-Colonel Moss. It returned to Winchester about three o'clock in the afternoon on Friday. Its commanding officer reported that at Cedarville, a place about twelve miles from Winchester, he encountered a large force of the enemy composed of cavalry, infantry, and artillery. It did not appear, however, that he had placed himself in a position to ascertain the number and character of the force which he had encountered, or exercised the usual necessary efforts to obtain that essential information. Officers of his command and reliable scouts who were present gave contradictory reports. This report was discredited by myself and by General Elliott, my second in command.[1]

[1] On June 12th, 7 P.M., Pleasanton telegraphed to Hooker from Warrenton Junction: "A colored boy captured on (Tuesday) 9th states that Ewell's corps passed through Culpeper on Monday last on the way to the Valley and that part of Longstreet's was gone also. A second negro across the river confirms the statement. I send a reconnaissance to find out the truth." The reconnaissance does not seem to have found out anything. On the same day Hooker told Halleck: "Brigadier-General Pleasanton, without additional cavalry, I fear will not be able to prevent the rebel cavalry from turning his right."

Hooker at that time did not seem to apprehend a movement against Milroy, although a negro had reported it and Ewell was then in the Shenandoah Valley. There was, however, still great uneasiness about a cavalry raid toward Washington. For this reason Reynolds on June 12th, with three corps, was sent to Bealeton to guard the railroad. His letter of instructions speaks of "the absence of any specific information as to the objects, movements and purposes of the enemy," which shows that Pleasanton had discovered nothing and that Hooker was still in the dark.

BRANDY

PLEASANTON TO HOOKER

June 13th, 9 P.M.

"The negroes say Ewell took the road to Sperryville. They were all travelling the same way. I am pushing reconnâissances in that direction. Ask Ingalls if he got my dispatch about Mosby."

When Pleasanton was writing this dispatch Ewell was closing around Winchester.

There was nothing in the report that indicated the presence of General Lee's army [in Culpeper]. It was supposed that the force on the Front Royal road could be no other than the enemy we had faced during the occupancy of Winchester, or *that the anticipated cavalry raid of General Stuart was in progress;* against either or both of which I could have held my position.[1] I deemed it impossible

[1] HOOKER TO HALLECK

June 12th, 1.15 P.M.

Learning that the enemy had massed this cavalry near Culpeper for the purpose of a raid, I dispatched General Pleasanton to attack him on his own ground. General Pleasanton crossed the Rappahannock on the 9th at Beverly and Kelley's Fords, attacked the enemy and drove him three miles, capturing over 200 prisoners and one battle flag. This in the face of greatly superior numbers was only accomplished by hard and desperate fighting by our cavalry, for which they deserve much credit. Their morale is splendid. They made many hand-to-hand combats, always driving the enemy before them.

HOOKER TO DIX

June 12, 1863, 1.30 P.M.

All of Lee's army, so far as I know, is extended along the immediate banks of the Rappahannock from Hamilton's crossing to Culpeper. A. P. Hill's corps is on his right, below Fredericksburg. Ewell's corps joins his left [Ewell was then in the Shenandoah Valley] reaching to the Rapidan, and beyond that river is Longstreet's corps with not less than 10,000 cavalry under Stuart. For several days past Lee has been at Culpeper.

that Lee's army with its immense artillery and baggage trains could have escaped from the Army of the Potomac, and crossed the Blue Ridge through Ashby's, Chester's, and Thornton's Gap, in concentric columns. The movement must have occupied four or five days; notice of its being in progress could have been conveyed to me by General Hooker's headquarters in five minutes, for telegraphic communication still existed between Baltimore and Winchester. . . . Telegraphic communication with my headquarters continued till 12 noon Saturday (13). The Blue Ridge screened the operations of Lee's army from me. *I had always relied with implicit confidence upon receiving timely notice by telegraph of its advance in my direction.*" [Italics mine.]

In his review of the records of the Court of Inquiry in Milroy's case, Judge-Advocate-General Holt says: "It is singular to observe up to how late a period the movement of Lee in advancing upon Winchester and down the Valley remained undiscovered by those in authority. It appears that soon after June 1 intelligence had been received and it was generally understood that the rebel general, Stuart, had collected a large force (about 12,000) of cavalry in Culpeper for the purpose of making an extensive *raid*. In a telegram of May 29 General Halleck had warned General Schenck that his forces must be on the alert in anticipation of an attack; and that on June 8, he telegraphed to the latter general the particulars in reference to Stuart's force, etc. It was observed by Milroy that after June 1st the enemy in his front was becoming bolder, and this was attributed to the fact that Stuart was assembling his cavalry in force and that a raid was impending. In his telegrams to General Schenck up to the evening of the 13th, especially those of the 12th and 13th, he reports the troops as having severe skirmishes with the enemy, whom he represents to be in force, *but he conveys no intimation, nor had he been able to obtain any information, that Lee's army was advancing.* [Italics mine.] On the contrary, he expresses the opinion that the attack on Winchester (which he supposed to be made by the usual Valley force somewhat increased) *is but a feint to cover the raid of Stuart.* Nor does General Schenck's information from Kelly up to the evening of the 13th suggest the advance of Lee through the mountains, but on the contrary tends to allay any apprehension of such advance. On the 9th the latter General telegraphs that his scouts have returned from Snicker's Gap and saw no enemy. On the 12th he telegraphs that his scouts are in and have neither seen nor heard of an enemy. . . . Meantime (on the 10th), the Secretary of War telegraphs to General Schenck that Pleasanton had sharply engaged Stuart at Beverly and thinks the latter too much crippled to make his raid into Maryland very soon. [Not a word about Lee, Longstreet, or Ewell]. . . . It was on the 14th also, about noon, Schenck received a telegram from the General-in-Chief in final answer to his of the 12th. This telegram, which was dated from the War Department at 10.30 A.M., is as follows: 'It is reported that Longstreet's and Ewell's corps have passed through Culpeper to Sperryville towards the Valley.' This, General Schenck testifies, was the first and only information received by him from General Halleck that any of Lee's force had gone to the Valley."

On this opinion Abraham Lincoln endorsed: "The disaster, when it came, was a surprise to all." So it appears that if Pleasanton found out that Lee, Longstreet, and Ewell were in Culpeper, he kept it a secret. By his report from Culpeper he had given Milroy a cup of kind Nepenthe. He put him to sleep.

General Lee's headquarters were near Culpeper Courthouse. He rode to a hill on the field and witnessed the combat from the Barbour house. Although it was known that the attacking force was both cavalry and infantry, he supposed it was only a reconnaissance to discover if his army was there. Of course he would, as far as practicable, conceal from the enemy what they wanted to find out. But there was a probability that it was a real attack by Hooker's army and he wanted to provide for that contingency. If it were a reconnaissance, he would not allow it to proceed beyond Brandy, for it might disclose the presence of Longstreet and Ewell. Rodes' division of Ewell's corps was in camp four miles from the field on the Rixeyville road. It was therefore ordered to march to a point to be in convenient supporting distance of the cavalry in case of necessity. It halted on the Botts' farm two miles off, but was kept out of sight. The emergency for using it never arose, nor did Gregg, or any of his officers, discover its presence or report seeing it. Gregg said a train-load of infantry came up to Brandy, but it was imaginary. Why would General Lee display a train-load of infantry at a point near where he had a division of infantry concealed behind a hill? Rodes says: "On the 9th, anticipating an order to do so, I moved the division towards Brandy Station to the support of General Stuart's cavalry. Halting, under General Ewell's orders, at Botts' place, I subsequently under orders advanced to Barbour's house in advance of the station, but did not get in reach of the enemy, he having apparently been repulsed by the cavalry."

General Junius Daniel, whose brigade of Rodes' division approached nearest to Brandy, reports: "On the morning of the 9th firing was heard in the direction of Brandy Station and I received orders to proceed in that direction. About twelve o'clock I arrived near Brandy Station and received orders from General Ewell and General Lee to proceed in person to the station and report to Brigadier-General Hampton. Upon arriving at the station I reported to General Hampton and was by him placed in line of battle about one mile in advance of the station, to support some cavalry that had fallen back before the enemy; their skirmishers being at that time a little in advance of their position, and their artillery firing upon the enemy at long range. A short time after this I received orders from the Major-General commanding the division to throw out skirmishers to the front and move my line some half mile to the rear. After remaining in this position a short time, the enemy began to retire and I received orders to advance my skirmishers and retire my line still further to the rear; *keeping my troops con-*

cealed behind the hills during the movement. The enemy retired before my line of skirmishers. About 5 P.M. I received orders to call in my skirmishers and move to a wood near Botts' house and there go into camp." It is clear that the infantry was concealed from view by the hill on which the Barbour house is situated. Gregg never saw them. The infantry was kept in reserve; the Confederate cavalry was between them and the enemy, and won a great victory. The following dispatch from General Lee to Stuart on the field shows what was his opinion of the operation, and his anxiety to conceal the presence of infantry:

June 9th 1863.

MAJOR-GENERAL STUART, COMMANDING:—

GENERAL: General Lee desires me to say that he has your dispatches by the couriers and from the signal station. General Longstreet has a division looking to Stevensburg, and General Ewell on the other side (of the railroad) looking to Brandy Station. He desires you not to expose your men too much but to do the enemy damage when possible. As the whole thing seems to be a reconnaissance in force to determine our force and position, he wishes these concealed as much as possible and the infantry not to be seen, if it is possible to avoid it.

I am, etc.,

C. S. VENABLE,

Major, etc.

Duffie went to Stevensburg but never saw or heard of Longstreet. Hood and McLaws were a few miles ahead of him; Pickett's division had not yet arrived.

LEE TO SEDDON

CULPEPER, June 9th, 1863.

The enemy crossed the Rappahannock this morning at 5 A.M. at the various fords from Beverly's to Kelly's, with large force of cavalry, accompanied by infantry and artillery. After a severe contest till 5 P.M., General Stuart drove them over the river.

It is true that no effective pursuit of the enemy to the Rappahannock was made, but it is was not because Stuart's cavalry was too much crippled. Robertson's brigade had not been engaged and was intact; Munford's had crossed Hazel River and arrived on the field after Buford's repulse at St. James' Church; only three of his squadrons were engaged late in the afternoon as sharpshooters. Hampton, however, did pursue. His report says in reference to Gregg's retreat from Brandy Station: "In conjunction with this charge of the enemy in front I moved the First Carolina and the Jeff Davis Legion so as to turn his right. The leading regiments (Cobb's Legion and the First South Carolina) charged gallantly up the steep hill upon which the enemy was strongly posted, and swept them off in a perfect rout without pause or check. Their guns were abandoned and many of their men killed and captured. In the meantime, as the enemy attempted to escape down the railroad, the two regiments which were with me met the head of their fleeing column and dispersed it in every direction. The First North Carolina, which was in front, took many prisoners and the colors of the Tenth New York regiment. The capture of the force which had been driven from the hill would have been almost certain but that our own artillery, which had been again posted on the hill we had recovered, opened a heavy and well directed fire at the head of my column. The delay rendered necessary to make this fire cease enabled the enemy to gain the woods in his rear." The principal reason why there was not a more vigorous pursuit was that the infantry with Pleasanton covered the cavalry. This reversed the usual order of these two arms on a retreat. Since the invention of long range and repeating fire-arms the use of cavalry in attacking infantry is obsolete tactics. Stuart had of course resisted, and had repelled the combined attacks of infantry and cavalry in the morning near Beverly's. Colonel Newhall speaks of his having deployed infantry to cover Buford's crossing at Beverly's Ford. Buford made no report of Brandy; if he had had any success that day I suppose he would have reported it. He made several reports during the campaign. That night Pleasanton sent the following dispatch to Hooker, and Hooker repeated it to Washington. If it had given any definite information about Lee's army, it would have been communicated to Schenck at Baltimore, and Milroy at Winchester.[1]

[1] Pleasanton's report, which is dated June 15, states that he conducted what he calls "the expedition" in accordance with Hooker's instructions of the 7th, but says nothing about a reconnaissance. At the date of his report he had heard that Ewell had stolen a march on Milroy and of course he then knew a great deal about Lee's army that he did not know on June 9. He says he halted at Beverly Ford but that he was holding it to hear from Gregg. The plan was for him and Buford to unite with Gregg at Brandy and move on to Culpeper Court-house. But this operation was reversed; Gregg fell back and joined Buford and retreated with him over the Rappahannock. Gregg's report says: "I moved my command [from Brandy] in the direction of Rappahannock bridge and soon united with General Buford's left." Pleasanton reported a total loss of 907; of this 75 of the killed and wounded were in the infantry; and that his total effective force was 10,981. Stuart's loss was 575. Of his five brigades Robertson's took no part in the action,

and only three squadrons of Munford's were engaged. Stuart captured
6 flags and 3 pieces of artillery. How little information Pleasanton
carried back is shown by Hooker's dispatch to President Lincoln the
next day.

June 10th, 1863, 2.30 p.m.

"General Pleasanton, by telegram forwarded to the Major-General
[Halleck] commanding the army this morning, reports that he had an
affair with the rebel cavalry yesterday near Brandy Station which resulted
in crippling him so much that he will have to abandon his contemplated
raid into Maryland [No raid had been contemplated] which was to have
started this morning. I am not so certain that the raid will be abandoned from this cause. It may delay the departure for a few days.
[Elwell started to Winchester that morning.] I shall leave the cavalry,
which is all that I have mounted, where they are near Bealeton, with
instructions to resist the passage of the river by the enemy's forces. If
to effect this he should bring up a considerable force of infantry [the
infantry had already been brought up to Culpeper, but Hooker did not
know it] that will so much weaken him in my front that I have good
reason to believe that I can throw a sufficient force over the river [at
Fredericksburg] to compel the enemy to abandon his present position.
If it should be the intention to send a heavy column of infantry to accompany the cavalry on the proposed raid [when the movement began the
cavalry accompanied the infantry] he can leave nothing behind to interpose any serious obstacle to my rapid advance on Richmond. . . . At
present the enemy has one corps of infantry at Gordonsville with the
advance at Culpeper, with the manifest tendency of other corps to drift
in that direction. I now have two bridges across the Rappahannock,
ready to spring over the river below Fredericksburg, and it is this, I
believe, that causes the enemy to hesitate in moving forward."

All of which shows how little Hooker knew about the situation of
Lee's army. Ewell was then drifting to the Shenandoah Valley.

June 9th, 1863, 8 p.m.

Major-General Hooker: —

A short time after my last dispatch to you, General Gregg with
his infantry and artillery joined me about two miles from the river, to
which point I had driven the enemy. He reported that he had encountered a much superior number of the enemy's cavalry and had a

severe fight. Also, that a train of cars had been run up to Brandy Station filled with infantry who opened on his men. I also received information from letters and official reports captured in the enemy's camp, as well as from his prisoners, that the enemy had upwards of 12,000 cavalry (which was double our own force of cavalry) and twenty-five pieces of artillery. I also learned from contrabands and prisoners that a large force of infantry had been sent for from Culpeper, as well as Longstreet's command at Ellis' Ford. Having crippled the enemy by desperate fighting so that he could not follow me, I returned with my command to the north side of the Rappahannock. Gregg's command crossed at Rappahannock Bridge. To-morrow Stuart was to start on a raid into Maryland, so captured papers state. Rest satisfied he will not attempt it. Buford had a long and desperate hand-to-hand encounter with the enemy, in which he drove before him handsomely very superior forces. Over two hundred prisoners of war were captured and one battle-flag. The troops are in splendid spirits, and are entitled to the highest praise for their distinguished conduct. Lee reviewed the whole of Stuart's cavalry yesterday.

A. PLEASANTON,
Brigadier-General.

If Gregg saw infantry on the train at Brandy, he should, as a reconnoitering officer, instead of retreating, at least have made a demonstration against it with both his cavalry and infantry. This would have compelled the force, if there, to show its strength. Nothing of the sort was done, which looks as if General Gregg was not seeking information. He says nothing about the number of the infantry, whether it was a brigade or a company. The failure of a reconnoitering force to discover the presence of an enemy and making a false report often results in great damage to his own side. It is said that such a failure was the cause of the surprise at Shiloh. Hooker's reply showed that he did not attach much importance to Pleasanton's dispatch. He said: "I am not so certain as you appear to be that the enemy will abandon his contemplated raid. With this impression I have felt a little hesitancy about withdrawing the infantry. Will you be able to keep him from crossing the river with his cavalry and batteries with you?" Not a word about Confederate infantry.

At that time Longstreet's corps was camped about Mount Pony in Culpeper; Pleasanton thought it was at Ellis' Ford on the Rappahannock; Ewell was then marching to the Shenandoah Valley; Hooker thought he was about Fredericksburg. Pleasanton was almost close enough to see the dust from Ewell's columns. Stuart's cavalry was stretched out as a screen along the Rappahannock; Pleasanton had never penetrated the screen.

At 2.30 P.M., on the 10th, Hooker telegraphed Mr. Lincoln that he had so crippled Stuart that he would abandon his contemplated raid into Maryland. "I am not satisfied," he said, "of his intention in this respect, but, from certain movements in their corps, I cannot regard it as altogether improbable. . . . At present the enemy have one corps of infantry at Gordonsville, with the advance at Culpeper, with the manifest tendency of the other corps to drift in that direction." He again proposed that, as a part of Lee's army had left his front, he should move towards Richmond. Mr. Lincoln disapproved it. On the 11th and 12th he telegraphed that Hill and Ewell were still in his front on the lower Rappahannock, and that Longstreet, with Stuart's cavalry, was in Culpeper. Ewell was then in the Shenandoah Valley within twelve miles of Winchester. Pleasanton had sent him some reports about contrabands (negroes) and deserters having reported that Ewell had gone towards the Blue Ridge, but evidently he placed no reliance in them. He must, therefore, have been thunderstruck when, on the 13th, Mr. Lincoln asked him if it was possible that Ewell could be at Winchester. Hooker immediately issued orders that set his army in motion for Manassas Junction. The next day his headquarters were at Dumfries on the Potomac. He there received a characteristic dispatch from Mr. Lincoln. It said: "So far as we can make out here, the enemy have surrounded Milroy at Winchester and Tyler at Martinsburg. If they could hold out a few days longer could you help them? If the head of Lee's army is at Martinsburg and the tail of it on the plank road between Fredericksburg and Chancellorsville, the animal must be very slim somewhere. Could you break him?" Hooker did not seem to think he could.

Critics may object that the horse artillery were too much exposed by being so near the picket line at Beverly Ford. Such criticism is mere pedantry; the operations of war cannot be reduced to maxims and formulas. The result shows that it was fortunate for the Confederates that their guns were in the place where Pleasanton found them. They were therefore in the right place. As a general rule, a battery in action has the support of infantry or cavalry. When Pleasanton's column was only chasing a picket, as they supposed, and almost in the artillery camp, a gun in the road suddenly opened fire on it. The column halted for fear of an ambuscade. It was natural to conclude, as Pleasanton did, that the gun had been masked and was there in anticipation of his crossing the river and had a strong support behind it. There was a similar ruse by the German cavalry at Sedan. Colonel Bonie, in his account of the operations of the French cavalry in the war of 1870, says: "The Colonel of the Prussian Hussars, who came to take over Sedan, stated that for several hours the 200 guns which caused such damage were supported by his regiment alone. His anxiety for a long time was intense, as, had anything happened, he could have afforded but little help. Accordingly, in order to convey the impression that he had a large body of troops at his disposal, he showed himself along the crests of the various heights, and thus displayed a continuous line that seemed to extend for some distance. What a splendid success might have been achieved had our cavalry been launched against the regiment that supported those guns?"

The misinformation which Pleasanton brought from Culpeper tended to quiet the fears of an aggressive movement. A similar false report by an officer sent to make a reconnaissance came near being the ruin of Bonaparte in Italy. On the 13th of June he went to Marengo, a village situated on the east bank of the Bormida, a tributary of the Po; he was looking for Melas, whose communications he had severed; the Austrians had been at Alessandria, a few miles below on the other bank of the river. A force was sent to reconnoiter; it reported that no Austrians were there and that there was no bridge on the river. Bonaparte concluded that Melas had escaped and was retreating to Genoa; he accordingly directed Desaix with his division to move to Novi to intercept him. Bonaparte's forces were scattered; he was not prepared to receive and he was not expecting an attack. Victor was left in observation at Marengo; Bonaparte slept that night several miles away; he was in no condition for battle the next morning.

According to Bourrienne, Bonaparte was as badly deceived by the staff officer who made the reconnaissance for him, as Hooker and Milroy were by Pleasanton. He says: "On the 13th, the First Consul slept at di Galifolo. During the evening he ordered a staff officer to ascertain whether the Austrians had a bridge across the Bormida. A report arrived very late that there was none; this information set Bonaparte's mind at rest and he went to bed well satisfied; but early the next morning, when firing was heard, he heard that the Austrians had debouched on the plain where the troops were engaged; he flew into a furious passion, called the staff officer a coward, and said he had not advanced far enough."

Both Lee and Stuart had known for several days that Pleasanton's cavalry corps was massed on the river. It is hard for a cavalryman who served under Stuart to realize that an army of 30,000 Austrians was at Alessandria on the opposite bank of the river, only five or six miles away, and that Bonaparte's Chief of Cavalry had not found it out. As is well known, Victor was surprised by an attack at daybreak in the morning; the French were defeated and driven several miles until they met Desaix's division; he had turned back and marched without orders to the sound of the cannon, and arrived just in time to snatch a victory from defeat. Although he was surprised, no other battle is more associated with the glory of Napoleon; on his coffin was spread the cloak he wore at Marengo.

II

GETTYSBURG

On June 14, Longstreet's corps was in camp in Culpeper, near Pony Mountain. General Lee's headquarters were near the Court-house. At midnight orders were issued to the division commanders, Hood, Pickett, and McLaws, to be ready to move the next day on the road to Winchester. News had been received that Ewell had cleaned the Valley of Milroy's forces. The route was afterward changed and Longstreet's corps marched along the eastern base of the Blue Ridge to Ashby's and Snicker's Gaps. They remained in the vicinity of the Gaps from the 17th to the 24th. General Lee's object was to perplex Hooker as to the destination of his army. He wanted Hooker to think that he intended a blow east of the Ridge on the Orange and Alexandria Railroad.

In anticipation of such a movement, Hooker kept the bulk of his army massed along the railroad, while Ewell, who had crossed the Potomac on June 15, with his corps and a strong force of cavalry under Jenkins, was roaming around unmolested over Maryland and Pennsylvania. The militia always scattered when he got close to them. Hooker detached no troops to follow Ewell. Lee had the initiative; Hooker conformed to Lee's movements and turned around on the inner circle so as always to cover

Washington. Of course it was expected that he would pursue Lee if he crossed the Potomac; otherwise Washington would be uncovered. When Ewell left Culpeper on the day following the combat at Brandy Station, Stuart's cavalry remained where it had been for some weeks. If it had gone with Ewell its absence would have disclosed the movement to the enemy and attracted their attention to the Shenandoah Valley. As the cavalry stayed in the same place, it was natural to conclude that the infantry was somewhere behind it on the Rapidan or Rappahannock. Jones' brigade of cavalry had been brought the week before from the Valley. The withdrawal of Jones' brigade had deceived Milroy and the authorities at Washington. It relieved them of all fear of an offensive movement in that direction. Milroy woke up one morning and found himself surrounded by Ewell's corps. Stuart, with a part of his cavalry corps as a veil, moved on Longstreet's right flank to screen it from observation. As the chief of cavalry of an army — as a commander of outpost service in masking his own side and unmasking the other — Stuart never had an equal.

Pleasanton's cavalry withdrew from the Rappahannock along the line of the railroad on the day that Stuart crossed it. Hampton's and Jones' brigades were left on the river; they followed the next day.

Hooker was moving north. On the night of June 16, in company with Fitz-Lee's brigade, which was under the temporary command of General Munford, Stuart went into bivouac near Piedmont Station in Fauquier.

General Lee's headquarters remained in Culpeper until the 16th; I suppose he was waiting for A. P. Hill's corps to come up from Fredericksburg. Hill was kept there until it was certain that Hooker was moving to the Potomac. At 3.30 P.M, on the 17th, General Lee was at Markham, near Manassas Gap, where he spent the night. From there he went on to the Valley and had his headquarters for a week at Berryville.

Notice of the northern movement of the Confederate army had not been formally given to me, but there were many signs of it. I had heard of Milroy's rout and expected it would be followed by our whole army. On the 16th I went on a scout and discovered Hooker's camps; he was then moving toward Washington. When I returned I heard where Stuart was and early the next morning went to see him. His tent was in Miss Kitty Shacklett's front yard near the roadside. He greeted me cordially; our last meeting had been at Culpeper, when I carried General Stoughton to him as a prisoner. He was in his usual gay humor — I never saw him at any time in any other. Always buoyant in spirits, he inspired with his own high hopes all who came in contact with him. I felt the deepest affection for him — my chief ambition was to serve him. He was the rare combination of the Puritan and the knight-errant; in his character were mingled the graces of chivalry with the strong religious sense of duty of a Round-head. He felt intensely the joy of battle, and he loved the praise of fair women and brave men. I served under him from the beginning of the war until he closed his life, like Sidney, leading a squadron on the field of honor; yet I do not remember that he ever gave me an order.

There was always so much sympathy between us, and I felt so much affection for him, that he only had to express a wish and that was an order to me. To Stuart I owe my first commission to raise a Partisan corps, and the promotion I afterwards received as Captain and Lieutenant-Colonel. All came unsolicited. There is no allusion to me in the published records of the war so gratifying as the endorsement he made on a report I made to him in February, 1864, in which he said: "Since I first knew him in 1861 he has never once alluded to his own rank or promotion; thus far, it has come by the force of his own merit." Perhaps some may say that the promotion came through Stuart's partiality. Maybe it did. I certainly owe to him whatever I was in the war. The work in which I had been engaged for several months in Northern Virginia made me capable of rendering a service at that time which he acknowledged in his report of the campaign.

After we had talked over the situation it was arranged for me to meet him at Middleburg in the afternoon. Seeing he was badly mounted, I gave him a fine sorrel we had captured from a Michigan lieutenant. A few days afterward the horse was killed under him. My men were waiting for me at the rendezvous a few miles away and I rode off to join them. We then went on to Middleburg and found Stuart there ahead of us. Colonel Munford, with his brigade, had just passed on to Aldie, a village on the pike a few miles below in a gap of the Bull Run

Mountains. Stuart was dismounted, standing in the street.

"Grim visaged war had smoothed his wrinkled front"; the young ladies of the town had surrounded and captured him; the scene looked like a dance around a Maypole. It lasted an hour or so until they were startled by the roar of guns at Aldie. In our conference I told him I was going again over the Potomac at Seneca. It had only been a week since I was there, but I thought they would not expect me back so soon.[1] Neither of us knew that the heads of Hooker's columns were so near.

Washington City, and the North generally, were in such a panicky state that I knew that my presence north of the Potomac would create an alarm as it had done the week before, altogether out of proportion to the size of my force, or the damage we could do. It would at least create a diversion in favor of General Lee. This was the first time, in fact the only time, that Stuart ever saw

---

[1] Colonel Jewett, commanding at Poolesville, reported: "The enemy dashed rapidly up the canal, driving in the patrols, and attacked Captain Dean's Company I, Sixth Michigan Cavalry, on duty at Seneca locks. Captain fell back towards Poolesville, forming line three times and only retreating when nearly surrounded. The enemy followed to within three miles of Poolesville, when he rapidly retreated, destroying the camp of Captain Deane and re-crossing the river where he had crossed. Our loss is four men killed, man wounded and sixteen men missing [and over twenty horses]."

HEINTZELMAN TO LOWELL, WASHINGTON, JUNE 12

"Consult your own discretion in your direction. Go where you please in pursuit of Mosby. A squadron from Winchester will probably pass Middleburg or Aldie to-day. It has been notified to be on the lookout for Mosby."

my men in a body. As they passed him in the street he made a jocular remark that the Yankees, when they saw them, were like the coon up a tree when he saw Captain Scott — the coon called out, "Don't shoot, I'll come down." The men moved on and I remained for some time with him. When we parted I told him that he would hear from me soon. After going a mile down the pike, I overtook my men and we turned off toward the Potomac. It was a hot day; the command had halted in a valley at the foot of the mountain to rest in the shade and drink some buttermilk a farmer named Gulick had brought us. We were not dreaming the enemy were so near us until we heard the artillery firing over the hills in the direction of Aldie. The enemy had unexpectedly come in collision with Munford. This showed that they must be in strong force ahead of us. In an instant every man was in the saddle. Ascending the hill we could see clouds of dust that indicated the roads on which Hooker's army was marching. Going on for two or three miles, we learned from prisoners we captured that Hooker's people were all around us.

But we were in the woods and they were not looking for small game. The prisoners were sent back to Stuart, with a dispatch giving him full information about the force in front. He got it before dark. I now determined not to go to the Potomac; I thought I could be more useful by operating against the enemy on the turnpike leading from Fairfax to Aldie, which I knew must be their line of communication. In this way I could annoy them and communicate with Stuart. That night I placed my command in the woods, and with three men — Joe Nelson, Charlie Hall, and Norman Smith — rode to the pike which was a few hundred yards off. The Union troops were passing in a continuous stream, but we did not attract their attention; in the dark they could not distinguish the gray uniforms from the blue.

The house of a Northern man named Birch, with whom I was well acquainted, was near. His front yard gate opened on the pike. We saw three horses standing there; a soldier was holding them. I concluded that these were officers' horses and an orderly. When we rode up the orderly no doubt thought I was a big officer with his staff. In a tone of authority I asked whose horses these were. The soldier respectfully replied that they belonged to Major Sterling and Captain Fisher, and that they were just from General Hooker's headquarters. He told me that the headquarters were in Fairfax and that the officers had gone into the house to get something to eat. After pumping him dry, I told him to come close to me; he did not hesitate and had no suspicion as to who I was. I leaned over, took him by the collar and told him my name. He was an Irishman; he misunderstood me and thought I called him "Mosby," and answered indignantly: "You are a d—d liar, I am as good a Union man as you are." It was clear that an exhibition of force was necessary to subdue him; so I drew my pistol; he saw it in the starlight. I now felt sure of a prize, and as happy as a Florida wrecker when he sees a ship drifting ashore in a storm. The Irishman stood perfectly quiet — all doubt of my personality had vanished.

I then told my companions to dismount and be ready to receive the officers whom we saw walking to the gate. Joe Nelson approached Major Sterling and, extending his hand, asked for his arms. Major Sterling mistook the movement for a salutation and shook hands, as he thought, with a friend. Charlie Hall was equally polite to Captain Fisher. It was hard to convince them who we were. At first they thought it was a practical joke. I then ordered them to deliver their dispatches. Major Sterling handed me a large envelope.[1] It contained a letter of instructions to Pleasanton and with it a statement of the strength of Hooker's army.[2] He informed Pleasanton

[1] COLONEL RICE TO LIEUTENANT CLARK, A. A. G.

June 18th, 1863, 12 M.

In accordance with directions from the commanding officer of the brigade I report the facts in regard to the capture of Major Sterling and Captain Fisher, as related to me by the people of the house where they were taken. Major Sterling and Captain Fisher were on their way to communicate with [General Pleasanton, when they halted at the residence of Mr. Almond Birch for supper and to inquire how far it was to Aldie. Having finished their supper, they started for their horses which were left with their orderly at the yard gate. The horses and orderly had been removed and, before Major Sterling and Captain Fisher had reached the gate, 10 or 12 cavalrymen seized them and hurriedly mounted them and bore them off. This took place last evening at ten o'clock, about 400 yards from the picket outpost at the house of Mr. Birch on the Little River turnpike. Mr. Birch and his family are from Clifton Park, Saratoga County, N. Y. They are Union people known to some of the officers of our regiment.

[2] PLEASANTON TO BUTTERFIELD, CHIEF OF STAFF

June 19th, 1863.

Your dispatch of 10 A.M. received; I heard from an orderly, who escaped, of the capture of Major Sterling and judged he had something important so I have acted carefully. The pass taken from Longstreet's

that Stahel's cavalry would be sent on a reconnaissance to Warrenton and Culpeper the next day. As the dispatch gave notice to Stuart, he sent Hampton to meet Stahel; Hampton drove him back to Fairfax Court-house.[1] We then went to a house a mile off and got a light. I read the dispatch and then wrote Stuart all I had learned. The prisoners, the dispatch, and my letter were sent immediately to Stuart in charge of Norman Smith. He delivered them before sunrise. Captain Fisher was Chief Acting Signal Officer on his way to establish a signal station on the Blue Ridge.

This shows Hooker's ignorance of the whereabouts of Lee's army; Captain Fisher would have ridden into

---

infantry soldier is important, and, from the caution they are using to cover Upperville, I think they may attempt to mass their force there and throw it through Thoroughfare Gap by night. Thoroughfare Gap and Leesburg are the two points it is necessary to make strong in connection with this at Aldie; then the mountain range will do the rest.

[1] HOOKER TO PLEASANTON

June 19th, 1863, 11 A.M.

Inclosed is a copy of a dispatch captured with Major Sterling, probably on the 17th, which, we suppose, did not reach you. Since this was written you have further information, and General Slocum has gone to Leesburg. General Meade will with this be ordered to Aldie; Birney to Gum Springs. You will note the information that may have been received by the enemy, if they got the dispatch when they captured Sterling. What do you know of his capture? As early as possible, establish communication with General Slocum. Howard is at Trappe Rock crossing of Goose Creek. [Near the Potomac.] Nolan's Ford is held, or should be, by McKee, and the mouth of the Monocacy. As soon as you know that McKee can come on and reach you by Leesburg, order him to join you. Of course you will only order him up when you are sure that he can do so without danger to his command.

Longstreet's camps if he had gone on. In his report Captain Norton of the Signal Corps says, "On the 17th, Captain Fisher, Chief Acting Signal Officer, went out on a reconnaissance and in the evening was captured by the enemy near Aldie."[1] Stuart forwarded the captured dispatch to General Lee at Berryville. I remember saying in my note to Stuart, "The skies are bright to-night with the reflection of Hooker's camp-fires." Meade's corps was that night at Gum Spring in Loudon; we slept within half a mile of their camps; neither disturbed the other's slumbers. It was a midsummer night's dream:

"At the dead of the night a sweet vision I saw,
And thrice ere the morning I dreamed it again."

We were again on the pike early in the morning. After some captures we hurried back to Stuart. It was more important to carry him information than prisoners and horses. As before stated, I had left Stuart at Middleburg the day before; he too had had an adventure soon after we parted which caused him to move his headquarters four miles back to Rector's Cross-roads.

On the morning of June 17, Pleasanton's corps was camped about Manassa Junction. His orders to his

[1] DeForest's brigade was sent on the scout to Warrenton. This is his report:

DEFOREST TO HOOKER, FAIRFAX STATION

CENTERVILLE, June 19th.

I found a large force of rebel cavalry at Warrenton. I drove in their pickets to within one mile of the place. Two regiments attempted to flank me on each side. The number is said to be 5,000 or 6,000. A contraband said Stuart was to be there to-day.

two division commanders, Buford and Gregg, were to move to Aldie, a pass of the Bull Run Mountain, and camp there that night; the next day they were to go on to Noland's Ford on the Potomac, where an engineer was laying a pontoon bridge. Every army corps was marching that morning in that direction and expected to cross the Potomac the next day. Hill, Longstreet, and Stuart were still east of the Blue Ridge; Hooker and Pleasanton thought they were in the Shenandoah Valley to follow Ewell, who was then in Maryland. Their ignorance of the where bouts of Lee's army shows how well Stuart, with a curtain of cavalry, had screened its operations. Hooker was evidently greatly surprised when he heard of the collision at Aldie. Pleasanton had expected to stay one night there; he stayed a week. Hooker came to a halt. On the 17th, Butterfield wrote from Fairfax Court-house to Ingalls, Chief Quartermaster at Washington: "Since we were not allowed to cross and whip A. P. Hill, while Longstreet and Ewell were moving through Culpeper and Sperryville, we have lost the opportunity of doing a thing which we know to a certainty we could have accomplished. My impression is now that there is not a rebel, excepting scouts, this side of the Shenandoah Valley; that Lee is in as much uncertainty as to our whereabouts and what we are doing as we are to his; that his movement on the upper Potomac is a cover for a cavalry raid on the north side of the river and a movement of his troops further west, where he can turn up at e weak spot." He had not then heard from Aldie,   it we were inside his lines, and was still under the delusion that only a cavalry raid was contemplated by the Confederates.[1]

[1] BUTTERFIELD TO COMMANDING OFFICER, FORCES MOUTH OF THE MONOCACY

June 18th (Rec'd 9.10 A.M.)

Seize and hold Noland's and Hauling Fords. General Slocum's corps may be in that vicinity to-day, on that side of the Potomac.

BUTTERFIELD TO REYNOLDS

FAIRFAX STATION, June 18th, 3.30 P.M.

... [Colonel E. V.] White last night at Point of Rocks marching careless of our cavalry. Two regiments of infantry ought to have been at the mouth of the Monocacy last night. We have not settled where Lee with Longstreet and Ewell are yet. Headquarters at Fairfax Court-house to-night.

REYNOLDS TO BUTTERFIELD

BRADY'S HOUSE NEAR HERNDON.
June 18th, 4 P.M.

My two signal officers were within one mile of Leesburg this morning at 10.45 A.M. They report no force of any kind there, but Mosby's guerillas from there up to Point of Rocks.

BUTTERFIELD TO MEADE

They are getting sufficiently over their stampede to speak collectedly, coolly in Pennsylvania. ... White was at Point of Rocks with 400 men last night, destroying cars. Six hundred of our cavalry from Dumfries via Alexandria, should have reached the mouth of the Monocacy with a bridge and two regiments of infantry last night. Slocum is by this time in Leesburg (3 P.M.) We don't exactly settle where Lee is yet. Catch and kill any guerillas, then try them, will be a good method of treating them.

BENHAM TO HOOKER

WASHINGTON, June 18th, 8 A.M.

About 8 P.M. of the 16th I received an order to have a bridge of 1200 feet in the Georgetown canal by daylight of the 17th, which I at

But two hours later, at 10.30 P.M., he wrote to Pleasanton "Your dispatch by orderly received announcing that you had run against [Fitz] Lee's brigade at Aldie. The general desires that you push him up and find out what is behind him — whether it is the advance of Lee's army covering his movements. . . ." Gregg had ordered Colonel

once directed the whole command to prepare, it requiring much time to unload trucks and rearrange the boats for passing the locks. About 2 A.M. of the 17th I received a dispatch directing the bridge to be laid at Noland's Ford by noon of the 18th, and, it appearing necessary by that dispatch, I ordered 250 more men of the Fiftieth to accompany the bridge. . . . Captain Trumbull was fortunately up with all his boats in the canal about 6 A.M., and he wrote me that he was pushing them through the set of locks above there, which was what I expected and desired.

SCHENCK TO TYLER

June 18th, 11.30 A.M.

What have you done for guarding the Baltimore and Ohio Railroad against the enemy from Harper's Ferry to Point of Rocks or the Monocacy? Report, if you can, as to train captured and destroyed by [Colonel E. V.] White's cavalry near Point of Rocks last night, and as to capture of Captain Means' cavalry company. . . . Keep up your cavalry patrol constantly to the mouth of the Monocacy. Heintzleman's people patrol below that point.

J. W. GARRETT, PRESIDENT B. AND O. R. R., TO SECRETARY STANTON

"A train sent to Harper's Ferry yesterday A.M. with troops and supplies, which left Sandy Hook for Baltimore at 5 last P.M., has been captured and burned at Point of Rocks. It consisted of a first-class engine and 22 cars. Our operator reports that the enemy were 400 of White's cavalry, and that they also captured and carried off Captain Means with his entire company of cavalry. [A mistake.] I fear this destroys connections west of the Monocacy until re-opened by a strong force. . . ."

The pontoon bridges were afterward laid lower down the river at Edwards' Ferry, but the fords above were kept heavily guarded. At this time Stuart and Pleasanton were fighting about Middleburg.

Duffie with his Rhode Island regiment to move through Thoroughfare Gap to Middleburg, and to camp there that night. The next day he was to join the division at Noland's Ford on the Potomac. Gregg evidently thought that Stuart was in the Valley. Duffie drove off a picket of Chambliss' brigade at Thoroughfare and moved on to Middleburg. The picket at Thoroughfare did not give notice of the enemy's approach. Stuart did not hear of it until Duffie's advance guard chased a vidette into the village. He and his staff got away as fast as they could. In accordance with his orders, Duffie went into camp at Middleburg with 275 men, although he knew that Stuart had just left the place. Of course, if Stuart was there, his cavalry was near. Duffie's folly is an illustration of the truth of what I have often said — that no man is fit to be an officer who has not the sense and courage to know when to disobey an order. The Confederate cavalry soon came up, attacked, scattered, and captured most of Duffie's regiment. His report, dated the next day (18th), at Centreville, tells the tale of the catastrophe: "I returned here exhausted at 1.30 P.M. to-day, with the gallant debris of my much-loved regiment — 4 officers and 27 men. My colors did not fall into the hands of the enemy, but were destroyed when they could not be saved. The color-bearer was mortally wounded."

Duffie was ordered to Alexandria and laid up for repairs. It was said that he had served as a French cuirassier in Africa, and had had many encounters with the sons of the desert. He escaped capture by Abd-el-Kadir to be caught by my men in the Shenandoah Valley in 1864. *Exit* Duffie.[1]

We returned from inside Hooker's lines by an unguarded path over the Bull Run Mountain and found Stuart at his headquarters. I gave him all the information I had gained; immediately a courier was sent with a dispatch to General Lee. Stuart enjoyed greatly my account of our adventures the night before. My men were dispersed for rest, but I stayed at headquarters.

On the 21st Pleasanton, reinforced by Barnes' division of infantry, made a reconnaissance and pushed the cavalry back to the Blue Ridge. But he could go no farther; Ashby's Gap was held by McLaws' division of infantry, and Snicker's Gap by Hood's. Early the next morning Pleasanton retired to Aldie and there waited for General Lee to develop his purpose. It is well understood that Stuart rode that night to see General Lee at his headquarters. Ewell had crossed the Potomac some days before and Jenkins' cavalry brigade had gone into Pennsylvania. While Pleasanton was pressing Stuart back to the Blue Ridge, I moved my command around his flank and bivouacked that night on the path in the Bull Run Mountain where we had crossed three days before. We were then between Thoroughfare Gap, which was held by Hancock, and Pleasanton who was at Aldie. At daybreak we moved down the eastern slope. When crossing a field we saw a body of cavalry drawn up by a church.

---

[1] BUTTERFIELD TO PLEASANTON
June 19th, 1863, 4.15 P.M.
Colonel Duffie is here with 28 men and officers; 32 all told.

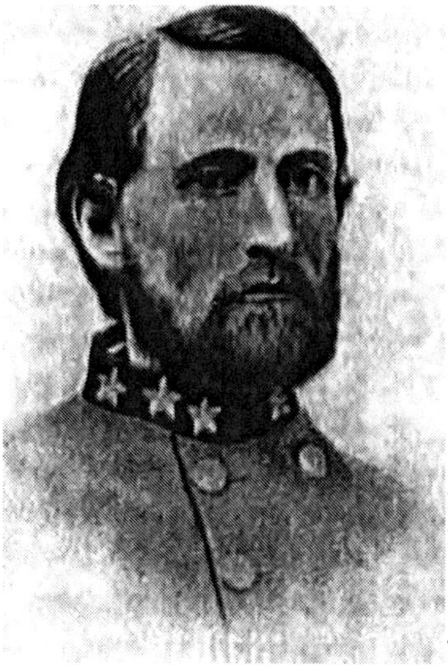

Jno. S. Mosby

Not suspecting that they were put there as a bait to draw us into a trap, I ordered my men to charge. The cavalry ran away when we got close to them, while a body of infantry, lying down in the church a few yards off, desecrated the sanctuary by firing a volley into us. We fell back to the woods at the foot of the mountain; no doubt it was thought that we had gone away — at least for that day. The force at the church returned to their camps near Aldie. Not one of my men or horses was killed; three were wounded. Ballard lost a leg, Mountjoy lost a finger, and Charlie Hall got a bullet in his shoulder. There was no pursuit of us; the party seemed satisfied with what they had done and went home. I sent the wounded back under charge of one of my most trusty men, Fount Beattie, and with about twenty men flanked around and kept on to the Little River pike. It was not long before we caught a wagon-train. Stuart's quartermaster was in need of mules; we furnished him with a fine lot. We had our revenge for getting into the ambuscade. The news of the capture of the wagons created a sensation in the camps and seems to have demoralized Hooker. A few hours before it had been reported to him that we had been routed and driven over the mountain. Another visit was not expected so soon. General Meade, who had put up the job on us at the church that morning, was very much disgusted with the performance. The following letter to Howard, written from Aldie, tells how he felt about it:

"June 22, 1863.

"Pleasanton, as I wrote you yesterday, drove the enemy through Ashby's Gap. He returned this morning and informs me that the Confederate army are in the Valley of the Shenandoah and Martinsburg; Lee and Longstreet at Winchester [both near Berryville]; A. P. Hill is coming up the Valley to join them. This is the substance of news as given by Pleasanton. He was yesterday opposed by only a brigade of cavalry and one battery, but the character of the country was so favorable for defense that it took him all day with his large force to drive them back some 12 [8] miles. I came near catching our friend, Mosby, this morning. I had intelligence of his expected passing a place about four miles from here at sunrise. I sent forty mounted men (all I had) and 100 infantry who succeeded in posting themselves in ambush at the designated spot. Sure enough, Mr. Mosby, together with 30 of his followers, made their appearance about sunrise, but I regret to say their exit also, from what I can learn, through the fault of both foot and horse. It appears Mosby saw the cavalry and immediately charged them. They ran (that is, my horses) towards the infantry posted behind a fence. The infantry, instead of rising and deliberately delivering their fire, fired lying on the ground but did not hit a rebel, who immediately scattered and dispersed, and thus the prettiest chance in the world to dispose of Mr. Mosby was lost."

Captain Harvey Brown, who commanded, reports a cavalry sergeant killed. He says they did not charge us because the ground was rolling. It was the same ground over which we had charged them. About the time that we captured the train on the pike that morning, Hooker told Heintzelman at Washington that Stahel had been sent on another reconnaissance to the Rappahannock. Hampton had driven him back on the one he had started to make two days before.

At 7 P.M. on the same day he heard of the loss of his mules, and telegraphed to Hancock at Thoroughfare to "direct General Stahel to return without delay to dispose his forces so as to catch the party inside our lines, if possible." Stuart's quartermaster then had his mules. Hancock replied: "I have sent your dispatch [by courier] to General Stahel by different routes." The dispatch overtook Stahel at the Rappahannock. He started back (in disgust he says), and on June 23d (the day after the capture) telegraphed Hooker from Gainesville: "In accordance with your orders I shall now scout the whole country from Bull Run Mountain towards Fairfax Court-house, and have ordered the rest of my command, and my train, to return to Fairfax, where I shall report personally to you."

Butterfield had also telegraphed to Hancock at Thoroughfare: "The General thinks you had better not send in any train until General Stahel's command comes in, and then move with them. A party of about 100 men of the enemy are inside our lines and have to-day attacked a train en route for Aldie."

In a report to the Secretary of War, Stahel said: "It was with feelings of bitter regret and disappointment I received this order, inasmuch as I was just crossing the Rappahannock with three brigades of cavalry and a battery of horse artillery, who were fresh from camp. . . . All of Lee's supplies had to pass between the Rappahannock and the Blue Ridge Mountains across the Shenandoah Valley, and my force was sufficient to have destroyed his entire trains and cut off General Lee completely from his supplies. . . . I was compelled by this order to abandon my movement and restrained from dealing so fatal a blow to the enemy, and return with my whole division to disperse about 100 guerrillas, who had escaped back of our lines before I ever received the order to return."

For more than a week Hooker's headquarters were at Fairfax and his army remained stationary; the seven corps were scattered over three counties — Fairfax, Prince William, and Loudon. The right was on the Potomac about Leesburg; the left twenty-five miles distant at Thoroughfare, and Pleasanton with his cavalry and Meade's corps in the center at Aldie. In the expeditions I had made inside their lines I had located each corps and reported it to Stuart. They were so widely separated that it was easy for a column of cavalry to pass between them. No corps was nearer than ten miles to another corps. On all the roads were wagon-trains hauling supplies. I pointed out to Stuart the opportunity to strike a damaging blow, and suggested to him to cross the Bull Run Mountains and pass through the middle of Hooker's army into Maryland. There was no force to oppose him at Seneca Ford about twenty miles above Washington — where I had recently crossed.

Hancock, with two divisions, was at Thoroughfare; his other division was at Gainesville, seven miles away. Hooker still had a suspicion that Lee meditated a blow against him on the railroad.[1] At Hopewell Gap there was nothing but a cavalry picket.[2] It would be easy to

[1] A division of the Sixth Corps was also kept at Bristoe on the railroad.
[2] WILLIAMS, A. A. G., TO HANCOCK

"June 24, 11.35 P.M.

"The commanding General does not think it necessary to have an infantry guard at Hopewell Pass. The cavalry guard there will answer."

flank Hancock on either side. No such movement was anticipated; that would make it safe. He could pass the Bull Run Mountains early in the morning and cross the Potomac early in the evening; in passing through the army he would sever communication between Hooker and Pleasanton. On the way a large portion of Hooker's transportation would be destroyed. His cavalry would be sent in pursuit of Stuart; that was the very thing Lee wanted him to do. It would relieve his army from the cavalry pressure and Stuart would be so far ahead that Pleasanton could never overtake him. *The best way to protect General Lee's communications was to assail Hooker's.* Small detachments from Stuart's main column could break up the canal to Edwards' Ferry on the Potomac, and railroad communication with Washington. The canal was the line of supply for the depot just established at Edwards' Ferry, where a pontoon bridge had been laid for crossing. This would create a panic in Washington; in all probability Hooker's army would fall back for supplies and to protect the capital. Ewell was in Maryland and Jenkins was making a raid into Pennsylvania; it was not then known that General Lee would follow him with Longstreet and Hill. Stuart would not, of course, expect to return by the same route by which he had gone into Maryland; but he could have easily joined Ewell somewhere north of the Potomac, as Hooker was still on the south bank. The truth is that General Lee was doubtful, as his correspondence shows, when he first reached the Valley, about following Ewell. When I got back from my trip inside Hooker's lines with my drove of mules, Stuart told me that General Lee was anxious to know if Hooker's army was moving to cross the Potomac. He did not ask me to go, but I volunteered to return and find out for him. With two men I re-crossed the mountain on the path where I had been bushwhacked the day before; and on the morning of June 23 was again riding between the camps of the different corps in Fairfax and Loudon. All was quiet; there was no sign of a movement. Hooker was waiting for Lee. During the day I sent two dispatches with some prisoners to Stuart by the men who were with me. I remember very well that one squad consisted of four lieutenants of Sickles' corps. I was now all alone. It must not be supposed that I was in disguise; I wore a Confederate major's uniform. The camps of the different corps were so far apart that it was easy to ride between them. After gathering the information which General Lee wanted, I turned my face late in the afternoon to the Bull Run Mountain. I knew that Stuart would be anxious to see me. In some way I lost my bearings and rode up to the house of a farmer named John I. Coleman and inquired the direction to the Little River pike. I told him who I was and showed him my gray coat and star. A light shower of rain was falling; an India rubber cape was thrown over my shoulders, not for disguise, but to keep me dry. I had been riding all day between the camps with the cape rolled up and tied to my saddle. The farmer had never before seen me; he could not conceive it possible that a Confederate officer would be there in uniform amongst the enemy's camps. Reynolds with the First

Corps was at Guilford about two miles off; the Third Corps (Sickles') was at Gum Springs about the same distance in another direction; while Meade's corps and the cavalry were six or eight miles away at Aldie. Hooker's headquarters were behind me in Fairfax. Coleman refused to tell me anything; he was sure that I was a Yankee disguised in a Confederate uniform. While I was trying to persuade him who I was I heard the tramp of horses behind me. Looking back, I saw two cavalrymen riding up; they took no notice of me but stopped to pick cherries from a tree. I rode back to them and asked who they were. They replied that they belonged to the Fifth New York Cavalry and were just from General Reynolds' headquarters.

They had ridden out from camp without arms. I demanded their surrender; there was nothing else for them to do. This transpired within sight of the farmer, who was now sure that I was not a Confederate soldier and that I wanted to trap him. We rode to the gate where he was still standing. I finally prevailed on him to point towards the turnpike. As I could not surround them, I then made the prisoners tie their horses together with a halter strap, and we rode away. It was not long before we were good friends; I told them who I was. My name was quite a familiar one in their camps at that time, and seemed to have put them under a spell. When we got in sight of the pike a long train of wagons with a large escort of cavalry was passing. To get to the mountain I would have to cross the pike. I knew I could not find the narrow path over it in the dark; it was near sundown; if

I waited for the train to pass out of my way it would be night. It was important for me to see Stuart. So I concluded to take the greatest risk that I took in the war — to ride with my prisoners through the wagons and column of cavalry. The rubber cape partly concealed my gray coat; but I did not put much reliance in the cape. It would attract no attention to see a man dressed in a gray suit riding in a column of blue-coats. He could not be a spy, as he was not in disguise; and it would be presumed that no Confederate soldier would dare to be there in uniform. But I chiefly relied on the prisoners to protect me from discovery. They rode by my side; there was nothing to indicate that they were prisoners; they appeared to be my companions, or an officer's escort. I held my pistol under my cape and warned the men against giving any sign to their friends. We rode on to the pike through a gap in the fence; I had calculated on going straight across, but there was a high fence with no gap on the other side.

I knew a road a hundred yards ahead that led from the pike. I determined to go on. It was my intention, if discovered, to dash speedily away. I was on a fast horse and I was afraid my prisoners would betray me if I dismounted to pull down the fence. So, ordering them to keep close to my side, we went on at a trot through the column and turned off on the road leading toward the mountain. In passing through the cavalry my right elbow jostled against a cavalrymen. He took no exception to my rudeness. If he had I would have said, "Excuse *me*," and ridden on. The prisoners seemed to be in a dazed condition. I remember that one of them asked me after we had passed through the column if those were our cavalry or theirs. It was now dark and I had not reached the foot of the mountain; I was afraid to sleep with my prisoners alone like the babes in the wood; so we stopped at a house. They signed their paroles and started to walk home. I got to Stuart early the next morning. He listened to what I told him, wrote a dispatch, sent off a courier to General Lee, and then laughed over my adventure. The information was that Hooker's army was still resting in the camps where it had been for a week. General Lee arrived at Berryville on the 18th; he was waiting for Hill's corps that had reached the Valley on the 21st and moved on to Charlestown.

On the 15th Rodes' division of Ewell's corps, with Jenkins' cavalry, crossed the Potomac at Williamsport; Jenkins went on to Chambersburg, but had returned to Hagerstown; Johnson's division followed, and on the 22d Early crossed at Shepherdstown and moved to Boonsboro at the foot of South Mountain — which is an extension of the Blue Ridge. Early's division had been kept back to threaten Harper's Ferry. The army was now closed up and Lee was ready to move. It has been represented by his biographer (Long) that Gettysburg was his objective point when he left Fredericksburg, and that he expected to fight a decisive battle there. The story has no more foundation than the legend of Romulus.

General Lee's cotemporaneous correspondence contradicts it. He had just won a great tactical victory at Chancellorsville, but he reaped no fruits from it. His report says that he took the offensive in order to compel the Northern army "to leave Virginia and possibly to draw to its support troops designed to operate against other parts of the country. In this way it was supposed that the enemy's plans of campaign for the summer would be broken up, and a part of the season of active operations be consumed in the formation of new combinations and the preparations that they would require."

If Gettysburg had been his objective point he would have marched directly there from Hagerstown on the road through the Monterey pass by which he retreated. A straight line is the shortest distance between two points. On June 8 he wrote from Culpeper to Mr. Seddon, Secretary of War: "As far as I can judge, there is nothing to be gained by this army remaining quietly on the defensive, which it must, unless it can be reinforced. I am aware there is difficulty and hazard in taking the aggressive with so large an army in its front intrenched behind a river where it cannot be advantageously attacked. Unless it can be drawn out in a position to be assailed, it will take its own time to prepare and strengthen itself to renew its advance upon Richmond and force this army back within the intrenchments of that city. This may be the result in any event; still I think it worth a trial to prevent the catastrophe. Still, if the Department thinks it better to remain on the defensive and guard, as far as possible, all avenues of approach and wait the time of the enemy, I am ready to adopt this course. You have, therefore, only to inform me."

Mr. Seddon concurred in these views, but called attention to the defenseless condition of Richmond at that time. There is no intimation in this letter of invasion; I do not think at that time General Lee had any more definite plan than to capture Milroy's force in the Shenandoah Valley, and manœuver the Northern army out of Virginia. All that he meant by aggressive action was a strategic, not a tactical offensive.

On the 19th, writing to Ewell, who was at Hagerstown, General Lee said: "I very much regret that you have not the benefit of your whole corps, for, with that north of the Potomac, should we be able to detain General Hooker's army from following you, you would be able to accomplish as much unmolested as the whole army could perform with General Hooker in its front. If your advance causes Hooker to cross the Potomac, or separate his army in any way, Longstreet can follow you. The last of Hill's divisions had, on the evening of the 18th, advanced a few miles this side of Culpeper Court-house *en route* to the Valley."

Ewell had not then been ordered to go into Pennsylvania, and it seems that Longstreet's following Ewell depended entirely on Hooker. Hooker did not follow Ewell, but kept between Lee and Washington. General Lee could not have expected that if his whole army crossed the Potomac, Hooker would stand still in Virginia. Some of his biographers and eulogists seem to think so — three of his staff officers say so.

From Berryville on June 23 he wrote to President Davis: "If an army can be organized under command of General Beauregard and pushed forward to Culpeper

Court-house, threatening Washington from that direction, it would not only effect a diversion most favorable for this army, but would, I think, relieve us from any apprehension of attack upon Richmond during our absence."

If it had been practicable to raise such an army, as the campaign closed the next week at Gettysburg, it could not have been assembled in time to render any assistance to General Lee in the Pennsylvania campaign. On the day (19th) that General Lee wrote to Ewell in what event Longstreet would follow him, he wrote again to Mr. Davis saying that — "Ewell, with two divisions, has advanced from the Potomac towards Pennsylvania. His Third (Early's) is retained near Shepherdstown for the present to guard his flank and rear. General Longstreet's corps on the Ashby's and Snicker's Gap roads threatens the enemy, who is massed between him and Washington. General Stuart's cavalry is operating in his front. I hope the First division of A. P. Hill's corps will reach here to-day, so that Early may be relieved and follow Ewell. All attempts of the enemy to penetrate the mountains have been repulsed by Stuart's cavalry, who yesterday again drove him from Middleburg, and by reports received last evening the enemy's infantry have evacuated Aldie. [Meade's corps had not left Aldie.] *Indications seem to be that his main body is proceeding towards the Potomac, whether upon Harper's Ferry or to cross the river east of it is not yet known.* The difficulty of procuring supplies retards and renders more uncertain our future movements." [Italics mine.]

It appears, therefore, that General Lee was aware that

Hooker was preparing to cross the Potomac; he could not then have been surprised when he heard he had crossed. Again, on the 20th, he wrote Mr. Davis: "Lieutenant-Colonel [E. V.] White of the cavalry has cut the Baltimore and Ohio east of Point of Rocks.[1] General Milroy has abandoned the south side of the Potomac, occupying Harper's Ferry with a picket, and holds the Maryland Heights with about 8000 (11,000) men. General Ewell's corps is north of the Potomac, occupying Sharpsburg, Boonsboro, and Hagerstown. His advance cavalry is at Chambersburg, Pennsylvania. The first division of A. P. Hill's corps will reach this vicinity to-day; the rest follow.

[1] Colonel White's report to Stuart says: "I crossed the Potomac last night (17th) about three miles above the Point of Rocks; broke the railroad and the telegraph wires at that point; then moved down to the Point of Rocks, at which place I attacked the enemy, killed 4, wounded 20 and captured 53, including three commissioned officers. I captured a train of cars and a number of wagons together with a large amount of baggage and camp equipage, which were burned."

Captain Semmes says: "On June 17 I was ordered by General Tyler, in company with Captain Vernon's company, to go to the Point of Rocks and hold the position. Before we got there we were attacked by White's battalion; we were overpowered and whipped."

This affair happened on the day that Stuart arrived at Middleburg. Point of Rocks is where the B. and O. railroad is located on the bank of the Potomac and is ten or twelve miles east of Harper's Ferry. After that affair, troops were sent there and to the mouth of the Monocacy. Longstreet's book says he wanted Stuart to cross at Point of Rocks. Stuart could not have crossed there. Point of Rocks is not mentioned in his correspondence with Stuart. He gave no such advice or order. He told Stuart to go through Hopewell Gap in rear of the enemy. But in going by Hopewell Stuart would have to go in an opposite direction from Point of Rocks; besides Point of Rocks was *between* and in *front* of *both* armies and in the rear of *neither*.

General Longstreet's corps, with Stuart's cavalry, still occupy the Blue Ridge between the roads leading through Ashby's and Snicker's Gaps, holding in check a large force of the enemy consisting of cavalry, infantry, and artillery. *The movement of the main body of the enemy is still toward the Potomac,* but its real destination is not yet discovered."

Again, on the 23d he wrote Mr. Davis: "*Reports of the movements of the enemy east of the Blue Ridge cause me to believe that he is preparing to cross the Potomac. A pontoon bridge is said to be laid at Edwards' Ferry, and his army corps, that he had advanced to Leesburg and the foot of the mountains, appears to be withdrawing.* Their attempts to penetrate the mountains have been successfully repelled by Genral Stuart with the cavalry. General Stuart last night was within a few miles of Aldie, to which point the enemy had retired. *Ewell's corps is in motion towards the Susquehanna.* General A. P. Hill's corps is moving [from Charlestown] towards the Potomac; his leading division will reach Shepherdstown to-day. I have withdrawn Longstreet west of the Shenandoah and, if nothing prevents, he will follow to-morrow." [Italics mine.]

These letters show that General Lee knew that it was Hooker's intention to follow him across the Potomac. The truth is, General Lee's fears of Hooker's crossing the river ahead of him, or that he was moving in that direction, were not justified by the information that Stuart had given him. The itinerary of the Army of the Potomac shows only a few slight changes in the positions of the seven corps between the 18th and the 25th of June.

Hooker's headquarters were at Fairfax. It is strange that no part of that army had been sent in pursuit of Ewell. I think it was because Hooker did not think that Lee would cross the Potomac. On the 22d Ewell received orders to move on to the Susquehanna. He was told that it would depend upon the quantity of supplies he found in the country, whether the Confederate army followed him or not.[1]

"If Harrisburg comes within your way," General Lee said, "capture it." This was not an order; it simply gave Ewell full discretion to go there, or not to go, according to circumstances. He further said: "General A. P. Hill arrived yesterday in the vicinity of Berryville. I shall move him on to-day, if possible. Saturday Longstreet withdrew from the Blue Ridge. Yesterday the enemy pressed our cavalry so hard with infantry and cavalry on the Upperville road that McLaws' division had to be sent back to hold Ashby's Gap. I have not yet heard from there this morning." "General Stuart could not ascertain whether it was intended as a real advance toward the Valley or to ascertain our position."

[1] In his report dated August 20, 1863, Stuart estimated Jenkins' cavalry brigade at 3800 men. General Rodes, in his report, speaks incidentally of Jenkins being 1600 strong. Stuart took command of Jenkins in Pennsylvania, and at the date of his report Jenkins' brigade was on duty with him at Culpeper. As Jenkins' returns were in his adjutant's office, it is not probable that he would greatly have overestimated his strength. In addition to Jenkins, there were with Ewell, Emack's Maryland battalion, White's and Gilmor's cavalry battalions, and Randolph's company. It is a low estimate to place the total of this force at 3000 cavalry. These operated on Ewell's right; on his left was Imboden's brigade of mounted infantry and cavalry.

It was only a reconnaissance that Pleasanton made on the 21st. Early the next morning he returned to Aldie. After hearing from Stuart that Pleasanton had gone back, General Lee at 3.30 P.M. on the same day wrote to Ewell: "I have just received your letter of this morning from opposite Shepherdstown. Mine of to-day, authorizing you to move towards the Susquehanna, I hope has reached you ere this. After dispatching my letter, learning that the enemy had not renewed his attempts of yesterday to break through the Blue Ridge, I directed General R. H. Anderson's division [of Hill's corps] to commence its march towards Shepherdstown. It will reach there to-morrow. *I also directed General Stuart, should the enemy have so far retired from his front as to permit of the departure of a portion of his cavalry, to march with three brigades across the Potomac and place himself on your right and in communication with you, keep you advised of the movements of the enemy and assist in collecting supplies for the army. I have not heard from him since.* [Italics mine.] I also directed Imboden, if opportunity offered, to cross the Potomac and perform the same offices on your left. I shall endeavor to get Early's regiments to him as soon as possible. I do not know what has become of the infantry of the Maryland line. I had intended that to guard Winchester."

This letter settles a question that has been raised whether Stuart's instructions required him to remain in Virginia and march north on the right flank of the two corps that were with Lee, or to move to Pennsylvania and join Ewell on the Susquehanna. General Lee's staff officers say that he was ordered to march into Pennsylvania on Longstreet's right flank between him and the enemy; the record says he was not. As they were widely separated he could not be with Longstreet and Ewell at the same time. When this letter was written, Ewell was marching north; Longstreet and Hill were still in Virginia and had received no orders to go to Pennsylvania. Stuart did not possess the power of the Genius of Aladdin's Lamp; he could not act as Ewell's Chief of Cavalry on the Susquehanna and watch Hooker with Longstreet on the Potomac. General Lee's staff officers say he ought to have done it. I do not think he possessed any such magical power.

This is General Lee's letter of instructions to Stuart:

June 22nd, 1863.

MAJOR-GENERAL STUART:—

GENERAL: I have just received your note of 7.45 this morning to General Longstreet. I judge the efforts of the enemy yesterday were to arrest our progress and ascertain our whereabouts. Perhaps he is satisfied. Do you know where he is and what he is doing? *I fear he will steal a march on us and get across the Potomac before we are aware.* [Italics mine.] If you find that he is moving northward and that two brigades can guard the Blue Ridge and take care of your rear, you can move with the other three into Maryland and take position on General Ewell's right, place yourself in communication with him, guard his flank, keep him informed of the enemy's movements and collect all the supplies you can for the use of the army. One column of General Ewell's army will probably move towards the Susquehanna by the Emmittsburg route, another by Chambersburg. Accounts from last night state that there was no enemy west of Frederick. A cavalry force (about 100) guarded the Monocacy bridge, which was barricaded. You will of course take charge of Jenkins' brigade and give necessary instructions.

At that time Longstreet's corps was at the Gaps of the Blue Ridge; Stuart was guarding the approaches from the east; he was brought into contact with Longstreet and, to some extent, under his orders. His correspondence with General Lee at that time passed through General Longstreet. This was to produce concert of action. The above letter of instructions to Stuart was sent to Longstreet and subject to his approval.

June 22, 1863, 7.30 P.M.

GENERAL R. E. LEE:—

GENERAL: Yours of 4 o'clock this afternoon is received. I have forwarded your letter to Géneral Stuart with the suggestion that he pass by the *enemy's rear* if he thinks that he may get through. We have seen nothing of the enemy to-day. [Italics mine.]

Most Respectfully,
JAMES LONGSTREET,
Lieutenant-General, etc.

MILLWOOD, June 22, 1863, 7 P.M.

MAJOR-GENERAL, J. E. B. STUART:—

GENERAL: General Lee has enclosed to me this letter for you, to be forwarded to you provided you can be spared from my front, and provided I think you can cross the Potomac without disclosing our plans. *He speaks of your leaving via Hopewell Gap [Bull Run Mountain] and passing by the rear of the enemy.* [Italics are mine.] *If you can get through by that route I think you will be less likely to indicate what our plans are than if you should cross by passing to our rear.* [Shepherdstown.] I forward the letter of instructions with these suggestions. Please advise me of the conditions of affairs before you leave and order General Hampton — whom I suppose you will leave here in command — to report to me at Millwood, either by letter or in person, as may be agreeable to him.

Most Respectfully,
JAMES LONGSTREET,
Lieutenant-General.

N.B. I think that your passage of the Potomac by *our rear* [Shepherdstown] at the present moment will in a measure disclose our plans. You had better not leave us, therefore, unless you can take the proposed route *in rear* of the enemy. [Italics mine.]

General Lee's letter of the 22d to Stuart, which was sent through Longstreet, simply directed him, in the event that the enemy "is moving northward," to leave two brigades to guard the Gaps, and, with the other three, to place himself on Ewell's right on the Susquehanna. It did not suggest by what route he should go. But Longstreet's letter, forwarding it to Stuart, says that General Lee, in a letter to him, spoke of his going through Hopewell Gap in the Bull Run Mountain; and he urges Stuart to go that route and around the rear of the enemy. In directing Stuart to join Ewell, if the enemy was moving northward, General Lee clearly did not mean that he was only to do so if Hooker's army was actually *in motion* to the north, but if he was satisfied that its general trend and direction were that way. There was a bare possibility that Hooker might turn his face toward Richmond; General Lee wanted Stuart to be on his back if he turned.

On the morning of the 24th, when I reported to Stuart the situation of Hooker's army, he had received another letter of instructions from General Lee. It differed[1] from the first in suggesting to Stuart to cross the Potomac in Hooker's rear. I suppose he did so because he had heard from General Longstreet that he wanted Stuart to go that way; and General Lee seems to have suggested in a letter to Longstreet that Stuart might go through the Hopewell Gap in the Bull Run Mountain. I have quoted Longstreet's letter to Stuart advising him "*to pass by the enemy's rear,*" if possible.

In conference with Stuart that day it was arranged that

[1] Dated June 3rd.

I should again cross the Bull Run Mountain with my small command and meet him the next day at a designated point on the Little River turnpike. There I was to take command of his advance as it moved on through Hooker's army to Seneca Ford. Ewell was then in the Cumberland Valley with Rodes' and Johnson's divisions. Early was moving north on a parallel line near the western base of South Mountain. Ewell had an abundance of cavalry with him.

Imboden with a considerable body of mounted troops moved on his left to Mercersburg. With Ewell's cavalry were two battalions commanded by Colonel Lije White and Major Harry Gilmor. They had been detached and sent with Ewell and Early because White and Gilmor were regarded as two of the boldest cavalry leaders in the Southern army; and many of their men were from Maryland and their homes were on the border. Gilmor was from Baltimore; Colonel White lived on the Potomac. Their knowledge of the country would make them valuable as guides and in procuring information. French's cavalry regiment and White's battalion went east with Early to York. Ewell arrived at Carlisle on the 27th. On the 24th Early halted on the pike leading from Chambersburg to Gettysburg and went to see Ewell. He received orders to move east through the Cashtown pass to York, cut the railroad between Baltimore and Harrisburg, to destroy the bridge over the Susquehanna, and then to join Ewell at Carlisle. Before he got to Cashtown, a village on the pike at the eastern base of the South Mountain (Blue Ridge), he turned to his left on the Mummasburg road, but sent Gordon's brigade to Gettysburg.

Gordon camped at Gettysburg that night and Early rode to the town to see him in the evening. If Gettysburg had been General Lee's objective point, as historians say, it is remarkable that he did not instruct Early to hold it when he had it; and that he should have marched such a roundabout way (*via* Chambersburg) to get there. His military secretary and biographer, Long, says that at Fredericksburg, just before the campaign began, General Lee traced the lines of march of his army on a map, and pointing to Gettysburg said there the great battle would be fought. This is fiction. I doubt if General Lee at that time had ever heard of such a place. It was of no strategic value. A military writer of high authority defines a strategic point as being "Any point or region in the theater of warlike operations which affords to its possessors an advantage over his opponent — every point in the theater of war, the possession of which is of great importance to an army in its military operations, is a strategical point. There are points which an army acting on the offensive strives to gain; the army on the defensive strives to retain." Gettysburg offered no such offensive or defensive advantages. On the day before the battle the commander of neither army wanted to get possession of it; and either was willing for the other to have it and hold it. Meade, who had superseded Hooker, held it simply as a cavalry outpost; General Lee had no thought of going there.

Some writers have said it was a place of military importance because it was the center from which so many roads radiated. That was the very thing that made it weak and untenable. It was so easy to approach it from any direction and to turn it. An army on the Ridge had a tactical advantage in an attack on its front; but the attacking force had the choice of turning its flanks. On the second day of the battle Meade was still doubtful about holding the position. He feared a movement around him toward Washington; which, it is said, Longstreet advised.

MEADE TO HALLECK

July 2, 1863, 3 P.M.

If not attacked, and I can get any positive information of the position of the enemy, which will justify me in so doing, I shall attack. If I find it hazardous to do so, or am satisfied the enemy is endeavoring to move to my rear and interpose between me and Washington, I shall fall back to my supplies at Westminster.

The great objection to Lee's army occupying the place, even if the enemy did not oppose it, was that its front did not cover its line of communication, or of retreat to the Potomac. It was compelled, in military language, to form a front to a flank. Such a formation is always avoided, if possible. This was McClellan's weakness on the Chickahominy; Lee took advantage of it and sent Stuart and Jackson to cut him off from his base on the Pamunkey, and force him to retreat by the flank to a new base on the James. A retreat under such circumstances is always a difficult and hazardous operation.

General Lee discovered this on his retreat to the Potomac with the enemy on his flanks. Historians have represented — notably Lee's staff officers, Colonel Taylor, General Long, Colonel Marshall and also Fitz-Hugh Lee — that it was owing to the absence of the cavalry that his adversary by celerity of movement got ahead of him; which implies that Gettysburg was their objective point. Now, on July 1, at 12 noon, when the battle was raging at Gettysburg (but Meade, who was fifteen miles away had not heard of it; neither had Lee), he sent a dispatch to Halleck, "I shall not advance any, but prepare to receive an attack in case Lee makes one. A battle-field is being selected in the rear, on which the army can be rapidly concentrated on Pipe Creek between Middleburg and Manchester, covering my depot at Westminster."

Meade had intended to move on July 1 away from Gettysburg and nearer the Susquehanna. In a letter to Pleasanton on June 30, Butterfield, his chief of staff, said that his "projected movement is towards the line of the Baltimore and Harrisburg railroad. His instructions require him to cover Baltimore and Washington, while his objective point is the army under Lee."

As Early was at York, Ewell at Carlisle with Jenkins' cavalry skirmishing in the suburbs of Harrisburg, while Stuart was moving to the east to join them with a long wagon-train he had captured, Meade concluded that Lee would concentrate somewhere on the Susquehanna. On the night of June 30, Reynolds with three corps was about Emmittsburg, ten miles from Gettysburg; the other corps were off to the east and heading for the Susquehanna. Early in the morning Reynolds, without hearing from Meade, moved in the direction of Gettysburg; not to fight a battle but simply in observation. Buford's cavalry division had occupied the place the day before. The news that the Confederates were falling back from Carlisle and York had not reached Meade on June 30. Stuart had cut the telegraph wire. But after Reynolds had received orders to move to Gettysburg, Meade got news from Harrisburg that the Confederates had evacuated Carlisle and York, and were apparently concentrating at Chambersburg. So he immediately issued a circular informing corps commanders that his object had been accomplished in compelling the enemy to withdraw from the line of the Susquehanna.

"If the enemy assume the offensive," he said, "and attack, it is my intention, after holding them in check sufficiently long to withdraw the trains and other impedimenta, to withdraw the army from its present position and form a line of battle with the left resting in the neighborhood of Middleburg and the right at Manchester, the general direction being that of Pipe Creek."

In a letter to Reynolds on July 1, the last he ever wrote him, Meade said, "The movement of your troops at Gettysburg was ordered before the positive knowledge of the enemy's withdrawal from Harrisburg and concentration was received."

Orders were immediately issued for the army to fall back if the Confederates advanced. But Reynolds was killed and never received Meade's order to withdraw to Pipe Creek. If he had received it that morning before starting from camp, no battle would have been fought at Gettysburg. Yet, according to historians, there was a race between Lee and Meade to get to Gettysburg. *So say General Lee's staff officers.* Reynolds had camped on the night of June 30, between Emmittsburg and Gettysburg. When he reached Gettysburg he found Buford's cavalry engaged with Heth's division that was advancing on the pike from Cashtown. Buford knew that Hill was at Cashtown, and that Ewell was ten miles north at Heidlersburg the night before. He could not have expected to do more than to hold the Confederates in check. Instead of forming his line of battle on Cemetery Ridge with Buford's cavalry on his flanks, Reynolds abandoned that strong position and moved two miles out on the Cashtown road with his infantry to join Buford. He then had Hill in his front and Ewell on his flank. The result of his tactical error was a defeat for which he paid the penalty of his life. His monument on the field perpetuates the memory of a heroic action and a great blunder. If Reynolds' object in leaving the Ridge and going to meet Hill had been to lure the Southern army to a place where it must fight at a disadvantage, then he would have reproduced Hannibal's stratagem of the battle on the Trebia. Mommsen says: "From the earliest hour of the morning the Roman light troops had been skirmishing with the light cavalry of the enemy; the latter slowly retreated and the Romans eagerly pursued it through the deeply swollen Trebia, so as to follow up the advantage which they had gained. Suddenly it halted; the Roman vanguard found itself face to face with the army of Hannibal drawn up for battle on a field chosen by himself; it was lost unless the main body should cross the stream with speed to its support." The main body crossed, but the Romans lost. Reynolds did by accident what Hannibal did by design.

On the morning of June 24, General Lee left Berryville with Longstreet's corps to unite with Ewell, who was then in Pennsylvania on the road to Carlisle; he crossed the Potomac the next day at Williamsport and spent two days in the neighborhood of Hagerstown. Maryland is only about ten miles wide where he crossed.

On the night of the 26th his headquarters were near the State line. His intention evidently was to keep in close contact with Hooker who was crossing the river east of the Blue Ridge at Edwards' Ferry on the same day. He did not want to get too far ahead of Hooker; he might turn back and march on Richmond as Sherman marched, after Hood left him, from Atlanta through Georgia. If he did, Lee would be close on his heels and would have the choice of pursuing him, or of taking Washington and Baltimore.

A. P. Hill, with Heth's and Pender's divisions, also crossed the Potomac on the 25th at Shepherdstown; Anderson's division had crossed on the 24th and had gone on to Boonsboro near South Mountain. Early had just left there and had marched north along the western base of the mountain. Anderson was sent to the Pass as a feint to create the impression that the Confederates were moving east. The object was to draw Hooker over the river in pursuit. General Lee here repeated the strategy that drew Hooker away from the Rappahannock.

On June 25, writing from Williamsport to Mr. Davis, General Lee said: "I have not sufficient troops to maintain my communications and have to abandon them. I think I can throw General Hooker's army across the

Potomac and draw troops from the South; embarrassing their plan of campaign in a measure, if I do nothing else and have to return. I still hope that all things will end well for us at Vicksburg."

This letter is not an afterthought written in despair when his plans had been defeated and his hopes were blasted, but a part of the *res gestæ* of the campaign and a key to his operations. It discloses the fact that he was manœuvering to draw Hooker out of Virginia and not invading hostile territory with any expectation of conquest or occupation; or of dictating a peace on Northern soil. His main object seemed to be to throw Hooker over the Potomac; the incidental advantage would be that it would create a diversion and cause troops to be brought from the South in defense of the North. By abandoning his communications he meant that as he had no base of supply he would subsist on the country and no line of communication would be necessary; as for ordnance stores and ammunition, he took with him all he expected to need.

That he was not in the least sensitive about his rear is shown by the fact that he had marched by Harper's Ferry and made no effort to compel the garrison of 11,000 men to abandon it. Yet up to the day of the battle there was continuous and uninterrupted intercourse between Lee's army and the Potomac. The reason was that Hooker had sent nearly all his cavalry after Stuart to defend his own communications with Washington. An English officer, Colonel Freemantle, a guest at Longstreet's headquarters, in his diary speaks of the spoils that Ewell was sending back.

"June 25. We took leave of Mrs. —— and her hospitable family, and started to overtake Generals Lee and Longstreet, who were supposed to be crossing the Potomac at Williamsport. Before we got more than a few miles on our way we began to meet the first fruits of Ewell's advance into Pennsylvania.

"June 26th. The town of Williamsport is on a bank of the river and we were now in Maryland. We had the mortification to learn that Generals Lee and Longstreet had quitted Williamsport this morning at 11 o'clock and were obliged to toil on to Hagerstown, six miles further.

"June 27th. After riding eight miles I came up with General Longstreet at 6.30 A.M., and was just in time as he was on the point of moving. Both he and his staff were most kind when I introduced myself and stated my difficulties. . . . General Longstreet is an Alabamian, a thick-set and determined looking man, forty-three years old. . . . He is never far from General Lee, who relies very much on his judgment. By the soldiers he is favorably spoken of as the 'best fighter in the army.' . . . This part of Pennsylvania is very flourishing, highly cultivated and, in comparison with the Southern States, thickly peopled. But all the cattle and horses have been seized by Ewell, farm labor had come to a complete standstill. . . . I entered Chambersburg at 6 P.M. . . . The women (many of whom are pretty and well dressed) were particularly sour and disagreeable in their remarks. I heard one of them say: 'Look at Pharaoh and his army going to the Red Sea.' . . . Others were pointing and laughing at Hood's ragged Jacks, who were passing at the

GETTYSBURG

time. ... They answered the numerous taunts of the ladies with cheers and laughter. One female had seen fit to adorn her ample bosom with a huge Yankee flag, and she stood at the door of her house, her countenance expressing the greatest contempt for the bare-footed Rebs; several companies passed her without taking any notice, but at last a Texan gravely remarked; 'Take care, madam, for Hood's boys is great for storming breastworks when the Yankee colors is on them.' After this speech the patriotic lady beat a precipitate retreat. ... I found Generals Lee and Longstreet encamped on the latter (Gettysburg) road, three quarters of a mile from the town (Chambersburg). ... Ewell, after the capture of Winchester, had advanced rapidly into Pennsylvania and has already sent back great quantities of horses, mules, wagons, beeves, and other necessities. He is now at or beyond Carlisle, laying the country under contribution and making Pennsylvania support the war instead of poor, used-up and worn-out Virginia. The corps of A. P. Hill and Longstreet are now near this place, full of confidence and high spirits. ... June 30. This morning, before marching from Chambersburg, General Longstreet introduced me to the Commander-in-Chief. General Lee is almost without exception the handsomest man of his age I ever saw. ... It is impossible to please Longstreet more than by praising Lee. I believe these two generals to be as little ambitious and as thoroughly unselfish as any men in the world."

On the 25th and 26th, while General Lee, with the corps of Hill and Longstreet, was resting in Maryland near the South Mountain (Blue Ridge), Hooker's army, after crossing the river below Harper's Ferry, was marching to seize the Gaps. The itinerary of the army of the Potomac shows that at that time two corps with cavalry had already reached Middletown and Jefferson in the Catoctin Valley near the eastern base of the mountain. Another corps was near at Point of Rocks. It must be presumed that the Confederate generals used every available means to discover the whereabouts and movements of the enemy. It would be proof of their incapacity if they neglected to do it. It is a conclusive presumption in law that a party has notice and that he has used due diligence to acquire knowledge of a fact when there are circumstances sufficient to put him on inquiry about it. General Lee was making manœuvers to throw Hooker over the river and he knew, as he says, that Hooker had thrown a pontoon over it; it is incredible that he did not have a vidette and a signal station on the mountain to inform him when his object had been accomplished. That he was guilty of such negligence I cannot believe — even on the testimony of the staff officers. The pontoon bridge was notice of Hooker's intention to cross, and should have put General Lee on inquiry to find out when he was crossing. With each army corps was a signal corps; from a mountain peak a scout, or a signal officer, could have seen a host in the Valley below, — "like the leaves of the forest when summer is green."

A cavalry force was not required to find this out; one man on the mountain could have done it as well as a thousand. Hooker made more use of his signal officers than of his cavalry to get information. I have spoken of the capture of one he had sent to establish a station on the Blue Ridge to overlook the Shenandoah Valley. On June 23, Tyler, at Harper's Ferry, telegraphed Hooker, who was then at Fairfax: "The signal officer reports that the atmosphere is clear and that he can see a line of troops ten or twelve miles long, moving from the direction of Berryville towards Shepherdstown Ford. It looks like Lee's movement towards Hagerstown in Pennsylvania."

It was Anderson's division, the advance of A. P. Hill's corps. On the 24th the signal officer discovered the movements of Longstreet's and Hill's corps, and Tyler again telegraphed to Hooker: "The following is just received from the signal station — 'the wagon train that was near Shepherdstown last night is now crossing the river near Sharpsburg. A large train extending as far as I can see on the Berryville road is passing Charlestown towards Shepherdstown. I see artillery with it.'"

General Lee was then marching to the Potomac. This premature movement of Longstreet's and Hill's troops in sight of the signal station on Maryland Heights, as disclosed in the above dispatches, made the Gettysburg campaign the Iliad of the South. It set Hooker's army in motion for the Potomac the next day. I shall refer to it again.

The following dispatch shows that Hooker's signal officer thought that the Confederates would have signal stations on the South Mountain as they had reached there first:

SLOCUM TO HOOKER

June 23rd, 1863, 10 P.M.

The signal officer at Point of Rocks reports a large force of the enemy at Shepherdstown, encamped on the south side of the river; they have not crossed yet.

TYLER TO HOOKER

HARPER'S FERRY, June 23, A.M.

Captain Daniels, the Signal officer, reports this morning as follows: view this morning is very fine. The enemy's camps are all gone in the vicinity of Sharpsburg and only a few troops left. But I can not see where they have gone. A long line of troops with wagon train can be seen coming towards Charlestown on a road south of the place.

CAPTAIN DANIELS TO MYERS, SIGNAL OFFICER

June 23, 1863.

Enemy that were in Sharpsburg yesterday have gone. Rear of the train is in sight, going north to Hagerstown. A wagon and artillery train is now passing through Charlestown towards Shepherdstown, 10 miles in length, accompanied by infantry and cavalry.

WILLIAMS, A. A. G., TO FRENCH, HARPER'S FERRY

FAIRFAX C. H., June 24th.

The General suggests that you keep the signal officers employed and order them to secure commanding points for observation.

BABCOCK (signal officer) TO HOOKER

June 24th.

I learn beyond a doubt that the last of Lee's entire army has passed through Martinsburg towards the Potomac. . . . The main body are crossing at Shepherdstown. . . . I can see them from the Mountain. . . . Large bodies of troops can be seen from South Mountain at Antietam Furnace by aid of a glass.

WILLIAMS, A. A. G., TO HOWARD, EDWARD'S FERRY

June 24th, 11.35 P.M.

The Commanding-General directs that your corps take up the line of march early to-morrow morning for Sandy Hook, in the vicinity of Harper's Ferry, reaching that place to-morrow afternoon.

GETTYSBURG

SAME TO FRENCH AT HARPER'S FERRY

The General [Hooker] suggests that you keep the signal officers employed and order them to secure commanding points.

HOOKER TO REYNOLDS, EDWARD'S FERRY
June 25th, 1863, 12.40 P.M.

Your dispatch, 9.45 P.M., received. General Howard has received orders directing him to report to you, and states that he has sent a staff officer to report to you. His headquarters to-night are at Jefferson. In Catoctin Valley near South Mountain.

OFFICE OF THE SIGNAL OFFICER,
WASHINGTON, June 25th, 1863

SIGNAL OFFICER, Maryland Heights: —
What has become of the immense trains reported from your station as moving through Charlestown to Shepherdstown?

ALBERT J. MYER.

HOOKER TO HANCOCK, THOROUGHFARE GAP
June 25th, 1863, 7 A.M.

On receipt of this order take up your line of march to Edwards' Ferry. Your best line will be via Sudley Springs and Gum Springs. The last named place you should reach to-night.

OFFICE OF THE SIGNAL OFFICER,
WASHINGTON, June 25th, 1863.

CAPTAIN L. B. NORTON, Chief Signal Officer,
Headquarters Army of the Potomac: —

If any considerable portion of the Army of the Potomac is moving north in Maryland, either in the Middletown Valley or east of the Catoctin Ridge, suggest to General Butterfield to keep the crest of the South Mountain and Catoctin Ridge clear of the enemy's scouts and signal officers by scouting parties of our cavalry. Send some of our [signal] officers with the cavalry.[1]

ALBERT J. MYER, Colonel and Signal-Officer.

[1] WILLIAMS, A. A. G., TO PLEASANTON
June 25th, 1863, 7.10 P.M.

The commanding general directs that you hold your command in readiness to march in the direction of Edwards' Ferry. Hancock will be at Gum Springs to-night. The First, Third and Eleventh corps will cross the river to-day. No supplies will be sent up to you to-day, unless you absolutely need them. You can draw at Edwards' Ferry.

On the other hand, it would have been much easier for the Confederates to keep the crest of the mountain clear of Hooker's scouts and signal officers. It was thought that the Confederates would do what they could do. I assume, until there is evidence to the contrary, that they did. But, to discover the presence of the enemy, it was not necessary to send out scouts and signal officers to the top of the mountain; by the 26th, Hooker's troops were occupying the Passes and in plain view. At 8.10 A.M., on the 25th — when Lee and Hill were crossing the river — Butterfield, chief of staff, who was still with Hooker at Fairfax Court-house, sent Reynolds a telegram saying: "Orders were telegraphed you early this morning to assume command of the Third and Eleventh Corps, in addition to your own (First). At the same time directions were given for a brigade of cavalry to report to you with two sections of artillery. All of these troops are under orders to cross the Potomac to-day at or near Edwards' Ferry, all but the Third Corps being convenient to that crossing at this moment. The cavalry and sections are ordered to report to you, that you may take possession of Crampton Pass and what is called South Mountain Gap (Turner's), as speedily as possible — if practicable, to-night; and that each cavalry column be closely followed by a brigade of infantry and a battery, and all instructed to hold these passes until further orders. Late last night the enemy had no force at either point. As their posses-

sion may be of importance in determining the future
operations of this army, the General desires that you will
take and hold them. You will direct your column in
the direction of Middletown on two lines, — should you
find it practicable,—and there encamp, should you receive no orders to the contrary. Please keep the General
informed of all your movements and those of the enemy
as soon as you can learn them; and especially advise him
the moment we are in possession of the Gaps. Two of
his staff officers will be sent you; also maps."

Hooker's army crossed the Potomac about as far below
Harper's Ferry as the Confederate army crossed above.
Reynolds, now commanding three corps, in pursuance of
orders, sent the following letter to Howard:

NEAR POOLESVILLE, June 25th, 1863, 9 A.M.

MAJOR-GENERAL HOWARD,

Commanding Eleventh Corps: —

After detaching the brigade and battery to support General De-
Forest's cavalry going to Crampton's Pass, you will move your command
in the direction of Middletown, as indicated, unless the passage of the
Pass be disputed, in which case you will move to the support of Colonel
DeForest. General Hooker will be here by 10 or 11 to-morrow morn-
ing.

STEINWEHR TO HOWARD.

BOONSBOROUGH GAP, June 27th, 1863, 1 P.M.

There is a monument placed upon a hill about one-half mile from
here, from which point an extensive and clear view is had of the whole
Valley including the towns of Sharpsburg, Williamsport, Hagerstown,
Boonsborough, and also the approaches to the Gaps south of us. In
this important position I have placed an intelligent officer, furnished
with a field glass, who will report to me whatever he may see of movements in the Valley, and which reports I shall forthwith transmit to you,
if of any importance.

HEADQUARTERS ARMY OF THE POTOMAC
June 25th, 1863.

JOHN C. BABCOCK, Frederick, Md.: —

General Reynolds goes to-day with three corps to hold, if possible, the South Mountain Gap (Boonsboro) and Crampton's Gap. Report.

REYNOLDS TO HOWARD
JEFFERSON, June 26th, 1863.

Let me know as soon as you get information about the passes — Crampton's and South Mountain. General Hooker is at Poolesville and very anxious to know if they are occupied. . . . My headquarters will be here to-night, and I will move up all the corps together, so as to concentrate at Middletown or in that neighborhood.

HOOKER TO BIRNEY
POINT OF ROCKS, June 26th, 2.30 P.M.

General Hooker directs that you report to General Reynolds at Jefferson, who will command the First, Third and Eleventh corps until the marches are completed as ordered.

REYNOLDS TO HOOKER
JEFFERSON, June 26th, 2.30 P.M.

The signal officers report that they can see nothing at Crampton's Gap. Howard has moved up to Middletown and my aide, Captain Wadsworth, went with General Howard to Middletown. General Birney (Third corps) is at Adamstown and I have sent him orders to move up here to-morrow and shall move Doubleday forward to Howard. It is called six miles to Middletown from here and also six or seven miles from Adamstown here. . . . General Stahl was at Frederick to-day and will be at Middletown to-night.

TYLER TO HOOKER

That portion of the rebel troops passing Boonsboro are evidently taking the route by Emmitsburg into Pennsylvania. A. P. Hill's division passed Sharpsburg this morning for Hagerstown. Anderson's division had gone to Boonsboro the day before. The next day it marched to Hagerstown.

At that time Jones' cavalry brigade was on picket duty on the Potomac in Loudon County, Virginia, having been placed there to observe the enemy. Hooker's troops crossed and marched up the river in sight of him. There was not a more vigilant officer in the army than Jones. I knew him well, and had been his adjutant. No one who knew Jones can believe that he failed to watch and report what he saw. A courier sent over the Blue Ridge could have carried the news in a few hours to Lee or Longstreet.[1]

Then the Twelfth Virginia Cavalry, one of the largest and best regiments in the army, was detached from Jones to picket the Potomac west of the Ridge from Shepherdstown to Harper's Ferry. The homes of many of the men were in the Valley and they knew the country. Baylor's company was from the neighborhood of Charlestown. He was an active partisan officer; with him were a number of men distinguished as scouts. Couriers were sent frequently from this regiment to General Lee. If Lee or Longstreet didn't know where the enemy were, he had only to send one of these scouts over the mountain to find out. Some historians — including some of Lee's staff officers — say that Lee, Longstreet, and A. P. Hill spent

---

[1] MEADE TO HALLECK
June 28, 1863, 7.25 P.M.

General Steinwehr, from the Mountain House, South Mountain, reports that his scouts inform him that 5,000 of Stuart's cavalry passed through Williamsport yesterday afternoon. General Sedgwick, on the march from Poolesville, reports that 3,000 of the enemy's cavalry, with some artillery, are in his rear. This is communicated to you for your information. My impression is that Stuart has divided his force with a view of harassing our right and left flanks.

two days in Maryland, in the shadow of South Mountain, and never suspected that Hooker's army was on the other side in the Gap; and that General Lee was seized with a panic and spoke of returning immediately to Virginia when he heard at Chambersburg that Hooker had crossed the Potomac.[1]

They do not seem to realize that they bring a grave charge of incompetency against their chief as a commander as well as against his lieutenants. Such Arcadian simplicity should not be imputed to these generals. Lee and Longstreet remained during the 26th about Hagerstown; that night they camped a few miles from there in Pennsylvania. I believe they exercised due vigilance and used the means they had to get information. Kershaw's brigade of Longstreet's corps was the rear of the column. He gives his itinerary as follows:

[1] Longstreet's chief signal officer was Captain J. H. Manning; he was from Loudon County, Virginia, near the Potomac. This gave him the advantage of having a local knowledge of the country. Longstreet's report says: "Captain Manning with his signal torches lighted us across the bridge" at Falling Waters; and again speaks of his having discharged the duties of his department "with zeal and ability." If Longstreet had any curiosity to know where Hooker was, all he had to do was to send Captain Manning on top the mountain. In the last fight of my command, a week or so before General Lee surrendered, Captain Manning happened to be at home on furlough; he volunteered to go in the charge at Hamilton and was severely wounded. I am sorry that he is not living now for I have no doubt he would be a witness to prove that Longstreet made use of his signal corps, when he was on the road to Pennsylvania. It would be a great reflection on Longstreet if he did not. Manning could have told him, and, I believe, did tell him, that Hooker was crossing on his pontoon at Edwards' Ferry while he and Hill were crossing the Potomac above.

"Twenty-sixth, crossed the Potomac River; encamped near Williamsport.

"Twenty-seventh, marched by way of Hagerstown, Middletown, Pa., and Greencastle, and encamped five miles from Chambersburg."

On that day Hooker's army was occupying the South Mountain Passes and looking down on the Confederate columns.

HOWARD TO REYNOLDS

MIDDLETOWN, MD., June 26th, 5.10 P.M.

I have learned from different sources that there is no enemy at Crampton's Pass, though my brigade commander sent there has not reported. Fifteen of my headquarter cavalry dashed into Boonsboro and went half a mile beyond, chasing out a squad of rebel cavalry. [I suppose they were some of the Twelfth Virginia on a scout.] The inhabitants there report that Longstreet encamped between Berryville and Sharpsburg last night and moved this morning towards Hagerstown. . . . Lee in person crossed the Potomac last night. His entire force came up yesterday — reported to be between 60,000 and 70,000 men.[1]

The Northern Generals seem to have had pretty accurate information about Lee's movements. They did not get

[1] STAHEL TO REYNOLDS

June 26th, 1863, 3.10 P.M.

"I have one brigade and one section of artillery at Crampton's Pass, patrolling thoroughly on the other side, but without meeting with any enemy whatever; they are supported by one brigade and two sections of artillery of the Eleventh Corps. I have one regiment in South Mountain Pass patrolling in that vicinity but without meeting any of the enemy. One brigade and two sections of artillery are at Middletown and two regiments about two miles from this place on the road leading to Lewiston. . . . There was a small force of rebel cavalry at Boonsborough this morning but there are none of them there now."

Of course the Confederate cavalry which was sent there to scout reported what they saw.

it from their cavalry, but from observation on the mountain. Pleasanton's cavalry corps did not cross at Edwards' Ferry until the night of the 27th, the day that Lee arrived at Chambersburg. It was kept as a rear-guard of the army because of the news that Stuart was behind it. According to the general rules of war, they would have been in advance, harassing Lee's flank. In this way Stuart protected Lee. During all that time Lee did not lose a wagon or a straggler. Stahel's division of cavalry from Fairfax had been sent to join Reynolds, but did not come up till the night of the 26th, after the Confederates had passed through Maryland. On the 26th, Reynolds at Middletown complained to Hooker that "The cavalry sent out by Stahel does nothing. They go into camp behind the infantry and send out small squads from them. General Stahel was at Frederick to-day and will be at Middletown to-night."

At Hooker's request, Stahel was relieved of command; Kilpatrick succeeded him. The conditions show that General Lee must have known on the 26th that several corps of Hooker's army had arrived near South Mountain when he was in Maryland; he would not in fact have advanced into Pennsylvania if he had not known it. He left the Gaps open to Hooker to pass. He must have calculated that Hooker might cross the mountain and get in his rear: I think he wanted Hooker to do it. He would have turned and finished Hooker.

As before stated, the main body of the Confederate army arrived in Chambersburg on the 27th; Longstreet and General Lee had their headquarters near the town;

GETTYSBURG 113

A. P. Hill, with Pender's and Anderson's divisions, moved several miles east on the Gettysburg pike and joined Heth's division which was in the advance at Fayetteville. The next day a part of Heth's division was sent to Cashtown at the eastern base of South Mountain. It is eight miles from Gettysburg. Heth followed with the remainder the next day.[1]

---

[1] An itinerary of the Confederate army in the Gettysburg campaign is published in "New York at Gettysburg," Vol. I, page 159. Pender's division is marked as "June 25th. Crossed the Potomac at Shepherdstown and marched to Fayetteville." Heth's is not mentioned on the 25th and 26th. Pender could not have marched all the way from Shepherdstown to Fayetteville on the 25th. Hill's corps certainly camped somewhere that night *en route* between Hagerstown and Chambersburg. Heth's division led the advance and no doubt arrived at Fayetteville on the 26th. On the 28th the itinerary says — "Hill's corps halted at Fayetteville." On the 29th — "Heth's division moved from Fayetteville to Cashtown." A part of Heth's division had gone a day or so before to Cashtown and had a picket at Fairfield several miles south. Buford ran up against it on the morning of the 30th.

Professor Jacobs of Gettysburg seems to have kept a diary at this time. It has these items:

June 28th, 1863.

"On this evening the camp-fires of an advance party of A. P. Hill's corps [Heth's division] then halting at Fayetteville, were to be seen on the eastern slope of the mountain about a mile above Cashtown."

June 29th.

"The rebel encampments, by the aid of a spy-glass, were seen to have been considerably enlarged. Hill had thrown a large portion of his corps, probably the whole of Heth's division, over the mountain."

If it had been General Lee's intention to go on North to Harrisburg (as his staff officer, Colonel Marshall, said in his address on Lee's birthday, January 19 (1896), he would not have halted at Chambersburg; nor would he have sent Heth's division east to hold the Cashtown Pass. But another staff officer and biographer, Long, contradicts Marshall.

If he had been going to Gettysburg and wanted, as Long says, to preserve his line of communication, he would have guarded the Monterey Pass through which his army retreated. The distances from Hagerstown to Chambersburg and to Gettysburg are nearly equal. Long, Lee's staff officer and biographer, says a spy came in on the night of the 28th that brought the first news that Meade had superseded Hooker; and also that the Union army had crossed the Potomac. He says that until then General Lee "was under the impression that the Federal army had not crossed." Taylor's biography makes no mention of the spy story; or of Lee's plan to go to Harrisburg. It did not occur to Long that as Meade assumed command at Frederick on the afternoon of the 28th, it was a physical impossibility for the spy to have reached Chambersburg that day. The Flying Dutchman might have done it. If General Lee thought that Hooker would stay on the south bank of the Potomac while he was ravaging Pennsylvania, then he was not fit to command an army. There was not a private under Lee who did not know better. Long's statement is the most derogatory thing ever said about Lee's military capacity. Lee's staff officers do not agree with each other.

Jacob Hoke, a citizen of Chambersburg, published a book, "The Great Invasion." It says:

Thursday, 25th.

"On the morning of this day General Ewell removed his headquarters from the Franklin Hotel in Chambersburg to a Mennonite Church, which stood in the midst of a beautiful grove one mile north of the town along the pike leading to Harrisburg. Hill's corps marched from Hagerstown and encamped one night between Greencastle and Chambersburg. General Early on this day rode from his encampment at Greenwood to Ewell's headquarters one mile north of Chambersburg, to consult with him as to his future course. He was directed to proceed on the following morning by way of Gettysburg to York, break up the Northern Central railroad, seize the bridge across the Susquehanna at Wrightsville and wait there for further orders. As soon as the Confederate force began to pass through Chambersburg, we saw the propriety of sending information of their number and movements to the authorities at Harrisburg. . . . Some of the scouts who made the perilous journey to Harrisburg had narrow escapes. In almost every case they were either chased, fired upon or captured in passing through the Confederate lines. When capture seemed inevitable they would chew up and swallow their dispatches. . . ."

Friday, 26th.

"This day was fraught with great events and stands marked in the history of Chambersburg. This will appear from the following facts: at an early hour in the morning of this day — Hill's corps being close at hand — Rodes' division left its encampment about Shirk's Hill, where it had been since the Wednesday preceding, and moved on down the Harrisburg road. . . . Johnson's division following Rodes moved but a short distance below Greenvillage. About eight o'clock in the morning Heth's division of Hill's corps entered the town, but instead of following Rodes and Johnson down the Harrisburg pike, turned east in the diamond or public square and proceeded out on the Gettysburg road and encamped near Fayetteville. Dismounting in the diamond and hitching his horse in front of a grocery store, the General entered into conversation with one of the citizens. . . . The citizen gave him whatever information he could and then inquired of him when he expected General Lee to arrive. Hill replied, 'I am expecting him every moment.' Casting his eyes up Main street he said, 'There he comes now. . . .' The two Generals — Lee and Hill — then rode a short distance away from the group and held a short, whispered conversation. As a large part of Heth's division of Hill's corps had already passed through Chambersburg, not following the divisions of Ewell's corps down the valley to Harrisburg but turning eastward and going out on the pike leading to Gettysburg, I concluded that if Lee followed in the same direction, Baltimore and Washington were his destination."

This conclusion was right. The other two divisions — Pender's and Anderson's — followed Heth's on the Cashtown pike. If General Lee had intended to take his army to Harrisburg, as Marshall says, he would not have turned to the east at Chambersburg, and would not have sent Heth on to Cashtown. Longstreet's report says a spy came in on the night of the 28th — he was evidently mistaken as to the date of the spy's appearance — but he does not intimate that the spy caused any change in Lee's programme, or that he ever had any purpose of going to Harrisburg. Lee's report follows Longstreet's as to the spy. Hill says he was ordered east to menace the communications between Harrisburg and Philadelphia. Long also says General Lee arrived at Chambersburg on the 26th. But admitting the spy story to be just as Longstreet tells it, if Gettysburg had been Lee's point of destination, as his staff officers say, he could easily have occupied it on the 29th. It is only 25 miles to Gettysburg from Chambersburg. On that day Hill with two divisions was camped 18 miles away from there; Heth's division was only 8 miles away. Longstreet was 25 miles distant, but by an easy march he could have arrived in supporting distance of Hill. Then if Lee had intended to go to Harrisburg he would not on the 27th have ordered Ewell back from Carlisle to Chambersburg. If on the night of the 28th the spy told Lee that Meade was then at Frederick, Lee knew that Meade could not be at Gettysburg the next day. Lee was much nearer to Gettysburg than Meade. Meade's itinerary shows that he did not leave Frederick until the 29th, and that he did not then move north towards Gettysburg, but in an easterly direction to intercept Lee on the Susquehanna. His report says: "June 28th was spent in ascertaining the position and strength of the different corps of the army, but principally in bringing up the cavalry which had been covering the rear of the army in its passage over the Potomac and to which a large increase had just been made from the forces previously attached to the defenses of Washington. Orders were given on that day to Major-General French, commanding at Harper's Ferry, to move with 7000 men of his command to occupy Frederick and the line of the Baltimore and Ohio Railroad, and with the balance of his force, estimated at 4000, to move and escort the public property to Washington." At that time there was no enemy in the Cumberland Valley to annoy General Lee in front or in the rear. Not a courier, a wagon, or a straggler had been captured between his army and the Potomac. The truth is that at that time Stuart was attracting more attention than Lee.

"Opening the door the officer entered alone — the soldiers crossing bayonets to prevent any one else from going in — and passing to the rear and out again, he ordered me to lock it up, saying, 'All right, now you will not be disturbed.' He did not go into the cellar where our groceries were stored. After these squads had reported at headquarters, our grocery, drug, book, stationery, clothing, boot and shoe stores were relieved of their remaining contents. In this work of plunder Major Todd, a brother of the wife of President Lincoln, took a prominent part and came near losing his life, for while attempting to enter the cellar of Dr. Richards, the doctor's daughter flourished an axe over his head and threatened to split it open if he persevered; when the miscreant ingloriously fled."

Hoke's "Great Invasion."

If Lee had intended to go on North to Harrisburg, he would not have recalled Ewell from Carlisle; nor would

A. P. Hill have been sent so far to the East on the Gettysburg pike; if he was going to Gettysburg Heth would not have stopped at Cashtown.[1] The following letter, dated June 28, 7.30 A.M., shows that as soon as Lee arrived at Chambersburg (27th), he wrote Ewell where Hooker's army was, and ordered him to countermarch to Chambersburg. I have read this letter in General Lee's letter-book which is now in possession of Colonel Gordon McCabe, of Richmond; it was copied by him for me directly from it. It appears in the letter-book in the handwriting of a staff officer, Colonel Charles Venable, and is attested by him. He was Professor of Mathematics at the University of Virginia. The hour and the minute of the day on which it is written are noted; General Lee understood the importance of dates in military dispatches. It must have been copied soon after the original was written as its place in the letter-book is in due succession of dates and pages. No doubt the dispatch was sent off in haste as it partly countermanded orders of the night before, and was soon afterward dictated to Venable by General Lee.

From memory—sketch of letter.
HEADQUARTERS ARMY OF NORTHERN VIRGINIA,
CHAMBERSBURG, June 28th, 1863, 7.30 A.M.
LIEUTENANT-GENERAL R. S. EWELL,
Commanding Corps:—

GENERAL: "I wrote you *last night*, stating that General Hooker was reported to have crossed the Potomac and is advancing by way of Middle-

[1] In his address on January 19, 1896, Lee's birthday, Marshall said that Lee had issued orders at Chambersburg to go on to Harrisburg, but after the spy appeared on the night of the 28th, Lee changed his plan and recalled Ewell. He had ordered Ewell back to Chambersburg twenty-four hours before it is alleged that the spy came in.

town, the head of his column being at that point in Frederick county. I directed you in that letter to move your forces to this point. If you have not already progressed on the road, or if you have no good reason against it, I desire you to move *in the direction of Gettysburg*, via Heidlesburg, where you will have turnpike most of the way and you can thus join your other divisions (Johnson's and Rodes') to Early's which is east of the mountain (at York).

I think it preferable to keep the east side of the mountains. When you come to Heidlesburg you can either move directly on Gettysburg or turn down to Cashtown. Your trains and heavy artillery you can send, if you think proper, on the road to Chambersburg. But if the roads which your troops take are good, *they had better follow you*."

    Official, C. S. VENABLE,   R. E. LEE,
        Maj. and A. D. C.   General.[1]

                  [Italics are mine.]

[1] Captain McCabe appends a note to the copy he furnished me of this letter, which says: "The above is a *verbatim* copy of the letter written down 'from memory' by Major (afterwards Lt. Colonel) Chas. S. Venable. The letter is in Colonel Venable's own hand-writing, which I know well as he was a correspondent of mine for many years. It cocurs on page 27 of the *original* 'Private Letter Book' of General R. E. Lee, now in my keeping. It is written *immediately after* a letter from General Lee to President Davis, dated Williamsport 25th June, 1865 (p. 25), and immediately before a letter from General Lee to General Imboden, pp. 27 and 28 of Letter Book."

                (Signed) W. GORDON McCABE,
                          Former Capt. Artillery,
                              3rd corps, A. N. V.

As will be seen from the following letter from Captain McCabe, the two letters immediately preceding and the one immediately succeeding Lee's letter from Chambersburg to Ewell are in the handwriting of Colonel Charles Marshall. He had this letter in his possession when he delivered his philippic on Lee's birthday in 1896 against Stuart; but he did not refer to it. In 1877 Colonel Walter Taylor, A. A. G., at the headquarters of the army of Northern Virginia (who is now living in Norfolk, Va.), published "Four Years with Lee." Of course he had access to Lee's letter-book if he wanted to see it. Marshall was then living in

Baltimore. Taylor and Marshall make the same complaint against Stuart. They make no mention of Lee's Chambersburg letter. Another staff officer, General Long, wrote the "Memoirs of Lee." He appears as ignorant as Marshall and Taylor about Lee's correspondence. Captain McCabe says that Lee's letter of 5 P.M., June 23, 1863, which directed Stuart to join Ewell on the Susquehanna and authorized him to go around Hooker, is in Colonel Taylor's handwriting; judging from Taylor's book he had forgotten all about it. It is strange that he did not examine the letter-book to see the orders he had written. Lee's letter to Ewell of June 22, ordering him to move on from Hagerstown into Pennsylvania, and informing him that Stuart would report to him with three brigades of cavalry, is in Long's handwriting. He and Taylor both censure Stuart for obeying the instructions which they wrote him at Lee's dictation. Captain McCabe further says that the letter immediately following Lee's Chambersburg letter, dated "Greenwood, July 1, 1863," and addressed to Imboden, is in Marshall's handwriting. It instructs Imboden about picketing the roads west of the mountain and concludes by saying: "My headquarters for the present will be *at Cashtown, east of the mountain.*" [Italics mine.] It is clear that when General Lee was writing this letter he had no idea of going to Gettysburg. Hill and Heth were fighting there then, but Lee didn't know it. Marshall copied the letter; but he was not a mere automaton; he understood its meaning — that the army would be concentrated at Cashtown that day.

In his address he stated that after the spy appeared at Chambersburg, Lee ordered the army to Gettysburg; which is contradicted by the letter to Imboden. The Homeric legend of the Lotus-eaters who lost their memories seems to be no longer a romance but a reality. Again, Colonel Taylor speaks of an interview between General Lee and A. P. Hill at Cashtown on the morning of July 1, before Hill started to Gettysburg. If this were true it would make General Lee responsible for the blunder of Hill and Heth. Now, as the letter to Imboden shows, General Lee was at Greenwood, west of the mountain and ten miles from Cashtown that morning. A. P. Hill's report says that Heth's division started to Gettysburg at 5 A.M., and was followed by Pender's. Hill went in command. General Lee certainly did not reach Cashtown before noon, long after General Hill had gone.

These are the letters from Captain McCabe of which I have spoken:

RICHMOND, VA., December 24th, 1905.

MY DEAR COLONEL MOSBY: —

I received your kind letter this evening and have at once copied the letter from Lee to Ewell *verbatim*, as it appears in p. 27 of the original "Letter-book" now in my keeping. The "sketch of letter," "from memory" is throughout in Colonel Venable's handwriting, which I know well as we corresponded for years and I still have many letters from him. . . .

Yours very truly,
W. GORDON McCABE.

I wrote Captain McCabe another letter asking him to state if Lee's Chambersburg letter appeared in the letter-book in due succession of dates and pages and received the following reply:

RICHMOND, VIRGINIA,
Jany 11th, 1906.

DEAR COL. MOSBY: —

Your letter of the 9th instant reached me on yesterday, and I have given close scrutiny to the letters in the "Letter Book" immediately preceding and immediately succeeding the letter written [by General Lee] at Chambersburg, 7.30 A.M., June 28th [1863.] I have taken six preceding and six succeeding, which will, I fancy, be quite sufficient for your purpose.

I. *Immediately preceding*

1. First letter immediately preceding letter of June 28, dated "Williamsport, 25th June, 1863," is in handwriting of Charles Marshall, Major A. D. C.

2. Next preceding, dated "opposite Williamsport, 25th June, 1863," is in same handwriting.

3. Next preceding, dated "Hd. Qrs. Army No. Va., 5 P.M., June 23rd, 1863," is in handwriting of W. H. Taylor, A. A. G.

4. Next preceding, dated "Headquarters A. N. Va. June 23rd, 1863," is in handwriting of C. S. Venable, Major A. D. C.

5. Next preceding, dated "A. N. V. Hd. Qrs. 23rd, 1863," is in handwriting of Charles Marshall, Major and A. D. C.

6. Next preceding, dated "Hd.Qrs. 22nd June 1863," is in handwriting of A. L. Long, Col. and Mil. Sec.

GETTYSBURG

II. *Immediately succeeding*

1. First letter (immediately succeeding letter of June 28), dated "Greenwood, 1st July, 1863," is in handwriting of Charles Marshall Major and A. D. C.

2. Next succeeding, dated "Headquarters A. N. V., 4th July, 1863," is in handwriting of C. S. Venable, Major A. D. C. . . .

Captain McCabe gives the dates and handwriting of four more succeeding letters.

My object is to show that Lee's letter to Ewell, dated 7.30 A.M., June 28, was written in the letter-book by Colonel Venable on the day of its date, and appears in its proper place in the book. The reports of Generals Ewell, Early, and Edward Johnson show that their movements conformed to these instructions; and that there can be no mistake about the date of the letter.

Lee's letter of June 28th to Ewell speaks of a letter he had written him "last night." That letter, which was not copied, could not have been written later than the 27th, as Johnson's division, in compliance with that order, left Carlisle, which is thirty miles from Chambersburg, on the morning of the 29th; and Early on the evening of the 29th at York (thirty-six miles distant) received a copy of it from Ewell. Ewell's trains must have left Carlisle on the evening of the 28th, before Ewell received the second letter; else all would have gone by the Eastern route.

Ewell's and Early's reports verify the correctness of the copy of the order in every respect. Ewell says; "From (Carlisle) I sent forward my engineer, Captain Richardson, with General Jenkins' cavalry, to reconnoiter the defenses of Harrisburg, and was starting on the 29th for that place when ordered by the general commanding to join the main body of the army at Cashtown, near Gettysburg. . . . On the night of June 30, Rodes' division, which I accompanied, was at Heidlersburg [nine miles north of Gettysburg,] Early three miles off on the road to Berlin, and Johnson, with Colonel Brown's reserve artillery between Green Village and Scotland [near the Chambersburg pike *west of* South Mountain]. At Heidlersburg I received orders from the general commanding to proceed to Cashtown, or Gettysburg, as circumstances might dictate, and a note from General A. P. Hill, saying he was in Cashtown. Next morning I moved with Rodes' division *towards Cashtown,* ordering Early to follow by Hunterstown. Before reaching Middletown I received notice from General Hill that he was advancing upon Gettysburg, and turned the head of Rodes' column towards that place, by the Middletown road, sending word to Early to advance directly on the Heidlersburg road. I notified the general commanding of my movements, and was informed by him that, in case we found the enemy's force very large, he did not want a general engagement brought on until the rest of the army came up. By the time this message reached me General Hill had already been warmly engaged with a large body of the enemy in his front, and Carter's artillery battalion of Rodes' division had opened with fine effect on the flank of the same body which was preparing to attack me, while fresh masses were moving into position in my front." [Italics are mine.]

Ewell must have received Lee's order of the 27th on the next day, as he says he was preparing to start to Harrisburg on the 29th, as he had been authorized by Lee's letter from Berryville on the 22d, when the order came arresting the movement. It is thirty miles from Chambersburg to Carlisle. General Edward Johnson's division with the reserve artillery and the trains must have been sent off by Ewell in accordance with his first order on the western route before he got the second order to march

GETTYSBURG 123

east of the mountains. The trains must have started on the evening of the 28th as they were passing Chambersburg at midnight of the 29th. Johnson's report says he left Carlisle on the 29th. He never would have started from Carlisle by such a circuitous route to Cashtown or Gettysburg. Chambersburg must have been Johnson's destination when he left Carlisle; no doubt an order overtook him to turn east by Scotland.[1] Ewell had then

[1] "In the evening of this day — Monday, June 29th — sometime after dark in company with two of our citizens I went up into the steeple of the Reform Church to take observations. From that elevated position we had an uninterrupted view for miles around us. . . . Some time in the after part of this night, probably about one or two in the morning, I was awakened by my wife who told me to come to the window for some important movement was going on amongst the Confederates. Peering cautiously through the half-closed shutters we saw a continuous stream of wagons driven hurriedly through our streets. They were coming back from the direction of Harrisburg and, turning east at the Public Square, drove out on the Gettysburg pike. Although these wagons were heavily loaded, as the grinding noise they made indicated, they were sometimes driven in a trot. A low, rumbling noise could be heard which sounded stronger in the stillness of the night, as if the whole valley was filled with moving trains. These wagons proved to be a part of Ewell's train and their rapid passage eastward was a part in the great drama of concentration about Gettysburg, which will be described fully hereafter."

"Tuesday, 30th.

"The hasty passage of the wagon-trains through Chambersburg on the night of the 29th convinced us that Lee was about concentrating his army and that no time should be lost in sending this important information to the authorities at Harrisburg. . . . The remaining division of Ewell's corps — Johnson's — retraced its steps from the neighborhood of Shippensburg to Green Village, six miles northeast of Chambersburg, and from thence went by the country road directly across through Scotland to Greenwood, where it remained over night. [Fayetteville is six and Greenwood seven miles east of Chambersburg.] General Johnson's wagon-train, instead of following him across the country, came up to Chambersburg and turning east in the public square, proceeded to Gettysburg. Part of Rodes' wagon-train also retraced its way to Chambersburg and, joining Johnson's, passed towards the same destination. . . . This was the train which passed through Chambersburg during the night, as previously stated, and these two when united were, according to the statement of General McLaws in 'Annals of the War,' page 440, fourteen miles long. Its importance may be inferred from the fact that it was given precedence over Longstreet's two divisions and it was the detention caused by it that prevented these two divisions from reaching the field of battle as soon as expected. The divisions of Generals McLaws and Hood, which were unable to proceed until Ewell's wagon-train had passed, were detained in their encampment about Fayetteville until the following afternoon, when by a forced march the former reached Marsh Creek, four miles from Gettysburg, a little after dark, and the latter got about the same distance at twelve o'clock at night [July 1st]. The artillery belonging to these two divisions did not get the road until the following morning [Thursday, July 2]."

"The Great Invasion."
By HOKE, a Citizen of Chambersburg."

received the second dispatch from Lee. The trains were passing at midnight of the 29th through Chambersburg and took the Gettysburg pike. If the letter dated 7.30 A.M., June 28; had been written on the 29th, Johnson with the trains would not have started from Carlisle before the 30th. As Ewell acted under both orders, he blends them in his report. If, as Ewell says, he notified General Lee from Heidlersburg of his movements, and received a reply that he did not want a general engagement brought on, he could not have received it before the afternoon, as they were twenty miles apart on the morning of July 1, and on opposite sides of the mountain.

Early's report is the most accurate of any made in the

campaign. He says that on the evening of the 29th, at York, he received from Ewell a copy of the order from General Lee to rejoin his corps *west* of the mountain, and that he started in obedience to the order the next morning and sent White's battalion on the pike towards Gettysburg; if he had understood that place to be his destination he would have marched directly there. As it is thirty-six miles from Carlisle to York, the copy of Lee's letter to Ewell, which Early received on the evening of the 29th, must have been the first letter (27th) to Ewell. He had not expected to meet Ewell east of the mountain; but Ewell had received Lee's second order to go that route. The report says: "On the evening of the 29th, I received through Captain Elliott Johnson, aide to General Ewell, a copy of a note from General Lee and also verbal instructions which required me to move back so as to rejoin the rest of the corps on the *western* side of South Mountain; and accordingly, at daylight, on the morning of the 30th, I put my whole command in motion, moving by Weiglestown and East Berlin in the direction of Heidlersburg, from which I could either move to Shippensburg or to Greenwood, by way of Arendttsville, as circumstances might require. At the same time I sent Colonel White's cavalry on the pike from York towards Gettysburg, to ascertain if any force of the enemy was on that road. . . . A courier from General Ewell met me here (East Berlin), with a dispatch informing me of the fact that he was moving with Rodes' division by way of Petersburg to Heidlersburg, and directing me to march in that direction. I encamped about three miles from Heidlersburg and rode to see General Ewell at that point, *and was informed that the object was to concentrate the corps at or near Cashtown, and received directions to move the next day to that point.* I was informed that Rodes would move by the way of Middletown and Arendttsville, but it was arranged that I should go by the way of Hunterstown and Mumasburg. Having ascertained that the road from my camp to Hunterstown was a very rough and circuitous one, I determined next morning (July 1), to march by the way of Heidlersburg, and thence to the Mumasburg road. After passing Heidlersburg a short distance, I received a note from you, written by order of General Ewell, informing me that General Hill was moving from Cashtown towards Gettysburg, and that General Rodes had turned off at Middletown and was moving towards the same place, and directing me to move also to that point. I therefore continued to move on the road I was then on towards Gettysburg, and on arriving in sight of that place, on the direct road from Heidlersburg, I discovered that General Rodes' division was engaged with the enemy to the right of me, the enemy occupying a position in front of Gettysburg, and the troops constituting his right being engaged in an effort to drive back the left of General Rodes' line."

On the 30th, General Lee, with Longstreet and Hood's and McLaws' divisions of his corps, marched eight miles east to Greenwood and went into camp about noon. The detention was caused by Johnson's long wagon train from Carlisle that was passing. A. P. Hill had advanced to Cashtown with Heth's and Pender's divisions. He had no orders to go farther. Longstreet's report says: "On the night of the 28th one of my scouts [spy] came in with the information that the enemy had passed the Potomac and was probably in pursuit of us. The scout was sent to general headquarters with the suggestion that the army concentrate east of the mountains and bear down to meet the enemy."

It has been represented that General Lee was greatly agitated by the news the spy brought that Hooker had crossed the river and was near South Mountain; and that it produced a complete change in his plan of campaign. I shall show that the story is as pure a fable as the Wandering Jew. It has been generally accepted as true. And I, too, once believed in the real presence of Santa Claus and had no doubts about the deeds of Jack the Giant-Killer. Nobody has tried to explain how General Lee could have expected Hooker to stand still on the south bank of the Potomac while he was foraging in Pennsylvania; or how he could have been surprised to hear that Hooker was following him. He ought to have been surprised to hear that Hooker was *not* following him.

Longstreet attaches so much importance to the spy that he dignifies him with his picture in his book and under it is the inscription, "The Confederate scout who brought to General Lee the first news of Meade's assignment to command and the positions of the corps of the Army of the Potomac." All this in and about Chambersburg on the night of June the 28th. The order relieving Hooker of command was brought from Washington to Frederick City by Colonel Hardie on the morning of June 28th.

His mission was kept such a secret that his traveling companion, General Sickles, a corps commander, did not suspect it. The general order announcing the change of commanders was not published until the afternoon. It is improbable, if not impossible, that the Texas spy could have heard it before it was announced to the corps commanders.

It is fifty-five or sixty miles from Frederick to Chambersburg; the road is over the South Mountain; every path and gap was closely picketed and patroled. The steed Mazeppa rode could not have carried the spy to Lee's headquarters in that time. It would have required a supernatural agency to do it. I admit that a spy did come to Longstreet, and that he brought the news that Meade had been placed in command. The news about Meade being in command is unimportant. But it was *after* General Lee had left Chambersburg, and on the 30th, at Greenwood, when the army was on the march to Cashtown. So the news brought by the spy could not have been the reason for the halt at Chambersburg, or the recall of Ewell from Carlisle. But Lee's letter to Ewell, dated 7.30 A.M., June 28, shows that at the time of writing he thought *Hooker* was still in command. It was therefore written *before* the spy came in.

He said to Ewell: "I wrote you *last night* stating that. *General Hooker* was reported to have crossed the Potomac and is advancing by way of Middletown" [Italics mine], and he ordered him back to Chambersburg. He did not mention *Meade*. It is, therefore, an anachronism to claim, as Longstreet and Lee's staff officers do, that the spy's appearance was the cause of a change in Lee's plan of campaign and his going to Gettysburg instead of Harrisburg.

In Troilus and Cressida Shakespeare commits a similar error and makes Nestor quote Aristotle. There was a change of plan, *but not till July* 1. The spy was not responsible for it. Colonel Freemantle has this item in his diary: "June 30, Tuesday. . . . We marched from Chambersburg six miles on the road towards Gettysburg and encamped at a village called (I think) Greenwood. In the evening General Longstreet told me that *he had just received intelligence that Hooker had been disrated and Meade was appointed in his place.* Of course he knew both of them in the old army and he says that Meade is an honorable and respectable man, though perhaps not so bold as Hooker."

So it was on the 30th and not on the night of the 28th — and at Greenwood, not at Chambersburg — when Longstreet first heard that Meade was in command. No doubt he heard it from a spy. Again Freemantle says: "July 1st. At 2 P.M., firing became distinctly audible in our front, but although it increased as we progressed, it did not seem to be very heavy. A SPY WHO WAS WITH US insisted upon there being a pretty bunch of blue bellies in or near Gettysburg, and he declared he was in their society three days before."

A spy, no doubt, did appear, as the diary, says at Greenwood and told Longstreet that Meade had superseded Hooker; but the news did not affect General Lee. The appearance of the spy in the drama has been antedated by historians and he has been transposed back to Chambersburg, and used as a *deus ex machina* to create the impression that he had performed for Lee the duty of his chief of cavalry. If General Lee did not know when he first arrived at Chambersburg — and if Longstreet did not know — that Hooker had crossed the Potomac, then neither was fit to command an army, or an army corps. Longstreet further says that when he sent the spy to Lee he suggested that the army concentrate east of the mountain and "bear down to meet the enemy." Since the war Longstreet has claimed that he advised General Lee only to fight a defensive battle. But that does not accord with the advice which the report says he gave General Lee, — "To bear down to meet the enemy."

That is the language of Nelson's order to Collingwood at Trafalgar — it is the essence of offensive tactics. As they were a short distance from the mountain it would have been more consistent with the military policy which he says he advocated, to have advised his chief to imitate Hannibal when he decoyed the Roman army into the Thrasymene Pass. It has been claimed that Lee was going on to Harrisburg, but that the spy made him so uneasy about his communications that he ordered his army to Gettysburg to deter Hooker from crossing the mountain. But I have shown that, as soon as he arrived at Chambersburg, and twenty-four hours before it is alleged that the spy came in, he informed Ewell that Hooker was in pursuit and ordered him to countermarch to Chambersburg. He afterward modified the order and directed Ewell to move east of the mountain in the direction of Cashtown.

General Lee put no obstruction in the Gaps south of Cashtown. They were left open to Hooker and he was invited to come over. There was apparently a fine opportunity for him to seize Lee's communications and strike him in his rear. That was Lee's own favorite manœuver; and no doubt he calculated that Hooker would follow his example; if so, he would flank Hooker and go on to Washington. He set a trap for Hooker with a bait — he did not practise the thing for which he prayed — "Lead us not into temptation." It was Hooker's intention to do what Lee hoped he would do, but Halleck interfered and Hooker indignantly asked to be relieved. On June 28th, at Frederick City, in the afternoon, Hooker was relieved of the command of the Army of the Potomac.

Before the Committee on the Conduct of the War Hooker said: "As soon as I ascertained that another corps of his (Lee's) was crossing the Potomac, I commenced crossing my own army, and by the time that I was over the whole of the rebel army was on the north side of the Potomac. From Edwards' Ferry, where I crossed, I directed General Reynolds to send detachments to seize the passes of South Mountain, Turner's and Crampton's, in order to anticipate the enemy passing through them and confine him to one line of invasion, and directed him to follow those detachments with the First, Third, and Eleventh Corps, and take position at Middletown. On the 27th of June the following instructions were communicated to the Twelfth Corps: 'Hold your command ready to march to-morrow at 4 A.M.' It was to march in the direction of Harper's Ferry, where I was going myself.

It had been placed under my command by the orders of the general-in-chief, and I directed the Twelfth Corps to march in that direction for the purpose of being joined by the garrison there and moving upon Lee's rear upon the Potomac. My object was to destroy his bridges, if he had them; to drive away the guard that was left upon the river and also to intercept the commerce that Ewell had established in flour, grain, horses and horned cattle, which he was constantly sending to the rear." . . . "In connection with this I may state that I was unwilling to send one corps upon Lee's rear, apprehending he might turn upon it and crush it. I had taken the further precaution to send three corps to Middletown, to be in position to attack in flank if it was attempted."

Hooker does not seem to have taken into account what Lee would have been doing east of the Mountain, while he, like Ajax, after he had gone mad, had turned to killing sheep, was capturing stragglers and horned cattle on the turnpike that Lee had traveled. If this turning movement had not been disapproved by Halleck, General Lee would have been in the position of Frederick the Great at Roosbach, and Napoleon at Austerlitz. The concentration at Cashtown shows that he was preparing to do what these great masters of the art of war did in similar circumstances — to flank the enemy that was flanking him. At Austerlitz, when the Allies were seen extending around his flank to gain the road to Vienna, which was his line of communication, Napoleon had to restrain the impatience of his marshals — they wanted to attack and stop the movement against their rear. Jomini reports him as saying: "I asked Soult how long it would take him to gain the heights of Pratzen; he promised to do it in less than twenty minutes. 'We will wait, then,' I replied; 'When the enemy is making a false movement we must be careful not to interrupt him.'"

General Lee· had no desire to interrupt Hooker if he wanted to go over the mountain; he anticipated he would do so and simply put himself in a position at Cashtown to take advantage of such a movement if Hooker made it. It would have been a grand anti-climax to his campaign if Lee had lost heart and been stampeded, as some of his staff officers have said, because Hooker had done what he had dared him to do. He was perfectly willing to trade Hooker the Cumberland Valley for Washington City. If Hooker had crossed the mountain and got behind him, then Lee would have been between Hooker and Washington.

In his work on "The Operations of War," Colonel Hamley says: "As it is impossible that hostile armies can be operated from the same base, it follows that an army which throws itself across the communications of an adversary cannot directly cover its own. In general, however, an army, thus cut from its base, will have two or three alternatives: first, it may march directly on the opposing force and try to drive it off the line, or rout it; second, it may march to one flank across the communications of the enemy [to Washington]; third, it may attempt, by a march to the other flank, to avoid a collision."

If Hooker had thrown his whole army west of the mountain between Lee and the Potomac, which, no doubt,

Lee wanted him to do, and which Hooker says he intended to do, then Lee would have done what Napoleon did at Austerlitz; he would have marched directly on Washington. If Hooker had divided his army, then Lee, having the interior line, would have debouched through the Cashtown Pass, struck and destroyed him in detail — as Bonaparte did the Austrians at Rivoli. I do not believe that General Lee could have been demoralized, as Colonel Marshall says he was, by hearing that Hooker was behind him. He held the card that could have won the game.

As I have before stated, Meade issued orders on the morning of July 1 for the army to retire to Pipe Creek, about fifteen miles south, if pressed by the enemy. The following letters show that Meade, like Lee, had no expectation of a collision that day.[1]

BUTTERFIELD TO HANCOCK

July 1st, 1863, 12.30 P.M.

The major-general commanding directs that in view of the advance of Generals A. P. Hill and Ewell on Gettysburg and the possible failure of General Reynolds to receive the orders to withdraw his command by the route through Taneytown, thus leaving the center of our position open, that you proceed with your troops out on the direct road to Gettysburg from Taneytown. When you find that General Reynolds is covering that road (instead of withdrawing by Emmittsburg, which it is feared he may do), you will withdraw to Frizellburg, as directed by the circular of directions for the positions issued this morning.

[1] TANEYTOWN, MD., July 1, 1863.

GENERAL BUFORD: —

General: The major-general commanding directs me to order you to fall back to Taneytown, and then to Middleburg, in case the enemy should advance in force upon you and press you hard. The cavalry will dispute every inch of the ground, and fall back very slowly to the point designated, and send in all information they can gather. By order of Major-General Pleasanton.

C. Ross Smith,
Lieut.-Colonel, etc.

P.S. This move is only to be made in case of great necessity. The same order was repeated to Gregg, Kilpatrick and Merritt.

At the same time Meade wrote Sedgwick, commanding the Sixth Corps:—

"Should such be the case and General Reynolds find himself in the presence of a superior force, he is instructed to hold the enemy in check and fall slowly back. If he is able to do this, the line indicated in the circular of to-day will be occupied to-night."

Hill's report says: "On July 1, at 5 A.M., Heth took up the line of march with Pegram's battalion of artillery, followed by Pender with McIntosh's battalion of artillery. Colonel Walker, with the remainder (three battalions) of artillery, being with General Anderson," who was then behind on the march from Fayetteville to Cashtown. About three miles from Gettysburg, Heth's leading brigade (Archer's) encountered the advance of the enemy, Buford's two brigades of cavalry, on Willoughby Run.

Meade had no idea of holding the place because it would be so easy for Lee to turn it and get between him and Washington. For that reason French was kept all the time in his rear at Frederick with ten or fifteen thousand men to guard his communications. In Meade's opinion of the necessity for it Hancock concurred. Heth's division, after leaving camp at Cashtown, soon came upon Buford's pickets. Buford fought his cavalry dismounted and notified Reynolds. He kept Heth in check until Reynolds arrived and deployed for action. Heth's report says:

"On July 1, my division, accompanied by Pegram's battalion of artillery, was ordered to move at 5 A.M. in the direction of Gettysburg. On nearing Gettysburg it was evident that the enemy was in the vicinity of the town in some force. It may not be improper to remark at this time — nine o'clock on the morning of July 1 — I was ignorant what force was at or near Gettysburg, and supposed it consisted of cavalry, most probably supported by a brigade or two of infantry. On reaching the summit of the second range of hills, west of Gettysburg, it became evident that there were infantry, cavalry, and artillery in and around the town. . . . Archer and Davis were now directed to advance, the object being to feel the enemy, *to make a forced reconnaissance and determine in what force the enemy were* — whether or not he was massing his forces on Gettysburg. [Italics mine.] Heavy columns of the enemy were soon encountered. Davis, on the left, advanced, driving the enemy before him and capturing his batteries. General Davis was unable to hold the position he had gained. The enemy concentrated on his front and flanks in overwhelming force.

"The brigade maintained its position until every field officer except two were shot down and its ranks terribly thinned. On the right of the road, Archer encountered heavy masses in his front, and his gallant little brigade, after being almost surrounded by overwhelming forces in front and on both flanks, were forced back. The service lost at this time that most gallant and meritorious officer, Brigadier-general Archer, who fell into the enemy's hands together with some 60 or 70 of his men. *The enemy had now been felt and found to be in heavy force in and around Gettysburg.* . . . The division was now formed in line of battle on the right of the road. . . . Davis' brigade was kept on the left of the road, that it might collect stragglers, and, from its shattered condition, it was not deemed advisable to bring it again into action on that day. It, however, did participate in the action later in the day. After resting in line of battle for one hour or more, orders were received to attack the enemy in my front, with the notification that General Pender's division would support me."

As Heth states that he went only to make a reconnaissance to find out if the enemy was in force in his front, the above account shows that he ought to have been very soon satisfied that the enemy was *in force* and ought to have retired. But the report, on its face, shows that he was not making a *reconnaissance*. Two of his brigades had been shattered and a brigadier-general captured. But Hill, instead of winning unexpected trophies, had been worsted; he did not want to go back to camp and meet General Lee with his plume torn and a black eye. So he ordered Pender in.

"The division (Pender's)" says Heth, "had not advanced more than a hundred yards before it became hotly engaged." Hill says he went there "to find out what was in my front." If that was his object, what Heth's division had suffered ought to have given him sufficient information to have satisfied his curiosity. He had lost a brigadier-general and a large part of a brigade. Pender was faring no better than Heth, and Hill's force would no doubt have been driven back to Cashtown, if Ewell, with Rodes' division, marching like Desaix at Meringo, to the sound of the cannon, had not come in on the flank and saved him. But even with Rodes' reinforcement the issue was doubtful until Early came in on the enemy's rear and gave the finishing stroke. Ewell's act in coming to Hill's support was purely voluntary; Hill had no right to expect help from Ewell. Hill says that his two divisions were so exhausted by six hours' fighting that he did not pursue when the enemy was routed. Anderson did not arrive with his division on the field until the battle was nearly over. He was not engaged. Hill had ordered him to Cashtown before he left that morning with Heth and Pender to perform what he no doubt thought would be a brilliant exploit; and Anderson, with his division and three battalions of artillery, halted there for further orders. It seems that General Lee rode from Cashtown at full speed to the field, and arrived in the afternoon about the close of the combat. He knew in the morning that the enemy were at Gettysburg, and he would have been in front with Heth's division, if he had ordered it to go there. But he never would have sent one or two divisions to encounter an unknown force with his army stretched out on the pike from Chambersburg to Gettysburg. If he had intended to go to Gettysburg he would not have stayed so long at Chambersburg. *Lee, Longstreet, and Stuart were all absent for the same reason on the first day because the army had not been ordered to Gettysburg and it was not their duty to be there.* They were in their proper places — Hill and Heth were not.

Nor would General Lee have committed such an error as to order his widely separated divisions to concentrate on a point so close to the enemy. A military writer of high authority says: "It is always a dangerous operation to attempt a concentration upon some designated place within or near the enemy's lines; for, as a rule, the enemy can mass his forces there more rapidly than can the commander of an invading army. In fact, many a campaign has failed because the commanding general has attempted to unite his scattered forces at some point within the territory held by the enemy. By so doing he gives the enemy a chance to assemble his forces between the separated columns of the attacking army and to bring superior numbers against each column in succession." This was Pleasanton's error at Brandy.

Hill and Heth, to excuse themselves for precipitating a battle without orders, said they were only making a reconnaissance. If this were true they would not be justified. A reconnaissance in force should only be made by the orders of the commanding general. It is a hazardous operation as it frequently brings on a battle prematurely. Its only object is to get information as to the position and strength of an enemy. For this reason, sufficient force, and no more, is applied to make an enemy display himself. The attacking force then retires. Captain Wagner says ("Security and Information"): "Reconnaissances in force are made only by the orders of the

Commander-in-Chief and the force generally consists of all three arms. They are often made before action for the purpose of discovering the enemy's strength and disposition and frequently lead to a battle. The reconnaissance is conducted in the same general way as a regular attack. . . . It is evident, therefore, that a reconnaissance in force is a difficult operation. It is open to three serious objections. (1) It often results in committing the troops so completely to action as to bring on a battle through the necessity of bringing up other troops to their assistance. At Worth, a reconnaissance by the Twentieth Prussian Brigade developed the enemy, and the other German troops, moving to the sound of the cannon, precipitated a battle a day earlier than the Crown Prince had intended. (2) The withdrawal of the troops, in pursuance to the general plan of the reconnaissance, may often present the appearance of defeat. In 1859, Ginlay caused a reconnaissance in force to be made by Stadion's corps. It developed Forey's division near Montebello and, although the Austrians withdrew in accordance with the plan of reconnaissance, the moral effect on both sides was that of a victory of a French division over an Austrian army corps. (3) It is always a costly means of gaining information."

If the combat which lasted nearly all the day of July 1 had been really a reconnaissance it would present all of this writer's objections to reconnaissances in force. It was without orders, and it did commit the Southern army prematurely to battle; its withdrawal leaving its killed and wounded on the field would have had the appearance of a defeat, and the adversary would have had the prestige and all the moral effect of a victory.

It compelled Lee to stay at Gettysburg and fight a battle under duress — or retreat — or at least appear to retreat. Hill and Heth in their reports, to save themselves from censure, call the first day's action a reconnaissance; this is all an afterthought. They wanted to conceal their responsibility for the final defeat. Hill said he felt the need of cavalry — then he ought to have stayed in camp and waited for the cavalry. But he felt the need of infantry a great deal more than of cavalry. No one ordered him, and there was no necessity for his going to Gettysburg. Ewell was near there; he had as much cavalry as Buford had. There were about 25,000 engaged on a side; the battle lasted nearly all day; Hill says his two divisions were exhausted; but he says they were only fighting to find out if the enemy was in strong force in front of him. He found it. On July 1, Stuart was on the Susquehanna; *where he was ordered to go.* But Ewell had left; Stuart was not to blame for that. General Lee was responsible for Stuart; he was not responsible for Hill and Heth.

On the morning of July 1, General Lee's headquarters were at Greenwood. Anderson's division from Fayetteville, and Johnson's from Scotland, where it had camped the night before, occupied the road — Anderson's in advance — so Longstreet's two divisions could not get off before the afternoon. General Lee, before leaving, wrote the following letter of instructions to Imboden. It appears in his letter-book in the handwriting of his staff officer,

Col. Charles Marshall. The letter conclusively confutes the statement made by Marshall in his address on General Lee's birthday on January 19, 1896, that at Chambersburg, after the spy reported Hooker's advance, Lee ordered his army to concentrate at Gettysburg. He would not concentrate his army at one place and have his headquarters eight miles off at another.

GREENWOOD, July 1st, 1863.

BRIGADIER-GENERAL I. D. IMBODEN: —

GENERAL: I have received your letter of 7 A.M. yesterday from Mercersburg. . . . Upon arriving at Chambersburg to-day I desire you to relieve General Pickett, who will then move forward to this place. You will of course establish guards on the road leading to your position and take every precaution for the safety of your command. Obtain all the flour that you can load in your wagons from the mills in your vicinity, and if you cannot get sufficient, I believe there are 700 or 800 barrels at Shippensburg, about 10 miles north of Chambersburg, on the Carlisle road. . . . Send word to General Pickett at this place to-morrow, which is eight miles from Chambersburg, the hour when you will arrive here in order that he may be prepared to move on your arrival. *My headquarters for the present will* be at Cashtown, east of the mountains. [The italics are mine.]

General Lee was then less than ten miles from Cashtown; he expected to stop there that evening. All the divisions of his army — infantry, cavalry, and artillery — were marching on that point and would be there, or in supporting distance, by sundown. If his army had been ordered to Gettysburg he would have told Imboden that his headquarters would be with the army. There is a tone of confidence in his letter and no anxiety is expressed about his rear.

If he had felt any uneasiness about it he would probably have sent Imboden's cavalry to make a reconnaissance toward the Potomac. As there was uninterrupted communication with Williamsport by couriers west of the mountain, he knew that the Northern army must be to the East. He certainly knew that Meade was at Frederick several days before and he knew that Meade wouldn't stop there. He certainly had no expectation of fighting a battle that day; yet, at the time when he was writing, A. P. Hill and Heth were fighting at Gettysburg. They had gone off early that morning without orders, or notice to Lee, for an adventure, and expected to return to camp with their spoil that evening. Hill had five battalions of artillery at Cashtown; he took only two with him. The others were left behind with his *impedimenta*. In this way a battle was precipitated where Lee never expected to fight one. During the day (about noon, Freemantle says), in company with General Longstreet, General Lee left Greenwood for Cashtown. The Chief of Artillery, General Pendleton, rode with him. In his report, Pendleton says, that when they were crossing the South Mountain "cannon shots were heard, but its significance, however, was not fully understood. It might only be a passing skirmish; it might be more serious. After a brief pause near Cashtown, to see how it would prove, the commanding general, finding the cannonading to continue and increase, *moved rapidly forward*. I did the same and, at his request, rode near him for instructions."

Although General Lee had written Imboden in the morning that Cashtown would for the present be his headquarters, he paused there for only a few minutes, and then galloped on to the field of battle. *He never saw Cashtown again.* If he had given Hill and Heth authority to go to Gettysburg, he would have known the significance of the firing when he heard it. He knew the enemy held the place; Hill says he had informed him the night before; and he was in communication with Ewell, whose cavalry was in contact with Buford. It was therefore at *Cashtown*, and not at Chambersburg, where Lee was surprised and found his plan broken up.

I have said that Heth's division had gone in advance to Cashtown. A. P. Hill came on afterward with Pender's. He had left Anderson's division at Fayetteville on the 30th with orders to follow the next day. Anderson's report says: "Soon after daylight, on July 1, in accordance with the commands of the Lieutenant-general, the division moved from Fayetteville in the direction of Cashtown. Arrived at the latter place early in the afternoon, and halted for further orders. Shortly before our arrival at Cashtown, the sound of brisk cannonading near Gettysburg announced an engagement in our front. *After waiting an hour at Cashtown, orders were received from General Hill to move forward to Gettysburg.*" [Italics mine.] If Hill had started to Gettysburg to occupy the place, Anderson would not have had to wait for orders to go on; and, as General Lee must have passed Anderson's division on the march to Cashtown that day, he would have ordered him to move to Gettysburg if he had known that there was to be a battle there. The instructions he had sent to Imboden that morning for picketing the roads in every direction west of the mountain and parking the trains in the Pass, and the statement that his headquarters for the present would be at Cashtown, show that he then had no idea of going to Gettysburg. Yet he was there overlooking the battle-field that evening. As General Lee says he knew that General Meade was at Frederick City on the 28th, he must have expected his army to be not far behind Buford's cavalry. He could not expect it to be stationary; Gettysburg is little more than a day's march north of Frederick. No doubt he was surprised when he heard the sound of battle at Gettysburg; for he had given no orders to any one to go there. Before Hill arrived at Cashtown with Pender it seems Heth had sent a force on picket to Fairfield, about seven miles south. It was probably two Mississippi regiments. Buford's cavalry crossed the Potomac in rear of the army and then moved on west on the night of the 27th from Edwards' Ferry, to Middletown. On the 29th he passed through Boonsboro Gap and thence along the western base of the mountain — re-crossed at Monterey Gap, and bivouacked that night near Fairfield. He did not approach Lee's line of march, or capture a wagon or a soldier. Buford kept so close to the mountain that he never saw a Confederate during the day, and did not know that he had slept so close to their camps that night until he started early to go on to Gettysburg and unexpectedly ran against the picket. He felt the picket, but withdrew, and took the route by Emmittsburg.

He arrived near Gettysburg on June 30, about the time that Pettigrew's brigade, that Heth had sent out to get some shoes he had heard were there, came in sight. Pettigrew saw Buford and returned; he reported to Hill that the enemy were at Gettysburg. Hill says he immediately sent a courier with the information to General Lee. Yet Heth, in a published letter after the war, said that on account of the absence of the cavalry he ran like a blind man against Buford and *stumbled* into a battle. If Hill and Heth had stood still, they would not have stumbled. Pettigrew had worn out a good deal of shoe-leather but he got no shoes. It is not probable that Gordon's and White's men, who were camped there the night of the 26th, left any but children's shoes for the barefooted Confederates. No doubt Buford thought that Stuart's cavalry corps was on Lee's right flank. In no other way can his feeble operations on the 29th be accounted for. On the day before, General Steinwehr had reported from the mountain that 5000 Confederate cavalry had crossed the Potomac and had passed through Hagerstown. It was not true — but it did us almost as much good as if it had been true. The imagination is a powerful factor in war.

Buford expected to meet Kilpatrick, who had been put in command of Stahel's cavalry. But he and Gregg had been sent off after Stuart, who was riding around Meade, cutting his lines of communication and destroying his trains. Buford did not know that Stuart had crossed at Seneca. Meade was like a ship without a compass drifting in a fog. He had to have as strong detachments to guard his communications as if he had been in the enemy's country. On the contrary, General Lee had no trouble about his. He lived on the country where he camped.

He knew that Meade had cavalry at Gettysburg as an outpost and that his army could not be far behind. Ewell and Early had a strong force of cavalry and some of our best cavalry officers to do their scouting.

Early sent Colonel Lije White on the morning of the 30th from York on the Gettysburg road to gather information for him. No doubt he reported to Early that evening. In a letter from Gettysburg to Pleasanton on the 29th, Buford says: "I entered this place to-day at 11 A.M. Found everybody in a terrible state of excitement on account of the enemy's advance upon this place. He had approached to within half a mile of the town when the head of my column entered." In a letter to Reynolds on the night of the 30th, Buford said: "I am satisfied that A. P. Hill's corps is massed just back of Cashtown about nine miles from this place. Pender's division of Hill's corps came up to-day. . . . *The road, however, is terribly infested with prowling cavalry parties.* . . . Near Heidlersburg to-day one of my parties captured a courier of Lee's. Nothing was found on him. He says Ewell's corps is crossing the mountain from Carlisle, Rodes' division being at Petersburg in advance." [Italics mine.]

In another letter to Pleasanton on the night of June 30th, Buford said: "There is a road to Cashtown running through Mumasburg and Hunterstown on to the York pike at Oxford which is terribly infested with roving detachments of cavalry." Buford did not seem to think that the Confederates were deficient in cavalry. Hill's report of the campaign cannot be reconciled with the movements of his own corps, or with the reports of Lee, Early, and Ewell. It is dated in November and says that on the morning of June 29, he was in camp at Fayetteville and was directed to move in the direction of York and cross the Susquehanna, menacing the communications of Harrisburg with Philadelphia, and co-operate with Ewell. But the staff officers say that he was ordered on the 29th, after the spy came in, to Gettysburg. It is hard to believe that such an order was ever given. If it was, why did Hill stop at Cashtown? Why did he not move on to York? There was no enemy then in his way at Gettysburg.

But if he had gone to York he would have crossed Ewell marching away from the Susquehanna to Cashtown, and he would have met Early on the road coming back from York. Why would General Lee call Early away from the Susquehanna and send Hill there; or how could Hill co-operate with Ewell if they were marching in opposite directions? General Lee had not then ordered any corps of his army to Gettysburg. He never did till after the close of the first day's fight. On July 1, General Lee's and Longstreet's headquarters were ten miles from Cashtown. Hill was there with two divisions; his third was marching to join him; Ewell's three divisions started that morning for Cashtown. Longstreet's orders to his division commanders, Hood and McLaws, were to follow General Edward Johnson's division and trains that were then passing on the pike and "camp on the other side of the mountain." Pickett was left at Chambersburg. He was ordered to follow Hood as soon as relieved by

Imboden, and, when he arrived at Greenwood, to relieve Laws' brigade, which was on picket at New Guilford; Pickett was told that his own division would be relieved by Imboden. The instructions to Longstreet's three division commanders and to his chief of artillery are to "camp on the other side of the mountain." Gettysburg is not mentioned. Yet that evening the following dispatch was sent by Longstreet's order:

SORRELL, A. A. G., TO WALTON, CHIEF OF ARTILLERY

NEAR GETTYSBURG, PA., July 1st, 5.30 P.M.

The commanding General desires you to come on to-night as far as you can without distressing your men and animals. Ewell and Hill have sharply engaged the enemy to-day and you will be wanted for to-morrow's battle.

The same order was sent to Hood, Pickett, and McLaws. Laws did not wait for Pickett to relieve him; Longstreet ordered him to come on; he arrived in time to be in the next day's battle. Pickett left in a hurry; he marched through Greenwood and never halted. He left no picket behind in place of Laws' brigade. General Lee was, of course, *surprised* when he reached Cashtown and heard that Hill and Heth had gone off on an excursion and were fighting a battle eight miles away at Gettysburg. Lee was dragged to his doom and resolved to make the best of the situation. *But no one can show that the absence of a part of the cavalry with Stuart had anything to do either with bringing on or losing the battle.* If Lee had needed cavalry he had an abundance with Ewell at his call. No doubt he felt the need of Stuart in whom he placed great reliance; and that he expressed anxiety to hear from him. He didn't then know what had detained Stuart. Stuart was absent on duty obeying Lee's orders; he heard from him that day.

There have been complaints, but no one has proved that Lee did anything, or left anything undone, for want of information that cavalry could have brought him. In fact he did know all that cavalry could tell him. Longstreet says the spy told him *more*. The two generals who precipitated the battle are responsible for the disaster; they attempted to shift the blame on Stuart because his absence on the first day gave color to the charge, and had the assistance of certain staff officers at headquarters.

Stine's History of the Army of the Potomac (1893) and the Southern Historical Papers (1877), have letters from Heth in which he imputes to Stuart the whole blame for the loss of the battle; his description of the combat of July 1 conflicts with his own and Hill's official reports.

Of course, Heth's motive was to divert attention from himself; he admits that he proposed the trip to Gettysburg to Hill. His report says nothing about their going to Gettysburg on July 1 for shoes; but that they went on a *reconnaissance* and fought all day to find out if there was an enemy in front of them. They fought hard and found him.[1]

---

[1] General Lee's second report contradicts Heth; it says: "General Hill arrived [at Cashtown] with Pender's division in the evening, and the following morning [July 1st] advanced with these two divisions accompanied by Pegram's and McIntosh's battalions of artillery, to ascertain the strength of the enemy, whose force was supposed to consist chiefly of cavalry. The leading division, under General Heth, found the enemy's videttes about three miles west of Gettysburg and

There is nothing in their reports about General Lee being present and giving orders on the field, or of Heth's getting permission from him to take his division into the fight to help Rodes who was hard pressed. If Heth had said so, General Lee would have sent his report back to him for correction; he was not responsible for what Heth did that day. The record evidence proves the reverse — that Rodes came into the fight several hours after it began and after Heth's division had been knocked to pieces. Heth's letters since the war say he was hunting for shoes; his report says he was hunting a fight. A. P. Hill's report does not mention shoes. Heth's *letters* say nothing about making a reconnaissance. "Rodes," says Heth, "hearing the firing at Gettysburg, faced by the left flank and

continued to advance until within a mile of the town, when two brigades were sent forward to reconnoiter. They drove in the advance of the enemy very gallantly, but subsequently encountered largely superior numbers and were compelled to retire with loss, Brigadier-General Archer commanding one of the brigades being taken prisoner. General Heth then prepared for action, and as soon as Pender arrived to support him was ordered by General Hill to advance. The artillery was placed in position and the engagement opened with vigor. General Heth pressed the enemy steadily back, breaking his first and second lines and attacking his third with great resolution. About 2.30 P.M., the advance of Ewell's corps, consisting of Rodes' division, with Carter's battalion of artillery, arrived by the Middletown road and forming on Heth's left, nearly at right angles with his line, became warmly engaged with fresh numbers of the enemy. Heth's troops having suffered heavily in their protracted contest with a superior force, were relieved by Pender's, and Early coming up by the Heidlersburg road soon afterwards, took position of the left of Rodes when a general advance was made. The enemy gave way on all sides and was driven through Gettysburg with great loss."

And to cover up this blunder it is called a reconnaissance.

approached the town; he became heavily engaged and, seeing this, I sought for and found General Lee, saying to the General: 'Rodes is heavily engaged; had I not better attack?' General Lee replied: 'No, I am not prepared to bring on a general engagement to-day; Longstreet is not up' [which implies that Longstreet had then been ordered up]. Returning to my division I soon discovered that the enemy were moving troops from my front and pushing them against Rodes. I reported this fact to General Lee and again requested permission to attack. Permission was given. My division numbered 7000 muskets. . . . Nor do I see how there could have been any systematic plan of battle formed, as I have, I think, clearly shown that we accidentally stumbled into the fight."

Now Heth's story is contradicted by A. P. Hill, the commander of the corps, whose report says that he put Pender's division in to support Heth's that was in distress; and that about 2.30 in the afternoon, Ewell, with Early's and Rodes' divisions, came in and formed a right angle to his line and the field was won. Just as true an account of the battle as Heth's letters can be found in the Pickwick papers. Rodes' report shows that Heth's story is a fable. Now the truth is, when Heth early in the morning went into the action, General Lee was ten miles away, west of the mountains. Pendleton's report says they heard the firing when they were on the western slope and that General Lee did not understand it. When Rodes arrived on the field, Heth's division was in fragments.

In the same volume of the papers with Heth's letter is

one from General Long, who was a staff officer of General Lee and his biographer. Long says: "An engagement ensued which continued with great spirit until about four o'clock in the afternoon, when the Federal forces were signally defeated and almost annihilated. General Lee arrived on the scene near the close of the action."

Heth says he *stumbled* into the fight; he ought to have said he *blundered* into it. He says that, had the cavalry been in position, General Lee would have known of Reynolds' approach to Gettysburg and would have occupied the place and made it impregnable. But the absence of cavalry (if they had no cavalry) was no reason for Heth's going there on a raid; it might have been a good reason for his staying in camp. This statement assumes that Gettysburg was Lee's objective; it was not. Lee was as willing for Meade to be at Gettysburg as anywhere else; he had no idea of going there before he heard the firing; he went to the rescue of A. P. Hill and Heth. Lee had known for a week that Meade was moving north from Frederick and that he must be in the vicinity of Gettysburg. As a cavalry division was already there, he knew, without being told, that Meade's army must be near. He selected and held the Cashtown Pass as his point of concentration because nature had made it impregnable. He would have a mountain wall to cover his flanks, and the rich Cumberland Valley behind him. If he had ordered the army to Gettysburg he would have been with the leading division, and would have occupied the place several days before, instead of halting Hill's corps at Cashtown.

There was just as much reason for censuring Lee for

being absent on the first day as Stuart. It is impossible to believe that General Lee ever professed the ignorance of the movements of Stuart which Heth and Long and his staff officers have attributed to him. If he had done so it would have been affectation. He knew that his and Longstreet's orders would carry Stuart for a while into a state of eclipse around the enemy, out of sight, and out of communication with him.

Heth delivered the judgment in his letter that — "The failure to crush the Federal army in Pennsylvania . . . can be expressed in five words — *the absence of the cavalry.*"

I would rather say it was due to the presence of Heth. In another letter in the *Philadelphia Times* of December 27, 1877, Heth professes to have read in General Lee's letter-book his instructions to Stuart to keep in close contact and communication with him and Longstreet. Now the contents of the letter-book have since been published and I have read the original copies in the book. Heth's account of what he read in the letter-book is pure fiction. Instead of ordering Stuart to keep on Longstreet's flank, he ordered him to leave Longstreet in Virginia, cross the Potomac, and join Ewell on the Susquehanna, — a hundred miles away. It was all the same to Lee at what ford Stuart crossed the Potomac. Heth's letter was written to give information about the battle to the Count of Paris. It is the origin of his criticism of Stuart in his History of the War.

As for cavalry, there were as many with Ewell as there were with Reynolds that day. Buford fought his two brigades dismounted in the morning when Heth attacked him. There were no cavalry charges on either side. The Confederate cavalry simply guarded the flanks. If there had existed any necessity to make a reconnaissance, Lee's headquarters were near, and so were Ewell's cavalry.

The order should have come from the Commander-in-Chief. Hill and Heth never informed him of the exploit they meditated. He never would have sanctioned it. The object of a reconnaissance is not to gratify curiosity but to get information that shall be a basis of action — to be ready for an attack or a retreat. But the army could take no effective action before it was concentrated and Lee proposed to stand on the defensive. The concentration would have been completed that evening had it not been defeated by an act of subordinates. As General Lee was supposed to be responsible for the movement on Gettysburg that day, it has been a mystery why a man of his aggressive temper did not order a pursuit after the rout, but allowed the enemy to re-form in a strong position on Cemetery Ridge. Johnson's and Anderson's divisions that had just arrived on the field might easily have taken it. But we must not judge General Lee by what we know now, but in the light that was then before him.

It is very plain why he did not pursue. The battle had been brought on without his knowledge and against his orders. It was improbable that two of Meade's corps and a division of cavalry would not be in supporting distance of his army. The battle had lasted six hours and there was every reason to believe that fresh troops had arrived, or were near at hand. The only way to find out was to attack the enemy in force in his strong position.

The position of the enemy was almost inaccessible, even to infantry. No use could have been made of cavalry for a reconnaissance to find out the strength of the force holding the Ridge.[1]

[1] LEESBURG, VA., April 17, 1906.

HON. JOHN H. ALEXANDER,

MY DEAR COMRADE: According to promise I will give you for the benefit of Colonel J. S. Mosby a condensed statement of the operations of my Command at Gettysburg.

Gen. R. S. Ewell applied to Gen. Lee for my Command to go with him before he left the main army. I had scouted for General Ewell much. The application was referred to General Stuart who refused to comply with it, and Colonel French was sent. Before crossing the Potomac River General Ewell again asked for my Command, and his request was granted. I joined him at Chambersburg. The next morning I was ordered by Ewell to report to General Early, who was on the direct road to Gettysburg. In his dispatch to Early, General Ewell ordered to put me in front of Gordon's brigade. Colonel French, with a small portion of his Command was put on detached service; and the greater portion of his Command was placed under me and I was put in front of Gordon. But Colonel French's own regiment was not put under me, nor did I want them.

After we passed through Cashtown and arrived in about a mile of Gettysburg, I saw on my left from 700 to 900 of the enemy drawn up in line of battle. I reported this to General Gordon, and told him if he wished to see the fight to come up, which he did. My Command numbered 250. The fight was short and decisive. I captured 170 of them and would have captured more but for the fences which were numerous. I camped near Gettysburg that night. I was then ordered by General Early to go to Hanover Junction and break the railroad communications, &c. I started early the next morning. Nothing occurred on the way of any consequence, except that I captured a wagon load of jewelry. After supplying ourselves we buried the balance. We found Hanover Junction guarded by infantry. After a sharp fight we drove them away and burned the depot, bridges, &c. We camped that night not far from Hanover Junction, and joined General Early at York the next day. I was sent by Early in front of his Command, the next day,

GETTYSBURG 157

in the direction of Gettysburg. I gave Early valuable information which I gathered on the way, and joined Ewell at Cashtown. I was ordered by Ewell to make reconnoissance and report their number, position, &c. I did this and General Early made his attack on my report. Early ordered me to watch his left flank and I took my position on the left of Cemetery Hill.

After the first day's fight was over, and about dark, I saw the enemy leaving Cemetery Hill. I found General Ewell sitting on the ground near Gettysburg and reported to him what I had seen. At that time an officer from General Lee rode up and delivered General Lee's compliments to General Ewell for his great fight during the day, and said that General Lee said, 'if Ewell did not think his position strong enough he was to swing around to the right on Longstreet.' Early replied, "Tell General Lee I'll bet him fifty dollars in green backs we can whip them any way they come.' General Ewell, without replying, rose up and walked away and ordered me to follow. He asked me if I could find out for certain if my impression was correct that the enemy were retreating. Said that he would detach any number of men to go with me. I replied that if possible I would find out; but did not want any of his men, and wanted but few of my own. I promised him to be back by 3 A.M. I selected five men to go with me. We found the Yankees too thick around for us to ride through them; so I left our horses with three men in an orchard of very large trees, and took men on with me afoot. We had then gotten near enough to the pike to hear the noise of the troops moving over it; but could not distinguish whether they were reinforcements coming up or the army retreating. I finally reached the pike and listened attentively to all that was said, and learned that the whole army was up or coming up. The night had passed too swiftly for me. One of my men said, 'Colonel, the day is breaking.' We reached our horses, I know not how; but on the way we passed houses in which the Yankee soldiers were eating their breakfast, perhaps. When we reported to General Ewell that the whole army was up, or nearly so, he said, 'Hear that gun, it is too late; that means the opening of the battle. It is Longstreet's gun.'

I continued scouting for Ewell until General Stuart arrived on July 2nd, and was with General Stuart in his fight with the enemy on that day. On our retreat General Ewell ordered me to report to General Gordon and bring up his retreat. Gordon was in the rear on leaving Gettysburg. We had hard fighting all that day; and at one time Gordon had to come to our assistance. When night arrived I had scarcely a man or horse fit for duty.

I would be glad to answer any questions that Colonel Mosby may want to ask, and of which I am capable. I have gone but little into details. We inflicted considerable loss on the enemy in several small engagements, but also lost several men ourselves — especially while with General Stuart.

Respectfully,
E. V. WHITE (Signed).

But if immediate advantage was not taken of the panic the opportunity was lost — the tide must be taken at its flood that leads on to fortune. Steinwehr's fresh division with the reserve artillery occupied the commanding position of Cemetery Hill; and the troops that had been engaged were forming there on the reserve.[1] To judge

---

[1] Colonel Freemantle says: "July 2nd, Colonel Sorrell, the Austrian and I arrived at 5 A.M. at the same commanding position we were on yesterday, and I climbed up a tree in company with Captain Schreibert of the Prussian army. Just below us were seated Generals Lee, Hill, Longstreet and Hood in consultation — the two latter assisting their deliberations by the truly American custom of *whittling sticks*. . . . At 7 A.M. I rode over one part of the ground with General Longstreet, and saw him disposing of McLaws' division for to-day's fight. The enemy occupied a series of high ridges, the tops of which were covered with trees, but the intervening valleys between their ridges and ours were open and partly under cultivation. The cemetery was on their right and their left appeared to rest upon a high, rocky hill. The enemy's forces, which were now supposed to comprise nearly the whole Potomac army, were concentrated in a space apparently not more than a couple of miles in length. The Confederates enclosed them in a sort of semicircle, and the extreme extent of our position must have been from five to six miles at least. . . . Only two divisions of Longstreet's were present today, viz; McLaws' and Hood's; Pickett's being still in the rear. . . . At 2 P.M. General Longstreet advised me, if I wished to have a good view of the battle, to return to my tree of yesterday. . . . Every now and then a caisson would blow up — if a Federal one a Confederate yell

General Lee, we must put ourselves in his place; every general must be condemned if judged by any other rule. General Lee could not know by intuition that Meade's army was scattered, and a large part of it, including nearly all of his cavelry, had gone after Stuart.

Johnson's report says: "On June 29, in obedience to orders, I counter-marched my division [from Carlisle] to Greenvillage and hence easterly via Scotland to Gettysburg, not arriving in time, however, to participate in the action of the first instant." Johnson did not arrive at Cashtown before noon of July 1. Ewell, with Rodes'

would immediately follow. The Southern troops when charging to express their delight always yell in a manner peculiar to themselves. Their cheer is much like ours; but the Confederate officers declare that the rebel yell has a particular merit and always produces a salutary and useful effect upon their adversaries.

"Every one deplores that Longstreet *will* expose himself in such a reckless manner. To-day he led a Georgia regiment in a charge against a battery, hat in hand and in front of everybody. As soon as the firing began, General Lee joined Hill below our tree and he remained there nearly all the time, looking through his field glasses — sometimes talking to Hill and sometimes to Colonel Long of his staff. But generally he sat quite alone on the stump of a tree. . . . Soon after seven General Lee got a report by signal from General Longstreet to say 'we are doing well. . . . A long train of horses and mules got in to-day sent in by General Stuart and captured, it is understood, by his cavalry which had penetrated to within six miles of Washington.' [This was a supply train of one hundred and fifty wagons which Stuart had captured on its way from Washington to the army at Frederick.]

"At supper this evening General Longstreet spoke of the enemy's position as being 'very formidable.' He also said they would doubtless entrench themselves strongly during the night. . . . I have the best reason for supposing that the fight came off prematurely, and that neither Longstreet nor Lee intended that it should have begun that day. I also think their plans were deranged by the events of the first."

division, did not leave Carlisle until the 30th. I suppose he was waiting for Jenkins' cavalry, which was skirmishing in the suburbs of Harrisburg, to join him. In the meantime Ewell must have received Lee's second letter of the 28th to come the eastern route. Although Ewell started the day after Johnson left, yet he would have arrived at Cashtown ahead of Johnson if the note from Hill had not diverted him from his line of march, on the morning of July 1, to Gettysburg. This shows that Johnson marched about twice the distance that Rodes did. Johnson must have received orders at Cashtown to move on. Anderson says he received orders there to join Hill at Gettysburg. Colonel Freemantle passed both divisions on the road that morning — Anderson was leading. In his "Four Years with Lee," Colonel Taylor, Lee's A. A. G., says: "Major Edward Johnson, whose division reached the field after the engagement and formed on the left of Early, in a conversation had with me since the war about this circumstance [attacking Cemetery Hill on July 1st], in which I sought an explanation of our inaction at that time, assured me that there was no hindrance to his moving forward, but that after getting his own command into line of battle and before it became seriously engaged, or had advanced any great distance, for some unexplained reason he had orders to halt."

Of course the Commander-in-Chief, after he arrived on the field, became responsible for the conduct of the operations. Discretion to attack or not to attack could not be transferred to corps commanders. As Lee was present on the field his orders must have been absolute, if any were given. With the light before him I think General Lee had reason to think that Meade's whole army was on the Ridge in front of him. If he had ordered Hill and Heth to attack in the morning he would have kept up the pursuit in the evening. There were a thousand reasons for continuing the fight: there was no good reason for beginning it. This shows that he did not look with unalloyed pleasure on the trophies that had been won. Yet on the field of victory he condoned his lieutenant's offense; afterwards he was estopped from complaining of it. Colonel Freemantle's diary says: "At 4.30 P.M., we came in sight of Gettysburg and joined General Lee and General Hill [in the morning when General Lee heard the firing he rode rapidly forward and left Longstreet] who were on top of one of the ridges which formed the peculiar feature of the country around Gettysburg. We could see the enemy retreating up one of the opposite ridges, pursued by the Confederates with loud yells. The position into which the enemy had been driven was evidently a strong one. His right appeared to rest on a cemetery on a high ridge to the right of Gettysburg as we looked at it. . . . General Ewell had come up at 3.30 on the enemy's right (with part of his corps) and completed his discomfiture. General Reynolds, one of the best Yankee Generals, was reported killed. While we were talking, a message arrived from General Ewell, requesting Hill to press the enemy in front while he performed the same operation on his right. The pressure was accordingly applied in a mild degree, but the enemy was too strongly posted and it was too late in the evening for a regular attack. . . . The firing closed about dark, at which time I rode back with General Longstreet and his staff to his headquarters at Cashtown, a little village about eight miles from Gettysburg. . . . In the fight to-day nearly 6,000 prisoners had been taken and 10 guns. About 20,000 men must have been on the field on the Confederate side. The enemy had two *corps d'armée* engaged. All prisoners belong, I think, to the First and Eleventh Corps. . . ."

Lee had every reason to believe that the bulk of Meade's army was on the Ridge. His staff officer and biographer, Long, after the manner of Herodotus, gives a dramatic form to his narrative in an imaginary dialogue between himself and Lee that night. I say *imaginary*, because an analysis shows that he told Lee things that he and Lee could not have known then. This is another instance of an anachronism; Long antedated what he afterward learned. Long says: "The General, as if he had been thinking over his plans and orders, turned to me with the remark: 'Colonel Long, do you think we had better attack without cavalry? If we do so, we will not, if successful, be able to reap the fruits of victory.' In my opinion, I replied, it would be best not to wait for Stuart. It is uncertain where he is or when he will arrive. At present only two or three corps of the enemy's army are up and it seems best to attack them before they are greatly strengthened by reinforcements. The cavalry had better be left to take care of itself."

In the immortal dialogue of the Phædo, Plato puts imaginary speeches into the mouth of Socrates; while, as a fact, they were never spoken, still we know that they might have been spoken by the great martyr. General Lee would never have said what his staff officer here makes him say—he would have stultified himself. If Plato had introduced Lee in a dialogue, he would not have made him ask such a silly question; or give such an absurd answer if the question had been asked of him.

In modern war little use is made of cavalry except for strategic purposes — to screen its own side and unmask the other. The army had no Chief of Cavalry after Stuart was gone. Stuart, in fact, created a revolution in the use of cavalry. The improvements in fire-arms have made Murat's tactics in charging infantry squares as obsolete as the lance and the flint-lock. If not having cavalry to pursue and gather the fruits of victory was a good reason for not attacking Meade, it would have been an equally good reason for not attacking Hooker at Chancellorsville. There was no cavalry pursuit there; nor in any of the battles of Virginia. In fact in all of Lee's battles the work done by the cavalry was valuable but mostly preliminary — the cavalry cleared the way and guarded the flanks.

Then Long makes himself tell General Lee not to wait for Stuart — that they did not know where he was — and that only two or three of Meade's corps were up, and it was better to make an early attack. Now Major Venable, Stuart's staff officer, had reported to General Lee in person in the afternoon that Stuart was approaching and would soon arrive. Lee's report says so. He was on the ground the next day before Longstreet deployed a single brigade. Long also makes himself tell General Lee that only two or three corps of the enemy were on the ground. If Long knew it, General Lee knew it. But if Lee knew it, then he made a great mistake, and there is no excuse for his not having seized Cemetery Ridge on the evening of July 1. The only defense that can be made for General Lee's inaction is that he did not know then what we know now.

But if Stuart was not present, nearly all of Meade's cavalry was absent in pursuit of him. That was compensation to Lee — Meade would have had no cavalry to cover *his* retreat if defeated. Then, if General Lee knew that only a small part of Meade's army was in his front, he knew that they would be gone before daybreak or that Meade's army would be on the Ridge by sunrise. There are many things a man of sense knows without being told.

Before any blame can be attached to Stuart for the loss of the campaign it must appear, — (1) that he was guilty of disobedience of orders and improperly absent; (2) that in consequence of it there was an imperative necessity for Hill and Heth to move to Gettysburg on July 1. It is immaterial whether they went to get information, or to get shoes. It is a coincidence that in the October following, General Lee on the Rapidan again took the offensive and moved to strike Meade on the flank; and that Hill and Heth should have been again in advance at Bristoe, and have repeated the blunder of Gettysburg.

But no one would suspect it from reading General Lee's

report. It says: "General Hill arrived first at Bristoe where his advance [Heth's division] consisting of two brigades became engaged with a force largely superior in numbers posted behind the railroad embankment. The particulars of the action have not been officially reported, but the brigades were repulsed with loss and five pieces of artillery with a number of prisoners captured." This is a very mild statement of the case. Hill says he "ran up against the enemy's line of battle behind the railroad embankment (Second Corps) and of whose presence I was unaware. . . . In conclusion I am convinced that I made the attack too hastily [as he had done on July 1] and at the same time that [if there had been] a delay of half-an-hour there would have been no enemy to attack. In that event I believe I should equally have blamed myself for not attacking at once." Hill and Heth, in their haste to attack with two brigades the Third Corps that had crossed Broad Run, were ambuscaded by the Second Corps, under Warren, that had not crossed the stream, and was lying near in a railroad cut behind an embankment on their flank.

A few skirmishers would have developed Warren and saved Hill from the surprise. I do not think Hill would have had any reason to blame himself if he had taken time to reconnoiter, as Warren could not move off by daylight with Hill close on his flank without great loss; Warren says he did not leave until nine o'clock that night. Anderson's division was brought up and a part of it engaged. On Hill's report are the following endorsements:

General Hill explains how, in his haste to attack the Third Army corps of the enemy [in his front] he overlooked the presence of the Second [on his flank] which was the cause of the disaster which ensued.

R. E. LEE, General.

NOVEMBER 24th, 1863.

Respectfully submitted to the President: —

The disaster at Bristoe Station seems to be due to gallant but over hasty pressing on of the enemy.

J. A. SEDDON.

Returned to the Secretary of War: —

There was a want of vigilance by reason of which it appears the Third [Second] army corps of the enemy got a position giving great advantage to them.

J. D. [DAVIS].

Hill's loss was 1378 killed, wounded, and captured, and five pieces of artillery, in an affair that probably did not last fifteen minutes. General Posey was mortally wounded. General Lee had passed through Greenwich in pursuit of Meade with Hill and Ewell's corps. When they arrived near Bristoe the Third Corps had just crossed Broad Run on the retreat to Centerville; Hill ordered Heth to cross and attack it; the Third Corps went on; the Second, under Warren, was intercepted; it had not reached the stream and was marching in column on the railroad. Warren immediately formed a front to his flank behind a railroad embankment and a deep cut. Heth overlooked it; this was the cause of the failure of the Bristoe campaign. With ordinary skill the Second Corps should have been destroyed.

I have heard persons who were present speak of the

emotion that General Lee exhibited when he rode up and saw the ground strewn with the dead and wounded of Heth's brigades — "Like the leaves of the forest when Autumn hath blown." Long, the staff officer and biographer of General Lee, says: "Meade had made the best use of the several unavoidable delays of the Confederate army, and though Hill, who was seeking to intercept the Federal retreat at Bristoe Station, made all haste in his march, he arrived there only in time to meet the rear-guard of Meade's army. He made a prompt attack on the Federal column, which was hastening to pass Broad Run, which the remainder of the army had already crossed. The assault proved unfortunate. . . . When General Lee reached the position of Hill's repulse, that officer, deeply mortified by his mishap, endeavored to explain the causes of his failure. The General listened in silence and as they rode together over the field strewn with dead bodies, replied with sad gravity: 'Well, well, General, bury these poor men and let us say no more about it.' The movement had evidently proved a failure." It ought to have been and came near being a masterstroke. Colonel Taylor of Lee's staff, in a note made at the time says: "On Wednesday we left Warrenton and reached this place [Bristoe] on the same day. Here Hill's advance met a corps of the enemy and at once engaged it. Our other corps [Ewell's] came up in good time and we should have punished the enemy severely, but matters were not properly managed and they all escaped and, what is worse, they got the better of us in what little fighting there was. . . . By unpardonable mismanagement the enemy was allowed to capture five pieces of artillery. There was no excuse for it as all our troops were well in hand and much stronger than the enemy."

In October, General Lee, writing to Longstreet, who had been sent west, said in reference to the Bristoe affair — "We struck his [Meade's] rear-guard three times. The last at Bristoe, where Hill with his advance of two brigades fell too precipitately on one of his corps and suffered a repulse and loss."

In his "Story of the Civil War," John C. Ropes, a Northern man, but certainly impartial in his judgment as between Confederates, in reference to the opening of the battles around Richmond in which the duty assigned to A. P. Hill was to co-operate with Jackson, who was to attack the enemy in flank and rear, says: "The Confederates under the lead of A. P. Hill, a daring and energetic but inconsiderate officer, pushed the Federals hard and their outposts retired to their intrenched lines behind Beaver Dam Creek, a little east of Mechanicsville, where they felt secure from any direct attack. In spite of the fact that nothing had been heard of Jackson, and notwithstanding the evident strength of the Federal position, Hill attacked fiercely and recklessly. He was repulsed with great slaughter, mainly by McCall's division of Porter's corps, without having made the smallest impression on the Federal lines."

And in his life of Stonewall Jackson, Colonel Henderson says: "It was the impatience of Hill, not the tardiness of Jackson, which was the cause of the Confederate repulse." And with equal justice it may be added that it was the impatience of General Hill at Bristoe and Gettysburg, and not the absence of Stuart, that caused the Confederate disasters. A. P. Hill fell on the lines at Petersburg on April 2, 1865, and gave his life in defense of a cause he had served not wisely but too well. Of him it may with truth be said, as it was of the Roman Consul who led his army into the fatal defile, that "Flaminius died bravely, sword in hand, having committed no greater military error than many an impetuous soldier, whose death in his country's cause has been felt to throw a veil over his rashness and whose memory is pitied and honored."

And now to return to Stuart. I have said that on the morning of June 24 I reported to him when I came back alone from a scout inside Hooker's lines. I was leading the horses of the two prisoners I had captured and paroled. Stuart's headquarters were in Loudon at Rector's crossroads — a few miles in front of the Gaps of the Blue Ridge. General Lee was about fifteen miles away at Berryville in the Shenandoah Valley. Stuart was anxiously waiting to hear what Hooker was doing. He must then have received General Lee's order of 5 P.M., of the 23d, to start the next day and put himself on Ewell's right on the Susquehanna. It gave him the choice of routes — through the Valley by Shepherdstown, or by Hooker's rear. The news I brought of the situation in Hooker's army determined him to take the latter route. I told him that Hooker was quiet, waiting on Lee; there was no sign of movement, no change in the location of the camps — the different corps were still all far apart. General Lee controlled the situation. Hancock was on the extreme left at Thoroughfare; Slocum's corps was at Leesburg, near Edwards' Ferry. Stuart chose to go the shortest and most direct way to Ewell. If he passed through the Shenandoah Valley by Shepherdstown it would be a zigzag march over the Blue Ridge and then back again east over the South Mountain. He could not watch Hooker with the mountain between them. Longstreet urged him to go the route he took. But to a soldier of Stuart's energy and enterprising spirit the most powerful motive would be to go where he could do the most damage to the enemy on the march. The eastern route would offer the opportunity. Its safety — like Jackson's flank march at Chancellorsville — lay in its boldness. It would not be anticipated. On all the roads were wagon-trains, and on the canal which he would cross were boats carrying supplies to the army depot above. He would cripple Hooker by destroying his transportation. After hearing my report Stuart wrote a letter to General Lee — the most of it at my dictation — giving him the information which I had brought. He, of course, would acknowledge receipt of Lee's letter of instructions of 5 P.M., of the evening before, and inform General Lee when he would start and the route he would take. The courier with the dispatch must have overtaken General Lee during the day; he left his headquarters with Longstreet that morning and spent the night between Berryville and Williamsport. For a week he had been receiving dispatches regularly from Stuart; these suddenly stopped coming. This was notice to General Lee that Hooker's army was between them. He knew that while the operation was going on it was a physical impossibility for Stuart to communicate with him without a balloon or a carrier-pigeon. Lee had studied astronomy; he knew the cause of an eclipse. Lee's order on the 23d to Stuart was to come over to the Valley the following day and cross the Potomac at Shepherdstown, if he did not go the other way. As he did not cross with Hill's corps at Shepherdstown on the 25th, this also was notice that he would cross east of the Blue Ridge. The possibility of crossing at Point of Rocks or any point east of the Ridge, except Seneca, was never considered because it was impracticable. All the other fords east of the Ridge, except Seneca in Hooker's rear, were strongly guarded. Colonel White had made a cavalry raid at Point of Rocks on the 17th; but it could not be repeated. It created an alarm about the communication between Harper's Ferry and Washington. Stuart's report says that early on the morning of the 25th, when he discovered Hancock's corps moving northward, he sent a dispatch to General Lee with intelligence of it. As Hancock was on Hooker's extreme left it indicated that his whole army was marching to the Potomac. The courier traveled inside our lines and could not have been intercepted. General Lee must have received the letter about Williamsport the next day, as there was a line of relay couriers to his headquarters. It is therefore a reflection on General Lee to suppose that he was surprised when he heard that Hooker had crossed the Potomac. He had written Mr. Davis that a pontoon bridge had been laid at Edwards' Ferry; could he have imagined that it was not laid there for Hooker to cross on? The great military advantage of Stuart's taking the eastern route was that it would divert attention to the defense of the capital; if successful, all communication would be cut off and Washington would be isolated. He was not conducting a raid, or an independent expedition of cavalry, but was assigned to perform a part of a combined movement of the whole army. Stuart performed his part in the grand drama. It is understood that Stuart, on the night of the 21st, when he was in Ashby's Gap, rode to General Lee's headquarters a few miles off. No doubt it was then agreed that Ewell, who was at Hagerstown, should move into Pennsylvania, and that Stuart should follow him with three brigades of cavalry and leave his other two brigades with General Longstreet.

General Lee, of course, knew the character of the commanders, and probably selected the two cavalry brigades that were kept with him. At that time neither Longstreet or A. P. Hill had been ordered to Pennsylvania. The advantages of the different routes must have been discussed by them, as Longstreet in a letter to Stuart the next day speaks of Hopewell Gap in the Bull Run as one suggested by General Lee in a letter to him, and he expresses his preference for it. In fact, he told Stuart *not* to go the other way. It is clear that General Lee at that time had no objective point. His object was to compel Hooker to withdraw his army over the Potomac. He also sent Longstreet at that time a letter of instructions to be forwarded to Stuart, if Longstreet approved them. The letter expressed a fear that the enemy would steal a march and get over the river first. Longstreet forwarded the letter to Stuart with the qualification that he must go around the enemy through the Bull Run Mountain. In his book Longstreet criticises Stuart for obeying his own orders, and says he ordered him to march on his right flank into Pennsylvania. If Stuart had passed through the Valley he would have left General Longstreet and General Lee behind him, and marched on to the Susquehanna. He could not, therefore, have stayed with Longstreet to watch Hooker unless he disobeyed General Lee's orders. Three of Lee's staff officers — Colonel Taylor, Colonel Marshall, and General Long — with the record before them in their own handwriting, make the same statement that Longstreet does. The ridiculous position in which they put their Chief does not seem to have occurred to them; his reputation survives because nobody believes them. They take no account of the fact that Ewell was far away from the other two corps and from General Lee. The selection of the route through Hooker's army was based on the theory that the conditions would be maintained as they were until Stuart got through. The preservation of the status in Hooker's army depended on Lee. At that time the design was perfectly practicable; his army corps were separated by many miles and the only obstruction on the roads were wagon-trains hauling supplies. Hooker would have been astonished to hear that Stuart had cut his army in two, but before he could have recovered from the shock the blazing meteor would have passed out of sight.

He would then have sent his cavalry in pursuit —

that ought to have been what General Lee wanted — they would have been too far off to hurt Stuart. My preference was to go by the Hopewell Gap in the Bull Run Mountains and thus pass between Hancock at Thoroughfare and Pleasanton at Aldie. There was only a cavalry picket at Hopewell. This shows how little Hooker suspected the blow that was meditated; Hancock felt secure on that flank. Stuart, for some reason, was induced to cross at Glasscock's on the other side of Hancock. The contemplated enterprise, if it had not been defeated by a cause that Stuart could not control, was far less difficult and involved far less hazard than the ride around McClellan on the Chickahominy. Hooker was now on the defensive — waiting for Lee to move. When Lee halted, Hooker stood still; McClellan, on the contrary, was engaged in an offensive operation to capture Richmond; Hooker was defending Washington. After sending the dispatch to General Lee with the information I had brought, Stuart made preparations to start that evening. I was delighted at the part that was given to me. It was agreed that with my small command of twenty or thirty men, I should meet the head of Stuart's column on the Little River Turnpike the next day, ten or twelve miles below Aldie, and then lead the advance to Seneca Ford. Some of my men lived in that neighborhood and would act as guides. Circumstances which I had not anticipated prevented Stuart from meeting me at the appointed rendezvous. I was there. On the night of the 24th we bivouacked on the western side of the Bull Run; at daybreak two men were sent ahead to look out for an ambuscade. I did not want to run into another on that road. We had stopped at a spring and were eating some canned goods captured from a sutler when we heard a volley on the top of the mountain. The men did not come back so we knew that they were either killed or captured. The party in ambush had done us the favor to fire and give us warning. In a letter to Hooker the evening before Pleasanton said: "I shall try Mosby to-morrow." I suppose this was his mode of trial. But the ambuscade did not stop us; we made a detour, were soon over the mountain and passed by Hancock's corps to the turnpike. We met Hooker's whole army in motion toward the Potomac; the marching columns were on all the roads. We heard artillery firing a few miles off; Stuart had run against Hancock's column about Haymarket, and was having a duel with him. Hancock's corps had the road and was marching between us; so Stuart could not get through. He turned towards Buckland; we spent nearly all day in the woods near the pike and retraced our steps about sunset. I supposed that Stuart had returned. Stuart's report dated August 20, 1863, gives a correct account of events at that time. It says: "I resumed [22d] my own position at Rector's Cross-roads and, being in constant communication with the commanding general, had scouts busily engaged watching and reporting the enemy's movements and reporting the same to the commanding general. In this difficult search the fearless and indefatigable Major Mosby was particularly active and efficient. His information was always accurate and reliable. The enemy retained one army corps (Fifth) at Aldie and kept his cavalry near enough to make attack upon the latter productive of no solid benefits, and I began to look for some other point at which to direct an effective blow. *I submitted to the commanding general the plan of leaving a brigade or so in my present front and passing through Hopewell or some other Gap in the Bull Run Mountains, attain the enemy's rear, passing between his main body and Washington, and cross into Maryland, joining our army north of the Potomac. The commanding general wrote me authorizing this move if I deemed it practicable* [June 22 and 5 P.M., June 23], and also what instructions should be given the *officers* in command of the *two* brigades left in front of the enemy. He also notified me that one column would move via Gettysburg and the other via Carlisle towards the Susquehanna, and directed me, after crossing, to proceed with all dispatch to *join the right* [Early] *of the army in Pennsylvania*. Accordingly three days' rations were prepared and on the night of the 24th the following brigades — Hampton's, Fitz-Lee's and W. H. F. Lee's — rendezvoused secretly near Salem Depot. We had no wagons or vehicles except six pieces of artillery and caissons and ambulances. Robertson's and Jones' brigades, under command of the former, were left in observation of the enemy on the usual front with full instructions as to following up the enemy in case of withdrawal and rejoining our army. . . . At one o'clock at night the brigades, with noiseless march, moved out. This precaution was necessary on account of the enemy having possession of Bull Run Mountains, which in the daytime commanded a view of every move of consequence in that region. Hancock's corps occupied Thoroughfare Gap. Moving to the right we passed through Glasscock's Gap without difficulty and marched for Haymarket. I had previously sent Major Mosby with some picked men through to gain the vicinity of Dranesville, find where a crossing was practicable, and bring intelligence to me near Gum Springs to-day [25th.] [Stuart is here slightly mistaken; I had already informed him that he could cross at Seneca where I had lately crossed.] As we neared Haymarket, we found Hancock's corps *en route* through Haymarket for Gum Springs, his infantry well distributed through his trains. I chose a good position and opened with artillery on his passing columns with effect, scattering men, wagons, and horses in wild confusion; disabled one of the enemy's caissons, which he abandoned, and compelled him to advance in order of battle to compel us to desist. . . . *I sent a dispatch to General Lee concerning Hooker's movements* and moved back to Buckland to deceive the enemy. . . . I had not yet heard from Major Mosby, but the indications favored my successful passage in rear of the enemy's army." Stuart did not hear from me because Hooker's troops were marching on all roads between us. As the artillery firing had ceased in the morning, I concluded that he had gone back and I did the same. He made a wide detour through Fairfax and crossed the Potomac the night of the 27th at Seneca, and went into bivouac on the Maryland shore. On the same night Pleasanton's cavalry corps, the rear-guard of the army, crossed ten or twelve miles above on the pontoon at Edwards' Ferry and marched on to Frederick. According to all precedents, it should have been in the advance harassing Lee. It had been kept back by the news that a heavy cavalry force was in the rear. So Stuart's movement at least neutralized Hooker's cavalry corps. Pleasanton did not know that Stuart was crossing the river below him. The report further says: "The canal, which was now the supplying medium of Hooker's army, soon received our attention. A lock gate was broken and steps taken to intercept boats. At least a dozen were intercepted and the next morning several loaded with troops, negroes, and stores were captured by Colonel Wickham, Fourth Virginia Cavalry, commanding our rear-guard. . . . I realized the importance of joining our army in Pennsylvania and resumed the march northward early on the 28th."

One benefit of Stuart's crossing at Seneca was that it practically eliminated French's corps in the campaign, and put it on the defensive, to guard the line of the Potomac and the rear of Meade's army. It had been the garrison — 11,000 — at Harper's Ferry, but, when the place was abandoned, it was added to Meade's command. But Stuart's appearance created such a sensation that Meade sent 4000 to guard the canal, and 7000 were kept at Frederick. They were no more help to Meade in the battle than if they had stayed above the clouds on Maryland Heights. As before stated, it was perfectly practicable on the evening of the 24th, when Stuart left Rector's Cross-roads, for him to pass through the Bull Run and ride through Hooker's army to the Potomac.

GETTYSBURG

The wagons on the roads would, of course, have been burned; the mules he would have taken with him. If Longstreet and Hill had rested one day longer in the Shenandoah Valley, Hooker would have done the same, and Stuart would not have found the roads blockaded by his columns marching to the Potomac. Early on the evening of the 25th Stuart would have crossed and bivouacked for the night at Seneca. Men and horses would have had a night's rest. No doubt Hooker's cavalry would have been sent in pursuit, but they would have been too far behind to give any trouble. A detachment might have been sent that night (25th) to break the communications between Washington and Baltimore. On that day General Lee was at Williamsport; he could not have expected Stuart to communicate with him while he was executing the movement, simply because Stuart was too far away and the Blue Ridge and Hooker's army were between them. Besides, Stuart knew that General Lee had retained two brigades of cavalry with Longstreet in front of the Gaps to observe the enemy; and his signal stations on the Ridge would command a view of the Potomac and the Loudon Valley. Stuart's orders did not permit him to turn west and join Lee after he got over the river, but to march north to join Ewell. Lee's staff officers seem to think that Stuart should have marched in both directions at the same time.

"In either case," said General Lee, "after crossing the river [at Shepherdstown, or Seneca] you must move on and feel the right of Ewell's troops, collecting information, provisions, etc."

Lee had informed Stuart that he would find Ewell on the Susquehanna. Stuart obeyed orders, and on the morning of the 28th moved in that direction. It would have been far better if the orders had been less rigid, and Stuart had been given discretion to operate independently of the main army. There was an abundant force of cavalry with Lee and Longstreet, as well as with Ewell; there was only a small force with Meade. Stuart's columns should have been allowed to turn east toward Baltimore. Hooker's cavalry would have been drawn after it and would have been engaged in repairing the damage Stuart had done. In other words, the body of cavalry under Stuart should have been made an independent, or containing force, to hold in check or put on the defensive greatly superior numbers in Maryland and around the Capital; while the Confederates were having as good a time in Pennsylvania as Hannibal with the Carthaginians had in the Valley of the Po. It is strange that Stuart should have camped the night of the 27th on the river between Edwards' Ferry and Washington and that it was not discovered. The next morning, with no suspicion of danger, the boats were sent up the canal; and a long supply train left Washington for the army at Frederick.

The boats were burned. Stuart found the wagons on the road on which he was marching and took them along. He expected to turn them over to Early at York. Some of the teamsters tried to get away and were chased into the suburbs of Washington. He met and routed several bodies of cavalry during the day. They carried the astonishing news to Meade at Frederick, who had taken command of the Army of the Potomac at 2.30 P.M. that day. He sent Gregg's and Kilpatrick's cavalry divisions in pursuit. Buford was kept close on his left flank to watch Lee, but one of his brigades (Merritt's) was detached to guard the trains in the rear. At Westminster a body of Delaware cavalry showed more valor than discretion and had to pay the penalty for it. The fugitives got up a great panic in Baltimore which soon spread over the country. Gunboats were ordered from different places to protect Washington, Annapolis, Havre-de-Grace, and the powder works. Stuart marched all night of the 28th, and early the next morning burned the railroad bridge and cut the telegraph at Sykesville, and broke communication between Meade and Washington. He spent the night of the 29th in the vicinity of Westminster, and moved on in the morning, expecting to meet Early at York. Gregg's cavalry division and the Sixth Corps were on his track and got to Westminster after he left; they went on east to Manchester and Hanover Junction. On the night of the 30th the Fifth Corps camped on the ground where Stuart had camped the night before. Meade had borne off to the east toward Baltimore because he was sure from Early's being at York, and Stuart's marching in that direction with a wagon train, that the Confederate army would concentrate on the Susquehanna. At Hanover Stuart ran into, or rather over, Kilpatrick's rear-guard. There was a short skirmish — it was his policy as far as possible, to avoid one — and he hastened on to find Early. The enemy's cavalry did not molest him on the march. Hancock with the Second Corps was moving on in rear of the Fifth. Meade was not then looking toward Gettysburg but to the Susquehanna. In a letter that day he said to Pleasanton that his "projected movement is toward the line of the Baltimore and Harrisburg road." Stuart's night march from Hanover was a severe trial to men and horses, but the enemy's cavalry in pursuit of him suffered just as much.[1] Early in the morning of July 1 he

[1] In the *Century* Captain W. E. Miller describes the hardship endured by Gregg's cavalry that followed Stuart:

"Our march to Westminster was one of unusual severity for the night was very dark and both men and horses were worn out. The men fell asleep in their saddles and whenever the column halted the horses would fall asleep too. As the officers were responsible for keeping the column closed up, they had to resort to all sorts of expedients to keep awake, such as pinching themselves, pounding their heads and pricking themselves with pins. When within about five miles of Westminster it was discovered that the left of the line was not up. A halt was ordered and, on sending back, the fact was discovered that the artillery men and battery horses were sound asleep, and that whilst a portion of the column in front of them had been moving on, that in the rear was standing still. At Manchester a halt of a few hours was made, during which the men consumed what was left of the rations procured at Mount Airy, gave their horses the last grain of feed they had with them and obtained a little sleep. Mounting again we moved north along the Carlisle pike for half a mile and then by the Grove Mill road to Hanover Junction (Pa.), on the Northern Central Railroad, where we arrived during the forenoon of July 1st. Our movements at this place illustrate to some extent the uncertainties of the campaign. After a short delay Gregg received an order to proceed south towards Baltimore. Scarcely was the division drawn out on the road when a second order came directing him to turn about and move north as rapidly as possible towards York. Just as we were starting in the latter direction the final order came to send Huey's brigade back to Manchester (Md.), and to march with McIntosh's and Irvin Gregg's brigade westward to Gettysburg."

reached Dover and learned that Early had marched west the day before. After a short rest Stuart moved on to Carlisle and arrived there in the evening. He knew that Ewell had been there; he did not know he had gone. At Dover Stuart had sent a staff officer, Major Venable, on Early's track with a dispatch for General Lee.[1] That

[1] SYKES TO WILLIAMS, A. A. G.

UNION MILLS, June 30th, 6 P.M.

Stuart, Fitz-Lee and Hampton staid last night at the house of a Mr. Shriver who owns the mills at this place.

WILLIAMS, A. A. G., TO HANCOCK

June 30th, 1 P.M.

General Sykes [5th corps] has been informed that you would support him at Union Mills in case of the presence of a superior force of the enemy.

PLEASANTON TO GREGG

June 30th, 11.30 P.M.

After arriving at Hanover Junction and finding no enemy, push a force to York, and in case that place has been evacuated, let it proceed towards Columbia on the Susquehanna River and communicate with General Crouch. Take the brigade from Westminster with you but have a regiment at Manchester with General Sedgwick to picket in that vicinity.

The following is from Major Venable, who was an officer on Stuart's Staff:

FARMVILLE, VA., March 8th, 1907.

COLONEL JOHN S. MOSBY,

DEAR SIR: On the Gettysburg campaign General Stuart's command arrived at Dover, Penn., during the night of June 30th, 1863, where, learning that General Early's command was marching towards Gettysburg, I was directed by General Stuart to take a detachment of thirty mounted men and go in the direction pursued by General Early, to learn the purpose of General Lee. I left Dover before daylight of

night at Carlisle he received an answer and immediately started off to Gettysburg. He arrived there in time on July 2 to cover Lee's flank from Meade's cavalry that had just returned from pursuit of him. He had scarcely reached the field when a severe but indecisive conflict occurred in which General Hampton had a personal encounter with a cavalryman and was severely wounded.

When that combat ended, the cavalry of the two armies stood off, rested, and watched the flanks. The field of Gettysburg would have been impracticable for cavalry operations even if the improvements in fire-arms had not made obsolete the use of cavalry against infantry. As I have said, Gettysburg was a place of no strategic value and neither side wanted to hold it. For this reason one of Early's brigades spent a night there and went away, and Meade, whose cavalry was there on July 1, as an outpost for observation, sent Buford orders to withdraw and let the Confederates have it. A great objection to the position, as I have said, was that Lee's front did not cover his line of communication; hence in the retrograde movement both flanks were exposed to attack. There never was a more difficult operation performed in war than then devolved on Stuart. Not since the shouts of the Ten Thousand were

July 1st with the detachment of thirty men and after skirmishing all day with a regiment which was pursuing us from Dover, we overtook General Early about 4 P.M., just approaching Gettysburg, where upon my arrival I reported to General Lee, and found him on the hill west of Gettysburg. On making my report, he ordered a squadron of cavalry to go in search of General Stuart at once.

     Very respectfully,
       A. R. VENABLE, Late Major, etc.

heard when they caught a glimpse of the Euxine — "Thalatta! — Thalatta! — the *Sea! — the Sea*," has an army escaped from such peril, or a retreat been covered with such masterful ability. Nor does the parallel end here. The hero who led the Greeks to the sea had to answer an impeachment after they crossed the Bosphorus — so had Stuart! It turned out to be fortunate that Stuart missed Early and went on to Carlisle. More cavalry was not needed at Gettysburg. General Couch, who had commanded a corps in the army of the Potomac, had about 15,000 troops at Harrisburg, and, as the following dispatch shows, was directed to co-operate with Meade:

HALLECK TO COUCH, HARRISBURG, PA.

WASHINGTON, June 28th.

You will co-operate as far as possible with General G. G. Meade, who now commands the Army of the Potomac, and who is authorized to assume command of all troops within his sphere of operations. This authority embraces your command. Any information of the enemy's movements in your vicinity will be immediately telegraphed to General Meade.

COUCH TO HALLECK

HARRISBURG, June 30th.

As telegraphed previously, part of the rebel forces, if not all, have fallen back towards Chambersburg [Johnson's division] passing Shippensburg last night in great haste. I expect every moment to hear that my cavalry, under General Smith, has occupied Carlisle. My latest information is that Early with his 8000 men went towards Gettysburg or Hanover, saying they expected to fight a great battle there.

HARRISBURG, PA., June 30th, 9 P.M.

ABRAHAM LINCOLN, President: —

The rebel infantry force left Carlisle early this morning on the Baltimore pike. Cavalry still on this side of that town. Early with 8,000 left York this morning, went westerly or northwesterly. Rebels at Carlisle and York yesterday a good deal agitated about some news they had received. I telegraphed news to General Meade, care of Secretary of War.

D. N. COUCH, Major-General.

COUCH TO MEADE

HARRISBURG, July 1st.

At 10 A.M., June 30th, Lee's headquarters were at Greenwood, 8 miles east of Chambersburg, on the Baltimore pike. Hill's corps lies east of Greenwood. Greenwood is 2½ miles from the mountain. Longstreet's corps lies south of *Greenwood*, towards Hagerstown. Ewell's corps probably concentrated yesterday near Gettysburg.

MEADE TO COUCH

HARRISBURG, July 1st., 12 M.

The enemy are advancing on Gettysburg — Hill from Cashtown, Ewell from Heidlersburg. Can you throw a force in Ewell's rear to threaten him, and at the same time keep your line of retreat open? If you can, do so.

HALLECK TO COUCH

July 1st, 1863.

There seems to be a strong probability of a battle not far from Emmittsburg. It is hoped that you will assist Meade by operating on the enemy's left flank or left rear towards Gettysburg.

COUCH TO HALLECK

July 1st.

Dispatch received. I have sent out a force in the direction of Carlisle. It has been attacked by a body of cavalry at least, and just now things do not look well.

When Couch heard that Ewell had evacuated Carlisle he set his troops in motion to the south, in order, as he said, "to make a diversion in favor of Meade by attacking Lee's flank and rear." General W. F. Smith, with 3000 men, was in the advance and reached Carlisle in the evening of July 1. The other troops were following him. Soon after the arrival of Smith's troops, greatly to his surprise, the Confederates appeared and he received a demand for the surrender of the United States barracks which he was then occupying. The demand for surrender was refused and Stuart's artillery opened fire on them. The shells set fire to the buildings and they were burned. The troops that were marching in the rear, thinking that Ewell had returned, started back to Harrisburg. The troops that were at Carlisle came without rations, expecting to get them there. The trains bringing provisions had not arrived; they were stampeded by the artillery firing and the troops could not leave hungry and without rations. So they did not get away until July 4, after the battle was over, and never got a sight of the Confederates, although they followed them down the Cumberland Valley to the Potomac. General Smith's report says: "General Ewell had passed through the town on the Baltimore Pike about one and one-half miles, and while going on to examine his position word came from scouts that a large cavalry force of the enemy was in the immediate vicinity on the York road, and turning back, before I entered the village, their guns had opened on us. . . . Under these circumstances I determined to content myself till morning with simply holding the town, but before I could get a line of skirmishers out a summons was sent by General Fitz-Hugh Lee to surrender the town or send out the women and children."

A memorandum attached to his report says: "Friday, July 3. The troops remained at barracks all day waiting for provisions, the supply trains having been prevented from arriving by the occupation of the road by the enemy on the 1st and 2d of July. The attempt to procure provisions from citizens was only partially successful. Supplies arrived by railroad Saturday, July 4. The whole command left Carlisle at 6 A.M., and moved by the Papertown road, six and one-half miles to Mount Holly. . . .

"July 6, all troops moved by different roads to Newman's Cut, on the turnpike between Gettysburg and Chambersburg, four miles east of Cashtown, where they were concentrated during the evening."

All of Lee's trains had been collected at Cashtown; Imboden's command was the only guard. On July 4, they started to the Potomac, and on July 6 were at Williamsport.

The loss of his supply trains near Washington on June 28 had a depressing effect upon Meade; during the whole campaign he was nervous about his rear. On the 29th he detached Merritt's brigade from Buford's division to guard the trains on the road from Frederick to Emmittsburg. Hence it took no part in Buford's combat on July 1. On July 2, when Buford's cavalry was covering Sickles' flank, a signal officer sent the following stampede report:

CEMETERY SIGNAL STATION,
July 2nd, 1863, 12.35 P.M.

GENERAL BUTTERFIELD: —

Numerous fires, apparently from the burning of wagons south southeast from here. A wagon-train can be seen in the same direction. I think our trains are being destroyed.

(Signed) BABCOCK, Signal Officer.

There was no truth in the report; Westminster, thirty miles from Gettysburg, was now Meade's base of supplies. Stuart had camped there on the night of June 29. On July 1 one of Gregg's cavalry brigades had been detached and sent to guard the depot. And now just in the opening of the battle Buford's whole division was sent off to Westminster. It is not probable that a Confederate soldier was in thirty miles of the place. The withdrawal of Buford left Sickles' flank in the peach orchard uncovered — "*in the air.*" Longstreet took advantage of it and struck him a stunning blow. Buford was ordered in pursuit when the retreat began, but he was so far off that he did not overtake the Confederates till they got to Williamsport. But he found them in line of battle ready for him with their trains parked; so Buford went back. His report says: "July 6. The whole division (the Reserve brigade [Merritt's] having joined the night before), marched at 4 A.M. towards Williamsport to destroy the enemy's trains which were reported to be crossing the Potomac into Virginia.... The expedition had for its object the destruction of the enemy's trains which were supposed to be crossing at Williamsport. This, I regret to say, was not accomplished. The enemy was too strong for me but he was severely punished for his obstinacy."

Writing to Mr. Davis from Hagerstown on July 7, General Lee said: "The enemy's cavalry force which attempted to reach our cavalry trains yesterday afternoon was a large one. They came as far as Hagerstown, where they were attacked by General Stuart and driven back rapidly towards Sharpsburg."

General Lee's report says: "Part of our train moved by the road through Fairfield [Monterey Gap] and the rest by Cashtown, guarded by General Imboden. In passing through the mountains in advance of the column, the great length of the trains exposed them to attacks by the enemy's cavalry, which captured a number of wagons and ambulances, but they succeeded in reaching Williamsport without serious loss. They were attacked at that place on the 6th by the enemy's cavalry which was gallantly repulsed by General Imboden. The attacking force was subsequently encountered and driven off by General Stuart and pursued for several miles in the direction of Boonsborough. The army, after an arduous march, rendered more difficult by the rains, reached Hagerstown on the afternoon of July 6, and the morning of the 7th. . . . Part of the pontoon bridge was recovered and new boats built so that by the 13th a good bridge was thrown over the river at Falling Waters. The enemy in force reached our front on the 12th. A position had been previously selected to cover the Potomac from Williamsport to Falling Waters and an attack was awaited during that and the succeeding day. This did not take place, though the armies were in close proximity, the enemy being occupied in fortifying his lines. Our preparations being completed, and the river, though still deep, being pronounced fordable, the army commenced to withdraw to the south side on the night of the 13th."

Meade remained at Gettysburg until July 7; the following dispatch shows that he was expected not only to follow but to attack and destroy Lee:

WASHINGTON, D. C., July 8th, 1863.
MAJOR GENERAL MEADE, Frederick, Md.: —

There is reliable information that the enemy is crossing at Williamsport. The opportunity to attack his divided forces should not be lost. The President is urgent and anxious that your army should move against him by forced marches.

H. W. HALLECK, General-in-Chief.

It is remarkable that the Army of the Potomac twice afterwards during the year retreated — in October from the Rapidan back to Fairfax, and in November from Mine Run — before the Army of Northern Virginia. Possibly if Stuart had burned the trains he captured on the march he might have arrived earlier and joined Early on the 30th. But none of Stuart's critics can show any bad results from his carrying the trains along with him. If he had arrived on the 30th, at York, he could not have communicated with General Lee. Lee was fifty-five miles away west of the South Mountain at Chambersburg. Then General Lee knew perfectly well at that time the direction in which Meade was heading his army, and that his cavalry occupied Gettysburg. Stuart could have told him no more. The instructions did not require him to report to General Lee, but to Ewell. All the critics overlook that fact. But I have shown that while Early and Ewell had no need of more cavalry, Stuart's presence at Carlisle on the night of July 1 defeated a combination by which a heavy force would have been thrown on Lee's flank and rear when he was in the agony of combat.

The route through Hooker's army was suggested on the theory that the initiative being with General Lee, Hooker would await his movements, and the conditions in his army would not be changed before Stuart got over the Potomac. But unfortunately General Lee, with Longstreet and Hill, moved toward the Potomac on the 24th — the day before Stuart started to pass through Hooker's army — in view of the signal stations on Maryland Heights; Hooker immediately got notice of it by telegraph and put his whole army in motion the next morning (25th). This defeated the operation which Stuart had so auspiciously begun. Stuart's cavalry and Hooker's army could not travel together on the same roads.

If Longstreet and Hill had stayed quiet a day longer, Stuart would have crossed the Potomac in advance of Hooker's army early in the evening of the 25th, and the fate of the Confederate cause might have been different. General Lee was with Longstreet. There was no pressing necessity for the movement. Hooker was inactive — Ewell was foraging in Pennsylvania with nothing but militia before him that always scattered at his approach. While this premature movement caused the failure of a brilliant operation it was not necessarily fatal to the campaign, and might have been retrieved but for Hill's and Heth's blunder in precipitating a battle at the village of Gettysburg. Hooker, Meade, and the authorities at Washington all misunderstood the significance of Stuart's movement. They thought it was only a force detached to harass their rear and that the greater part of the Confederate cavalry was on their left flank with General Lee. At 12.45 A.M., at Leesburg on the 26th, Pleasanton told Hooker that: "The telegraph operator of Hancock's corps reported last night a body of several thousand cavalry at Gainesville, from direction of New Baltimore. My dispositions cover that. I shall remain here till the crossing is accomplished." On the 27th, Howard at Middletown telegraphed Hooker: "I have reports from different sources that Stuart's cavalry, or a part, crossed the river at Shepherdstown last night." Stuart was then in Fairfax. Hooker was all in the dark about Stuart. Williams, his A. A. G., said on the 25th to Pleasanton: "General Hancock reports that the enemy have appeared in the direction of New Baltimore, with a force estimated from four regiments to 6,000 men with one battery. The commanding General directs that you at once send a brigade of cavalry to report to General Hancock. He is marching to-day from Thoroughfare to Gum Spring." Colonel Asmussen at Middletown told Hooker: "The main body of General Stuart's cavalry was encamped last night between Williamsport and Hagerstown; the head of the column of General Stuart's cavalry commenced passing through Hagerstown at break of day." Meade at Frederick on the 28th told Halleck: "General Steinwehr from the Mountain House, South Mountain, reports that his scouts inform him that 5,000 of Stuart's cavalry passed through Williamsport yesterday afternoon. General Sedgwick on the march up from Poolesville reports that 3000 of the enemy's cavalry with some artillery are in his rear. This is communicated to you for your information. My impression is that Stuart has divided his force with a view of harassing our right and left flanks."

Meade then had no idea that Stuart was between him

and Washington and would soon break his communications. The first he heard of it was a telegram from Halleck dated June 28, 12.30 P.M. It said: "A brigade of Fitz-Hugh Lee's cavalry has crossed the Potomac near Seneca Creek, and is making for the railroad to cut off your supplies. There is another brigade of rebel cavalry south of the Potomac which may follow. [There was no such brigade south of the river then, but the specter had just the same effect as if there had been.] We have no cavalry here to operate against them. General Hooker carried away all of Heintzelman's cavalry."

Meade to Halleck: "Dispatch received in relation to crossing of enemy's cavalry at Seneca Creek. Have ordered two brigades to proceed at once in search and pursuit." Meade sent two divisions after Stuart and kept one, Buford's, with him.

In the *Philadelphia Weekly Times*, of December 15, 1877, I published a reply to a letter of General Heth in which he severely criticised General Stuart for being absent on the first day at Gettysburg and charged him with disobedience of orders. The War Records had not then been published and I only had Stuart's report as a guide, which I knew was correct, to quote as evidence against him. I contended that Stuart was absent under orders. I had then seen General Lee's first report, which states that at Chambersburg he had ordered the army to Gettysburg, and on account of the absence of the cavalry had run unexpectedly against the enemy. My article was written on the hypothesis that this statement of the report was true. As from my intimate relations with Stuart in the campaign I knew that his orders had required him to leave General Lee in Virginia and join Ewell in Pennsylvania, and that he had full authority to pass through Hooker's army and cross the Potomac at Seneca, I maintained that if General Lee was embarrassed by want of cavalry the blame must attach to General Robertson who had been left with Longstreet with instructions to do the very work which it was alleged was not done. I had not then seen Lee's instructions to Stuart; and Stuart's to Robertson. They are in the published records and sustain me in every particular and contradict Heth. With the evidence now before me that the army was never ordered from Chambersburg to Gettysburg; that General Lee never intended to go there, and that his plan was defeated by Hill and Heth, I modify the terms of that letter to the extent of saying that in my opinion no blame can be imputed to Robertson and Jones, and that the whole should fall on A. P. Hill and Heth. I said this much in *Belford's Magazine*, October, November, 1891, and in the *Richmond Times* in March, 1896. Heth was then living in Washington; he made no reply. Heth's rejoinder (*Philadelphia Times* of March, 1878), in behalf of Robertson to my letter of December, 1877, reiterates the charge against Stuart, but in defending Robertson he unconsciously condemns General Lee when he says: "General Lee was in daily communication with Robertson and knew exactly where he was. If he had not been in position, if he was not doing the work he was ordered to perform, why was he not ordered into position? No message or orders by couriers to Robertson that he was out of position. Some days as many as three couriers were sent by General Lee to General Robertson." Now if as many as three couriers a day passed between Robertson's and Lee's headquarters they must have carried dispatches about the movements of the enemy. It is not conceivable that these dispatches did not inform General Lee that Hooker had crossed the Potomac. On the morning of the 26th, Hooker's army moved across the front of Jones' and Robertson's brigades to the pontoon bridges — and they retired to the Gaps. It is *literally* true that General Lee heard nothing from *Stuart* about it, and he had no right to expect to hear from *him; but his report does not say that couriers from Jones and Robertson did not bring him the news.*

Heth insists that Jones and Robertson were ordered to remain at the Gaps for further orders after Hooker had crossed into Maryland. Stuart's instructions to them now published say just the reverse and sustain Stuart's report. If Jones and Robertson received such orders they must have come from Longstreet, or General Lee. My opinion is that Jones and Robertson informed General Lee as soon as they discovered that Hooker was moving towards the Potomac. If they had not there would have been an official complaint against them for gross neglect of duty, and they could not have held commissions in the Confederate army after such delinquency. Heth's qualifications to be a military critic can be judged by the following: "Colonel Mosby has been led by some one into a very grave error. When referring to the opening of the fight at Gettysburg (July 1), he says, 'Here Buford fought two hours before any infantry support came to him'; I can assure my friend, Colonel Mosby, that the author of this assertion has not a shadow of truth to sustain him; and of all the preposterous assertions in connection with the war, this is the most so that has ever come to my knowledge. As I opened the battle of Gettysburg — going to Gettysburg to get shoes, not to fight — I claim I should know as much about the opening operations and whom I fought as any man living. I did not have so much as a skirmish with General Buford's cavalry." If Heth ever knew anything about Gettysburg he never told it; his own report contradicts his letter. So do Buford's and A. P. Hill's. Heth's report does not say that he went after shoes; it says he went on a reconnaissance—to find out what force was in his front. *He found it.* When I wrote the letter in reply to Heth I did not know he had an interest in concealing the truth, and was trying to shift from himself on Stuart the responsibility for the loss of the battle. Heth and Hill, as their reports show, knew that the enemy were holding Gettysburg; how then could they have expected to get the shoes without a fight even if the shoes had been there? A. P. Hill does not mention shoes. Buford's report says: "By daylight on July 1 I had gained positive information of the enemy's position and movements and my arrangements were made for entertaining him until General Reynolds could reach the scene. Colonel Gamble [Eighth Illinois Cavalry] made an admirable line of battle and moved off proudly to meet him. The two lines soon became hotly engaged, we having the advantage of position, he of numbers. The First Brigade held its own for more than two hours and had to be literally dragged back a few hundred yards to a position more secure and better sheltered. The First Brigade maintained this unequal contest until the leading division of General Reynolds came up to its assistance and then most reluctantly did it give up the front." General Lee's second report also shows that Robertson and Jones were not left in Virginia by Stuart to guard the Gaps south of the Potomac after the enemy had disappeared. It says: "General Stuart was directed to hold the mountain passes *with part of his command as long as the enemy remained south of the Potomac, and with the remainder to cross the Potomac and place himself on the right of Ewell.*" At that time Ewell was marching away from Lee to the Susquehanna. I think it highly probable that Jones and Robertson did afterwards get instructions from Lee or Longstreet to wait at the Gaps for further orders. This is the only way I can account for no complaint being made for their remaining in their position after the enemy had left their front, from the morning of the 26th to the afternoon of the 29th, when the courier arrived from General Lee. Robertson made no report of the campaign; Jones made a brief one but it throws no light on the mystery of these cavalry brigades being kept so long in Virginia. At the same time I can see no damage that resulted from it, as the myth of General Lee having been surprised by meeting the enemy at Gettysburg has been exploded. Besides, Longstreet in his book says that the spy brought all the information that a body of cavalry could have brought. What more then was wanted? Why should two brigades of cavalry have been wasted to guard the Gaps and Lee's communications in Virginia against an imaginary enemy, when a hostile garrison of 11,000, a few miles farther north in the Harper's Ferry Gap, was left behind; and Crampton's, Boonsborough, and other passes north of the Potomac were unguarded while Hooker's army was in front of them? If Heth is right, General Lee should have kept one half his army guarding the Gaps. As Robertson is entitled to be heard I give his correspondence with Heth in reference to my article.

RICHMOND, VA., December 27th, 1877.
GENERAL B. H. ROBERTSON, Richmond, Va.:—

DEAR GENERAL: I send you to-day an article I prepared in answer to an article which appeared in the Philadelphia *Weekly Times* of December 15, 1877, by Colonel John S. Mosby, headed "Stuart at Gettysburg." Will you do me the kindness to say whether the statements I made *as to orders received by you after being detached from General Stuart's command with Jones' brigade and your own in June, 1863, are correct or not.* I have submitted what I have written to Major Walter K. Martin, Adjutant General of General William E. Jones' Brigade [Jones was killed], also to Captain Philip Haxall, Adjutant General of your brigade, and both inform me that the orders received by you and under which you acted are correctly stated by me.

Respectfully,
H. HETH.

Attention is called to the lines I have italicized. They raise a new issue. Heth had charged Stuart with carrying off all the cavalry which deprived Lee of his eyesight. My reply denied the charge and stated that two brigades of cavalry stayed with General Lee in front of the Gaps in Loudon with orders from Stuart to observe the enemy and report his movements to General Lee, or Longstreet, through a line of relay couriers; and I quoted Stuart's report in support of my statement. In his letter to Robertson, Heth refers, not to the instructions which *Stuart* had given him, but to "orders received by you *after* being detached from General Stuart's command." I had said nothing about such orders as I had never heard of them and they were entirely irrelevant to the issue; which was, what orders Stuart gave Jones and Robertson before they were detached. Any subsequent orders they received must have come from General Lee or Longstreet. If orders came to them to remain at the Gaps for further orders they were in conflict with Stuart's orders, and, of course, revoked them. So if Heth is right he has shifted the blame for the four days' inaction of these two brigades of cavalry on General Lee or on Longstreet. This is Robertson's reply:

RICHMOND, VA., Dec. 27, 1877.

GENERAL HETH, Richmond, Va.:—

DEAR GENERAL: Your letter of the 26th is before me and the alluded to article has been most carefully read. In spite of the repeated efforts I have not yet succeeded in finding the written orders under which I acted on the occasion referred to; but your statement corroborated by others in high position corresponds precisely with my recollection of said orders. My brigade, re-inforced by W. E. Jones', was left to guard the passes in the Blue Ridge Mountains — so as to protect the rear of Lee's army — with instructions to await further orders — then to sweep through the Shenandoah Valley, picking up deserters and stragglers, and join General Lee without delay. On the 29th of June I received orders from General Lee to leave one regiment of my command to picket south of the Potomac and report to him forthwith. I felt Ashby's Gap the same day in the evening (as soon as I could collect my command), and reached Gettysburg [Cashtown] on the morning of July 3rd, a distance which could not have been travelled except by rapid marching. *During the separation of my command from General Lee's army there was constant communication between us.* [Italics mine.] He was fully aware of my position and the specific duty I was then performing. That it met his entire approbation is proven by the fact that no complaint on his part or from any other source, was ever made against me or my command. Much more can be said but I deem it entirely unnecessary. I remain, etc.

B. H. ROBERTSON.

It will be observed that Robertson says he was in constant communication with General Lee. Of course then he communicated to General Lee the movements of the enemy — or nothing; that was the very thing he was there for. But it was not *Stuart's* orders for him and Jones to stay at the Gaps, but to follow Lee and watch Hooker. It is significant that General Lee expresses no disapproval of Jones and Robertson having waited so long in Virginia for orders. The following are Stuart's instructions to Robertson. They are dated the day he started around Hooker.

HDQRS. CAV. DIV. ARMY OF NORTHERN VA.
June 24th, 1863.

BRIG. GEN. B. H. ROBERTSON,
   Commanding Cavalry:—

GENERAL: Your own and General Jones' brigades will *cover the front* of Ashby's and Snicker's Gaps, yourself, as senior officer, being in command. Your object will be to watch the enemy, deceive him as to your designs and harass his rear if you find he is retiring. Be always on the alert; let nothing escape your observation, and miss no opportunity which offers to damage the enemy. After the enemy has moved beyond your reach, leave sufficient pickets in the mountains, withdraw to the west side of the Shenandoah, place a strong and reliable picket to watch the enemy at Harper's Ferry, cross the Potomac and follow the army, keeping on its right and rear. *As long as the enemy remains on your front in force, unless otherwise ordered by General Lee, Lieutenant General Longstreet or myself,* hold the Gaps with a line of pickets reaching across the Shenandoah by Charlestown to the Potomac. If, in the contingency mentioned, you withdraw, sweep the Valley clear of what pertains to the army and *cross the Potomac at the different points crossed by it*. You will instruct General Jones from time to time as the movements progress, or events may require, *and report anything of importance to Lieutenant-General Longstreet with whose position you will communicate by relays through Charlestown. I send instructions to General Jones which please read.* Avail yourself of every means in your power to increase the efficiency of your command, and keep it up to the highest number possible. Particular attention will be paid to shoeing horses and to marching off of the turnpike. In case of the advance of the enemy you will offer such resistance as will be justifiable to check him and discover his intentions, and if possible you will prevent him from gaining possession of the Gaps. In case of a move of the enemy upon Warrenton, you will counteract it as much as you [can, compatible with previous instructions. You will have, with the two brigades, two batteries of horse artillery.

Yours &c., &c.,

[The italics are mine.] J. E. B. STUART, Major-General, &c.

P. S. Do not change your present line of pickets until daylight to-morrow morning unless compelled to do so.

These are a model of instructions in outpost service. When they were written Robertson was about Middleburg in Loudon; Jones was some miles north, nearer the Potomac. The report of Colonel Massie of the Twelfth Virginia cavalry shows that Jones promptly obeyed Stuart's orders and sent his regiment to the Valley to picket on the Potomac. It is to be presumed that Jones, who was a strict disciplinarian, obeyed all his instructions about communicating with Longstreet. He certainly obeyed a part. In his report to Jones, Colonel Massie says: "On June 25 I received your order to establish a picket line fronting Harper's Ferry. It was executed that evening"; which was the day Stuart crossed the Bull Run Mountains to enter

Hooker's lines. Colonel Massie is now living and is a citizen of Rappahannock County, Va. In a letter to me dated March 27, 1907, he says: "Yours received. I am glad to give you any information I can. I was left with my regiment on the Virginia side of the Potomac in charge of a line of pickets to guard the river from Harper's Ferry to Williamsport, *and sent couriers daily to General Lee as I was ordered by General Stuart.*"

W. D. Briscoe (now dead), of the Twelfth Virginia cavalry, writes me: "On the 28th or 29th of June, 1863, Captain——Twelfth Cavalry, told me he wanted me to carry a dispatch to General Lee's headquarters. What the dispatch contained I do not know. I started immediately and crossed the Potomac at Williamsport, thence to Hagerstown and then to Greencastle and Chambersburg. . . . Stopped for the night and delivered my dispatch at General Lee's headquarters the next morning, a mile or two from the town." [1] See Lee's letter of 5 P.M., June 23d, instructing Stuart what orders to leave for the commanders of the two cavalry brigades.

---

[1] THE REPORTS AND CORRESPONDENCE

My criticism of General Lee's Report, which I believe he signed without reading, does not imply any criticism of him as a general. In fact it is a defence of the commander at the expense of his report, which does him great injustice. All criticisms of the campaign are based on the assumption of the correctness of Lee's report. It is to be regretted that General Lee ever signed the report, but it must be remembered that the first is dated a few days after the campaign closed, when he was suffering great pain from the disaster to his army. It is doubtful if he ever read it, or if it was ever read to him.

In defence of William of Orange for signing the order for the massacre of Glencoe, Macaulay says:

"An order was laid before him for his signature. He signed it but, if Burnet may be trusted, did not read it. Whoever has seen anything of public business knows that princes and ministers daily sign, and indeed must sign, documents which they have not read."

John C. Ropes, of Boston, author of the "Campaign of Waterloo," on December 14th, 1897, wrote me: "Thank you very much for your two letters of the 8th and 13th instants. Your views of the task which General Lee imposed on his cavalry in the Gettysburg campaign seem to me, as at present advised, correct, and I also share entirely in your view of the inaccuracy of Lee's Reports. I shall try to get it all into my 3rd volume. [The Story of the Civil War.] My second volume is about three-fourths done, and I think and hope to put it into the hands of the publisher this Spring." Unfortunately Mr. Ropes died before his third volume was completed. Two volumes had been published before his death.

General Lee's Report of July 31, 1863, says:

". . . In the meantime, a part of General Ewell's corps had entered Maryland and the rest was about to follow. General Jenkins with his cavalry, who accompanied General Ewell, penetrated Pennsylvania as far as Chambersburg. As these demonstrations did not have the effect of causing the Federal army to leave Virginia, and as it did not seem disposed to advance upon the position held by Longstreet, the latter was withdrawn to the west side of the Shenandoah, General Hill having already reached the Valley. General Stuart was left to guard the passes of the mountains and observe the movements of the enemy, whom he was instructed to harass and impede as much as possible should he attempt to cross the Potomac. In that event General Stuart was directed to move into Maryland, crossing the Potomac east or west of the Blue Ridge as in his judgment should be best, and take position on the right of our column as it advanced. By the 24th the progress of Ewell rendered it necessary that the rest of the army should be in supporting distance, and Longstreet and Hill marched to the Potomac. The former crossed at Williamsport and the latter at Shepherdstown. The columns reunited at Hagerstown and advanced thence into Pennsylvania, encamping near Chambersburg on the 27th. No report had been received that the Federal army had crossed the Potomac, and the absence of the cavalry rendered it impossible to obtain accurate information. In order, however, to retain it on the east side of the mountains, after it should enter Maryland, and thus leave open our communications with the

Potomac through Hagerstown and Williamsport, General Ewell had been instructed to send a division eastward from Chambersburg to cross the South Mountain. Early's division was detached for this purpose and proceeded as far as York, while the remainder of the corps proceeded to Carlisle. General Imboden, in pursuance of the instructions previously referred to, had been actively engaged on the left of General Ewell during the progress of the latter into Maryland. . . . Preparations were now made to advance upon Harrisburg, but on the night of the 28th information was received from a scout that the Federal army was advancing northward and that the head of the column had reached the South Mountain. As our communications with the Potomac were thus menaced it was resolved to prevent his further progress in that direction by concentrating our army on the east side of the mountains. Accordingly, Longstreet and Hill were directed to proceed from Chambersburg to Gettysburg, to which point General Ewell was also instructed to march from Carlisle. General Stuart continued to follow the movements of the Federal army south of the Potomac after our own had entered Maryland, and in his efforts to impede its progress advanced as far eastward as Fairfax Court-house. Finding himself unable to delay the enemy materially, he crossed the river at Seneca and marched through Westminster to Carlisle, where he arrived after General Ewell had left for Gettysburg. By the route he pursued the Federal army was interposed between his command and our main body, preventing any communication with him until he arrived at Carlisle. The march towards Gettysburg was conducted more slowly than it would have been if the movements of the Federal army had been known. The leading division of Hill met the enemy in advance of Gettysburg on the morning of July 1st. . . . It had not been intended to fight a general battle at such a distance from our base, unless attacked by the enemy, but finding ourselves unexpectedly confronted by the Federal army, it became a matter of difficulty to withdraw through the mountains with our large trains. . . . During the afternoon intelligence was received of the arrival of General Stuart at Carlisle, and he was ordered to march to Gettysburg and take position on our left."

The Report of January, 1864, says:

"General Stuart was directed to hold the mountain passes with part of his command as long as the enemy remained south of the Potomac, and with the remainder to cross into Maryland and place himself on the right of General Ewell. Upon the suggestion of the former officer that he could damage the enemy and delay his passage of the river by getting in his rear, he was authorized to do so, and it was left to his discretion whether to enter Maryland east or west of the Blue Ridge; but he was instructed to lose no time in placing his command on the right of our column as soon as he perceived the enemy moving northward. . . . It was expected that as soon as the Federal army should cross the Potomac, General Stuart would give notice of its movements, and nothing having been heard from him since our entrance into Maryland, it was inferred that the enemy had not yet left Virginia. Orders were therefore issued to move upon Harrisburg. . . . The advance against Harrisburg was arrested by intelligence received from a scout on the night of the 28th, to the effect that the army of General Hooker had crossed the Potomac and was approaching the South Mountain. In the absence of the cavalry it was impossible to ascertain his intentions; but to deter him from advancing further west and intercepting our communications with Virginia, it was determined to concentrate the army east of the mountains. . . . Hill's corps was, accordingly, ordered to move towards Cashtown on the 29th, and Longstreet to follow the next day, leaving Pickett's division at Chambersburg to guard the rear until relieved by Imboden. General Ewell was recalled from Carlisle and directed to join the army at Cashtown or Gettysburg as circumstances might require. The advance of the enemy to the latter place was unknown and the weather being inclement the march was conducted with a view to the comfort of the troops. General Hill arrived [30th] with Pender's division in the evening, and the following morning (July 1st), advanced with these two divisions, accompanied by Pegram's and McIntosh's battalions of artillery, to ascertain the strength of the enemy, which was supposed to consist chiefly of cavalry. As soon as it was known that the enemy had crossed into Maryland, orders were sent to the brigades of Robertson and Jones, which had been left to guard the passes of the Blue Ridge, to join the army without delay, and it was expected that General Stuart with the remainder of his command would soon arrive."

The discrepancies between the two reports, as well as with the correspondence, are many and manifest. There is no explanation why at Chambersburg, as stated, preparations were made to move on to Harrisburg *after* Ewell had been ordered to return from Carlisle; or why Hill was sent some distance on the Cashtown road and one of Heth's brigades was sent to the Cashtown Pass *before* it was alleged that the spy came in. Cashtown is east of Chambersburg; Harrisburg is north. Nor is it shown how it could be possible for Stuart to put himself on the right of Ewell on the Susquehanna, and at the same time march "on the right of our column" — *i.e.*, the main body with General Lee — as it advanced into Pennsylvania. The report says that the movement against Harrisburg was arrested by the intelligence brought by a spy on the night of the 28th, while Ewell's and Early's reports and Lee's order to Ewell show that it was arrested on June 27th, and that the army was ordered to concentrate at Chambersburg.

The first report says that after the appearance of the spy orders were issued for the concentration of the army at Gettysburg as the objective point. The second report says that A. P. Hill only went to Gettysburg to ascertain the force of the enemy. If so, Hill ought to have returned to his camp at Cashtown after he got the information he was seeking.

General Lee made two reports of Gettysburg. The first is dated July 31, 1863, about a week after he reached Culpeper. It is a general outline of the operations of his army; the second report, dated January, 1864, gives a more detailed account of the campaign. When the first was written it is not probable that he had received reports from either of his corps commanders except Longstreet; his is dated July 27; A. P. Hill's is dated in November; Ewell's has no date; Stuart's report is dated August 20, and is an answer to the complaints made against him in General Lee's report. Stuart evidently did not know at the time of writing his report of the manner in which a battle at Gettysburg had been precipitated against orders by A. P. Hill, and he evidently had not seen General Lee's letter of June 28 to Ewell to return to Chambersburg from Carlisle. He assumed that the report had correctly stated that at Chambersburg the army had been ordered to concentrate at Gettysburg. He seemed to have no suspicion that the apparition of the spy at Chambersburg was a ghost. If Stuart had known what we now know, he could have made a much more effective answer to the charge against him. But its mildness shows the appalling majesty of General Lee. The Confederate War Department immediately published Lee's report in the newspapers but suppressed Stuart's. The haste of the publication shows that the object was to forestall public opinion. Its partial and inaccurate statements that do so much injustice to the commander of the cavalry have been accepted as a judgment that estops all inquiry into the justice of the complaint. But in the Forum of History no judgment is final in the sense that it cannot be reviewed. After reading the report the public did not wait to hear the other side — it never does — but jumped to the conclusion that Stuart had gone off without authority with all the cavalry on a raid around Hooker's army; and that General Lee, having no cavalry, was left like a giant with his eyes put out. This is the illustration of his A. A. G., Colonel Walter Taylor. Stuart was thus made responsible for the loss of the battle and the charge has been re-echoed down the corridors of time. The report was thought to be conclusive and public feeling did not permit its statements to be questioned. In the South a superstition prevailed that it was as sacred as an oracle that had been uttered from the Pythian Cave. A scapegoat was needed, and a scapegoat was found. It is said that in the days of the Exodus the goat was sent to the wilderness loaded with sins; but in this case that precedent was not followed. Stuart held his high command until he fell on the field and left a void that was never filled.

He made no public defense against unjust criticism and was content to prove that his sword was still as potent as Arthur's

"To lift his country's fame above the polar star."

The report is understood to have been written by a staff officer, Colonel Charles Marshall, a great sophist, — an able and astute lawyer.[1] It is a fine example of special pleading, and the composition shows that the author possessed far more of the qualities of an advocate than of a judge. It is unfair to Stuart as it says nothing about Ewell having gone several days in advance into Pennsylvania; and that Stuart was ordered to join him with three

---

[1] In February, 1864, I was in Richmond and met Colonel Aleck Boteler, a member of the Confederate Congress, who had been a volunteer aide on General Stuart's staff. He told me that he had a resolution prepared thanking Stuart and the cavalry for their services, but was hesitating to offer it for fear of opposition from the prejudice against Stuart on account of Gettysburg. On January 8th the Congress had passed a resolution thanking General Lee and his army for their achievements and specially naming Gettysburg. It seems that to get the resolution passed Colonel Boteler had to make a compromise and omit all reference to Gettysburg, which was, of course, an implied censure. It recites the ride around McClellan on the Chickahominy, and around Pope, and many other exploits of the cavalry, including "the expedition into Pennsylvania." This last referred to Stuart's raid to Chambersburg, Pa. in October, 1862. It was a great mistake in Stuart's friends to accept it. They ought to have demanded praise for all he had done, or nothing. But as Stuart was then under a cloud from the effects of General Lee's report, it was thought that a vindication of Stuart would be a condemnation of Lee. None then suspected the part that A. P. Hill and Heth had taken in causing the disaster and that the report concealed it. If the Confederate Congress could thank General Lee for Gettysburg, they might have thanked Stuart for saving his army on its retreat to the Potomac.

brigades of cavalry; — or that Stuart had authority to cross the Potomac in Hooker's rear — or that he left two brigades of cavalry with Longstreet and General Lee to watch the enemy and guard the flanks of the main army as it moved north. Yet Lee's letters to Ewell and Stuart, and Stuart's report, all prove these omissions of the report. In an elaborate address on General Lee's birthday on January 19, 1896, the writer of the report threw off all disguise and openly charged what had been only inferred from it, that the disaster was due to Stuart's disobedience. The address was simply an expansion of the report. That Lee's campaign was broken up by somebody's disobedience nobody can doubt who will study the records; but the name of the responsible person is not hinted at in the report, or in Marshall's address. Why it should have been kept a secret no one has explained. It may be that by remaining on the field and continuing a combat which a rash subordinate had begun, General Lee thought that he had condoned the deed, and given it a sanction which he could not recall. If Hill had been censured after the battle by General Lee, no doubt he would have pleaded an estoppel against him. It does not seem to have occurred to historians to compare Lee's two reports with each other, or with the contemporaneous correspondence, and to note the discrepancies on material points between them. The truth has been revealed by the publication of reports and dispatches which show that the story of Gettysburg that has come down to this generation is a fable. The statement of the report that a spy came on the night of June 28, at Chambersburg, and brought the first news that Hooker had crossed the Potomac was never questioned until Longstreet and Marshall added their testimony that the spy also brought the information that Hooker had been superseded by Meade. As it was a physical impossibility for the spy to have brought the news so soon from Frederick about Meade, I became skeptical, and then doubted the whole story about the spy; and finally I discovered by Colonel Freemantle's diary that it was a fiction. Then the correspondence shows that on the day (27th) that General Lee arrived at Chambersburg, and twenty-four hours before it is alleged the spy came in with the surprising news, he wrote to Ewell, who was at Carlisle, telling him where Hooker was and directing him to return to Chambersburg. Nobody can reconcile this letter with the report. And now, since the methods of rationalism have superseded authority, no one believes that General Lee thought Hooker would stay on the bank of the Potomac while the Army of Northern Virginia was ravaging Pennsylvania.

In reference to Stuart, the first report says that he was left in Virginia to guard the Gaps of the Blue Ridge and to harass and impede the enemy in crossing the Potomac; in that event, it says, he was directed to cross into Maryland east or west of the Blue Ridge "and to take a position on the right of our column as it advanced." It also says that a part of Ewell's corps had entered Maryland and that Jenkins' cavalry had gone as far as Chambersburg; that Longstreet and Hill followed on the 24th, crossing the Potomac at Williamsport and Shepherdstown. "The columns reunited at Hagerstown," the report says, "and advanced thence into Pennsylvania, encamping near Chambersburg on the 27th." The inference from this is that the corps of Hill, Longstreet, and Ewell united at Hagerstown and marched in one column into Pennsylvania. They did not in fact unite until they reached Gettysburg. The truth is that on June 22, while General Lee with Longstreet and Hill was still in the Shenandoah Valley, Ewell, who was then at Hagerstown, got orders to move to the Susquehanna and was told that Stuart had been ordered to join him. Instructions to Stuart were sent the same day through Longstreet, and also at 5 P.M on the next day, to leave two brigades of cavalry with Longstreet and go to Ewell. Yet the report does not mention either the orders to Ewell, or the orders to Stuart. The orders contemplated Stuart's crossing the Potomac in advance of both armies — in fact, General Lee expressed to Stuart a fear that Hooker would get over the river ahead of him. Nor do the instructions to Stuart say a word about guarding the Blue Ridge Gaps, or harassing or impeding Hooker in crossing the Potomac. The fact is, the only effective impediment Stuart could have made to Hooker's crossing would have been by destroying his trains on the roads as he passed through his army. But this would have been only an incident of his march; the object was to go the most direct route to Ewell. Nor is there a word in Stuart's instructions about placing himself "on the right of our column as it advanced," — *i.e.*, the main body — for the plain reason that Stuart could not be with General Lee and at the same time far away with Ewell. Romance might impute such a miracle to Merlin. Neither is it true, as the report says, that Stuart followed the movements of the Northern Army after ours entered Maryland; or that he went as far east as Fairfax Court-house trying to impede its progress, for it would have been an act of folly to attempt it, and he had no such orders and no such motive. He went by Fairfax Court-house because he had found Hooker's army on the road by which he had planned to march to the Potomac on the 25th; and he was compelled to make this detour to get around it. In other words, Hooker's army detained Stuart. By concealing the fact that Ewell's corps had been detached and sent as an expeditionary force to the Susquehanna, and that Stuart was ordered to leave the army in Virginia and join him, a false impression of Stuart's conduct is created. It is natural to inquire how could General Lee expect Stuart to be at the same time on the Potomac and on the Susquehanna; or why he should rely on Stuart to report to him that Hooker had crossed the Potomac when there were two brigades of cavalry with him and Longstreet that had nothing else to do. The report makes no mention of these two brigades of cavalry, and gives no reason for not making them useful if needed. The complaint is against Stuart *personally* for not keeping the commanding general informed of the movements of the enemy; not against the cavalry as a body. But the complaint can have no reference to Robertson and Jones, as their brigades had been detached, and were directly under the orders of Lee and Longstreet. Now if they neglected to perform their duty and did not inform the commanding general when Hooker moved across their front to the Potomac, then they should not only have been censured in the commander's report, but they should have been shot. Yet there is nothing in the records to create a suspicion that they did not do their duty.

As General Lee had authorized Stuart to pass around Hooker, he does not explain how he could have expected Stuart to keep up communications with him while Hooker's army was between them. The report says that he expected it. In the accounts they have written of the campaign the staff officers have carefully followed the report and have been careful to conceal the orders to Ewell and to Stuart. It is the characteristic of staff officers to become merged in their Chief, and Lee's have shown themselves to be as subservient as Polonius was to his royal master:

Hamlet. "Do you see yonder cloud that's almost in the shape of a camel?"

Polonius. "By the mass, and 'tis like a camel, indeed!"

Hamlet. "Methinks it is like a weasel."

Polonius. "It's backed like a weasel."

Hamlet. "Or a whale."

Polonius. "Very like a whale."

The best evidence that the report is misleading is that all who read it were misled. Nobody can reconcile the orders with the report; their publication was a revelation; the staff officers seem to have at least forgotten them although they appear in their handwriting in Lee's letter-book. The gravamen of the complaint the report makes against Stuart is that the cavalry was absent, and that it was needed, not in the battle, but to make preliminary reconnaissances before the battle. If such was the case, General Lee was responsible for the absence of the cavalry with Stuart; but no one has shown that any harm resulted from it. He and Longstreet were responsible for the use of the cavalry left with them. Nor does the report explain why, if the cavalry was needed in Pennsylvania, the two brigades of Robertson and Jones were kept in Virginia after the enemy had gone; General Lee's second report says they were guarding the Gaps; and that after the spy came in he ordered them to join the army. This shows that he knew he had this cavalry at his call to use when he needed it. If Robertson and Jones remained to guard the Gaps it must have been by Lee's or Longstreet's orders. Stuart's orders to them were to cross the river when the enemy crossed; and to move on Longstreet's flank, and to watch and report to him.

As before stated, not the slightest complaint was made of Jones and Robertson. I suppose they stayed in front of the Gaps under the orders of General Longstreet, or General Lee. Robertson says that couriers were passing continually between his and General Lee's headquarters — Colonel Massie of the Twelfth Virginia Cavalry says the same thing. But what ought to be conclusive in favor of Robertson and Jones is that no charge of delinquency was made against them. The cavalry was about equally divided. Jones had the largest brigade; Robertson's was the smallest. While Robertson, the senior commander, who was a West Point officer, lacked the initiative and enterprise which are necessary to make an efficient cavalry officer, yet he was a good disciplinarian and could obey orders and perform routine work as well as anybody. Jones was regarded as a very efficient outpost officer. Stuart knew that Jones, although the junior in rank, would be the real commander of both brigades. As proof of this Stuart did not content himself with giving instructions to the senior officer and trusting him to instruct his junior; but he also sent written instructions to Jones, through Robertson, which he requested Robertson to read. I do not think there can be found in the war records another instance where instructions have been addressed directly to a subordinate who is under the immediate command of another. The rule is to direct the intermediate officer to instruct the subordinate. When General Lee told Stuart he must leave him and go to Ewell, he also told him what instructions he must give to the commanders — not alone the senior commander — of the two brigades left in Virginia. The principal reason was that the chief reliance was on Jones; another reason was that Jones' brigade was in Loudon, much nearer the Potomac than Robertson's, and Stuart wanted Jones to save time by communicating directly with Lee and Longstreet instead of sending dispatches by a circuitous route through Robertson according to official etiquette. On the morning of the 26th, Pleasanton's cavalry corps marched directly across their front, and in full view of Jones and Robertson, from Aldie to Edwards' Ferry. The movement was before their eyes and seen by them. Robertson's brigade then retired to Ashby's Gap, and Jones' brigade, which was twelve miles further north, to Snicker's Gap, in Loudon, where they remained until the afternoon

GETTYSBURG 217

of the 29th, when orders came from General Lee, and they started to Pennsylvania. The second report says:

"As soon as it was known that the enemy had crossed into Maryland, orders were sent to the brigades of Robertson and Jones to rejoin the army without delay, and it was expected that General Stuart, with the remainder of his command, would soon arrive." But Stuart could not have been expected to arrive at Chambersburg; he had never been ordered there. It will be observed that General Lee here speaks of Robertson and Jones' brigades not as a single, but as separate commands, and says he sent orders to *each*.

Ordinarily the orders would have been sent to the senior officer alone. No doubt both Jones and Robertson had each been sending dispatches directly to the army headquarters, and orders had in turn been sent separately to them. As General Lee says that Jones' and Robertson's brigades had been left to guard the passes of the Blue Ridge, it must mean that they were kept there by his orders. The orders to guard the Gaps until further orders must have come from Longstreet or General Lee; they certainly were not Stuart's. He left these two brigades some ten or twelve miles in front of the Gaps to observe the enemy and "report anything of importance to Lieutenant General Longstreet, with whose position you will communicate by relays through Charlestown." I have before stated that the Twelfth Virginia Cavalry in obedience to this order was sent to the vicinity of Charlestown. In the event of the enemy's moving to the Potomac, Jones and Robertson were instructed by Stuart to harass the enemy and follow the army. In reply to the objection that Stuart should have left a more enterprising officer in command of the cavalry, the answer is, it was done with the full knowledge and approval of General Lee — probably Robertson was his selection as he knew that Jones would be with him. But, as Stuart calculated that Hooker would send the most of his cavalry in pursuit of him, he did not think that the routine work that would devolve on the cavalry he left behind would require any extraordinary boldness or skill. Robertson, without the aid of Jones, had sufficient capacity to perform the ministerial duty of writing a dispatch and sending a courier with it. Most any private could have done that. If he had not sent the information he would have been guilty of a criminal negligence that would have demanded his dismissal from the army. Yet General Lee made no complaint of Robertson, and at his own request, when the campaign was over, sent him to take a larger command in South Carolina. Robertson had reported to him with two regiments from a camp of instruction a few days before the battle at Brandy. On that day he certainly showed he lacked the energy required in a cavalry officer. But no such high qualities were required to execute the plain duties which Stuart imposed on him. There was not a wagon-master or a teamster in the army that could not have done that work. Robertson says he did it. The report does not contradict him. The work was important but it does not necessarily follow that it was difficult. The second report differs materially from the first, although it renews the complaint against Stuart. The first does not state, as the second does, that Stuart had authority to cross the Potomac *in rear* of the enemy. It simply said west or east of the Ridge.

This was construed as meaning that he was authorized to cross east of Harper's Ferry but between Hooker and Lee. The first said nothing about Ewell's entering Pennsylvania some days in advance of Lee and Longstreet. The second admits that he did. The second also admits that two brigades of cavalry were left in Virginia, but erroneously says they were placed there to guard the Gaps. On the contrary, Stuart ordered them to leave when the enemy left and not a word was said about guarding Gaps. The second admits that Stuart was ordered to place himself on the right of Ewell, but then involves itself in the contradiction of saying that he was directed "to lose no time in placing his command on the right of our column as soon as he should perceive the enemy moving northward." By "our column" was evidently meant the main body with General Lee, as the report says: "It was expected that as soon as the Federal army should cross the Potomac, General Stuart would give notice of its movements, and nothing having been heard from him since our entrance into Maryland, it was inferred that the enemy had not left Virginia." The second report differs materially from the first in not stating with precision the objective point on which the army moved when it marched east from Chambersburg. The first stated that the three corps of Longstreet, Hill, and Ewell were immediately ordered to Gettysburg after the spy brought in the surprising news that Hooker had crossed the Potomac. But the second report only indicated the direction in which the army moved and says that Hill was ordered to move *towards* Cashtown, and that Longstreet followed him, while Ewell was recalled from Carlisle, and directed to go either to Cashtown or Gettysburg. Cashtown is only mentioned once in the first report, where it says a part of the trains on the retreat passed through that Gap. The first report, after stating that Hill was ordered to Gettysburg, says: "The leading division of Hill met the enemy in advance of Gettysburg on the morning of July 1," and further on it speaks of "finding ourselves unexpectedly confronted by the Federal army," but it does not intimate that Hill went there without orders, or to make a reconnaissance. But the second report, which conflicts with the first, was made to conform to Hill's that had come in after the first was written, and says that Hill went from Cashtown to Gettysburg to find out what was in his front. The first says he was ordered there from Chambersburg. Stuart was absent on the first day under orders; in my opinion the orders were right. I now repeat what I said in the *Richmond Times* in April, 1898, in reply to the strictures of Colonel Marshall in his address: "How could Stuart join Ewell on the Susquehanna, guard the Gaps of the Blue Ridge Mountains in Virginia, watch and impede Hooker's crossing the Potomac, and then place himself on the right of the column as it advanced with Lee into Pennsylvania unless he was inspired with ubiquity. Even Hercules could not perform all of his twelve labors at the same time. This is the Age of Reason; the Age of Faith has passed.

We wonder how a people as intellectual as the Athenians could believe that Theseus appeared at Marathon and led the last onset against the Persians; and yet we are now asked to believe that General Lee expected Stuart to surpass all the heroes of the Greek mythology." And I might have added, how could Stuart pass around Hooker and at the same time keep between Hooker and Lee?[1]

[1] On the day after the Confederate army recrossed the Potomac, General Robertson addressed the following letter to General Lee. It does not seem that General Lee had any fault to find with him.

HEADQUARTERS CAVALRY BRIGADE,
July 15th, 1863.

BRIG. GEN. R. H. CHILTON,
    Asst. Adjt. Gen., Hdqrs. Army, Northern Virginia: —

GENERAL: I have the honor to represent to the commanding general the fact that in consequence of casualties, detached service, sickness, &c., my command is reduced to less than 300 men. I consider it injustice to myself and the service to remain longer in my present position. Three regiments of my brigade were left in North Carolina and are now actively engaged there and upon the Peninsula. I volunteered to accompany the two regiments ordered to Virginia, but since their reduction I think my services would be of more avail elsewhere. I therefore respectfully request authority to rejoin my brigade, or else that I be assigned to a command commensurate with my rank.

B. H. ROBERTSON,
Brigadier-General, &c.

(Indorsement)
July 15th, 1863.

Respectfully forwarded and recommended that he be relieved from duty with this command accordingly.

J. E. B. STUART,
Major-General.

August 5th, 1863.

Respectfully forwarded to the Adjutant and Inspector-General's Office. In accordance with this request of Brigadier-General Robertson in and consequence of his being unfit for active duty at this time, he has been relieved from the command of these two regiments and directed to report to the Adjutant-General for orders. He was not ordered to take command of that part of his former brigade in North Carolina because it was thought possible some other disposition had been made of it since his removal from that department. I think it very important to establish a camp at some point in the rear where our cavalry can be recruited and I know of no one so well qualified for the post as Brigadier-General Robertson.

R. E. LEE, General.

Carl Schurz, who commanded the Eleventh Corps in the battle, in his autobiography says: "We did not know that we were marching toward the most famous battlefield of the war. Neither General Meade nor General Lee wished to fight a battle at Gettysburg. Lee wished to have it at Cashtown, Meade on Pipe Creek. Both were drawn into it by the unexpected encounter of the Confederate General, Heth, who hoped to find some shoes for his men at Gettysburg, and a Federal Cavalry general on a reconnaissance, both instructed not to bring on a general engagement, but rather cautioned against it." Heth sent Pettigrew's brigade on the 30th in search of shoes; probably the old ones which Gordon's and White's men had thrown away when they were at Gettysburg. Heth's report says: "On July 1st my division, accompanied by Pegram's battalion of artillery. was ordered [by A. P. Hill] to move at 5 A.M. in the direction of Gettysburg." Hill and Heth were not searching for shoes on July 1st.

THE END

CPSIA information can be obtained at www.ICGtesting.com
Printed in the USA
LVOW121305090613

337277LV00006BA/456/P